A True Story of Hope, Courage and Love

RUNNING
FROM
YESTERDAY

MARGARETTE ALLYN

ISBN 979-8-9864690-0-3 (hardcover)
ISBN 979-8-9864690-1-0 (paperback)
ISBN 979-8-9864690-2-7 (eBook)

First hardcover & paperback edition 30 November 2023.

Library of Congress Control Number: 2023920065

Edited by Cathryn Mora, Adina Edleman and Elizabeth Lyons
Cover illustration by Juliette Fogra
Cover typography by Miblart
Interior design by PB Design Studio
Author photo by Kate Holliday

Published by Margarette Allyn
www.margaretteallyn.com

DISCLAIMER

This is my story as I remember it, including the key relationships I had with those therein and how they impacted me throughout the years.

It is also essential to mention that some names and situations have been changed to protect those involved. At the same time, this is only my recollection of events and conversations. As any experienced cop will tell you, every single perspective of the same situation can be completely different. Others who were present may remember things differently than me, and I honor that too.

This book talks about alcoholism, suicide, and physical abuse. If you feel triggered by anything in this book, I strongly encourage you to seek professional assistance.

You don't have to struggle or do this alone. There is help available out there; you are worth it.

DEDICATION

I dedicate this book to you for reading it; cheers my friend.

To Grandma Sarah, who started it all.
"The spirit in me salutes the spirit in you."

- Mary and Carmen

CONTENTS

PROLOGUE

A charcoal black gun sits on the Pottery Barn table. Blaring sunlight spills into the room, highlighting the table's knife-like edges and the cream sofa's wooden trim. Despite the light, the gun remains dull, cold, and scratched.

I look at the gun on the table. What if I miss? What if I live? Will I feel the bullet tearing through my brain, or will it be over painlessly?

Shooting myself in the head had not been my original idea. I initially wanted to drink myself to death but kept coming to in sheer agony. I could credit the self-shooting idea with a suicide job I'd been called out to as a rookie. A female detective sat on a bench in Fort Tyron Park in Washington Heights at dawn and did it. The first shot didn't kill her. She was alive just enough to try again. And succeeded.

"I need you to stand by this walkaway entrance; some detective shot herself in the damn head," our lieutenant said, standing at the entrance to the park walkway. My partner ushered me in, unaware that my rookie status may not have prepared me for what I was about to see.

There she was on a bench, smack dab in the middle of morning car horns and bird song, slumped over.

"I have no idea why she would do something so crazy... I met her dad; they seem like a nice family. He's a mess over there..." the

1

lieutenant said as I surveyed the scene in front of me, the beauty of the surroundings in sharp contrast to the horror of the blood-stained sheet covering her body.

I remember how the break of sunlight made the park look peaceful. The trees slightly swaying in the breeze and birds swooping down then up, making perfectly curved waves in the air.

She is now lifeless and finally free of her demons, whatever they were. Her family would be left with the pain of her death, like a daily living punishment and reminder of what they had lost.

I wasn't shocked that she'd killed herself; I was more fascinated at the corpse being female. I was used to men getting killed, killing someone else, or taking their own lives. I'd known of illness taking a couple of close female friends, but I never knew of a woman taking her own life. So early in my career, I hadn't seen much of anything, *official that is*, and I certainly couldn't fathom I would one day use her exit to plan my own.

Now I'm sitting on my sofa embroidered with green flowers, curved back, and pedal legs. It reminds me of my summers spent in North Carolina, mixed with a little Victorian beauty. I bought it from a flea market on 74th Street and Amsterdam. *It will pretty up my space…* I'd thought. But not changing the wall color or adding any art to accompany the Victorian addition caused a visual break that traveled down to my heart, which was already shattered.

Beside the gun is a bottle of vodka, a bottle of wine, and a bottle half-filled with tequila. The glass had them all mixed in harmony; that's both my comfort and misery now. The gun sits there at the end of the table, like a morbid bookend, the big finale after I down the last drink.

Spotting the NYPD shirt buried in the pile of laundry makes my eyes focus like a rattlesnake about to destroy its prey. Gazing while suddenly daydreaming, I tilt my neck, take a breath, and rub my hazy head.

Many people feel worthy enough to wear that uniform. It's their dream. Or perhaps family lineage and obligation. Or the desire to feel something other than human. The day I stood in Madison Square Garden on graduation day, I felt as if God made me the star of a show. God was standing right next to me in the middle of a stage. I couldn't have been prouder. I felt I'd arrived,

I'd made it, and everything was going to be okay. No more paranoia over where I was going to live. No more office buildings. No more bad relationship choices. No more trying to fit in. And most of all, no more of the street life as I knew it. To that heartbroken little girl in me who needed so much love, it felt like it had taken so long to get here.

Looking at that uniform sends a seething anger through me. An anger that leaves me paralyzed with fear and regret. Not to mention I have long given up on the belief that God is still standing by me. I shake my head to unclog the constant pain in my ear and loosen the stinking thoughts swimming around in my brain. They are all soaked in spirit, and nothing is cohesive.

I slowly turn my head back to light a cigarette and inhale deeply, staring at *The Honeymooners* on the television that sits in an unfinished armoire, a Goodwill find. Most everything around me was acquired through some avenue of good will or flea markets or vintage luck. Attached to someone else at some point, now connected to me. There is no sound, just Ralph and Alice through the smokescreen. Being married to Ralph seemed like a headache. Alice is yelling something.

The bottle rattles against the glass like a woodpecker as I pour vodka to the top. I think of my mother for a moment. Like that detective's father, my mother would be left with only her memories of me. Others would only hear of me as a stranger: "that cop who killed herself"—just like the woman on the park bench.

The knots in my stomach grow into a single boulder. How did I get here? What used to be a perfect childhood soon turned to shit, a promising career in the corporate world morphed into pointless admin work, and then a gamble with the NYPD, which was supposed to solve everything, didn't pay off. None of it got me to a place of feeling good about myself and I know one thing to be undoubtedly real: Everything comes to an end. And maybe that's a good thing.

There is Christmas music from my neighbor's apartment. Ralph and Alice are becoming blurry. The gulp of my spirit mixture no longer burns as it coats the holes inside of me. I lay my head back, a tear rolling down my cheek, and slowly pick up the gun.

CHAPTER 1

I t's 1981. After church, Grandma, my sister, Shelly, and I go to our favorite restaurant, Reliable, on 145th Street between Amsterdam and Broadway. We sit in the back of the small space in a booth. The smell of collard greens, baked and fried chicken, black eyed peas, mashed potatoes, mac and cheese, stewed veggies, and sweets fills the air. Families file in, unbutton their pants, take off their flowery hats, drape colorful blazers and skirt jackets on the backs of chairs, place purses on the red cloth tables, and without further ado, the sounds of music and talk surround us.

I am eating my favorite meal: oxtail stew with mac and cheese and collard greens. Shelly is eating her baked chicken and green beans. I rush while talking because I won't be allowed a slice of peach cobbler if I waste the food.

I am eager to get Grandma's answers to all the questions I have following Sunday School. The Bible stories scare me and enthrall me at the same time, but Grandma always explains them in a way I understand.

"Why would God drown everyone and everything and save only Noah and his family? Those animals and people must have been very scared," I ask.

"Child, Noah's Ark is a story about faith. Faith is trusting in what you can't see and believing in its goodness even though you can't see any proof, and still believing, even when times are hard. Without faith, people make a lot of choices, do a lot of bad things, and the world gets crazy because of the crazy things people do. So, God started everything over with the one man and family who always followed goodness and mercy," she replies.

"What's crazy?" I wonder out loud.

"When someone does something to themselves or someone else that is hurtful, and they don't care; they feel they can because they are just as scared as anyone else, but they show it by being mean to others and doing whatever they want, over and over again," she explains.

"Will God drown us with a flood if we do something bad?" I ask.

"Why would God do that? If he is all good and love?" Shelly says as she chomps on her chicken.

"Well, God doesn't want to hurt people," Grandma reassures me. "We hurt us. God takes care of us as long as we believe in Him and in loving one another."

Having absorbed enough knowledge for the day, I innocently ask, "May I have peach cobbler now?"

My grandma's name is Sarah. She said her mother got it from the Bible. My grandma named me Margarette and said it is a French name that means daisy. When she first told me that, I didn't know what French meant, but she makes sure I always feel beautiful and wanted and loved.

Grandma Sarah and Grandpa James live with us—Mom, Uncle Allan, Aunt Kim, Shelly, and me. Grandma is the first person Shelly and I see almost every morning and most of the time, the last person to kiss us at night. She is the center of my world.

Grandma is short when she states a command and wants something done, and long and lyrical when she gives compliments. "Never let someone put you down. You don't have to stoop to their level, but never let them think they are a level above you." What that means, I have no idea. I am a free thinking and acting child. There is not a slither of fear or doubt in my mind. What it takes to be a grown up eludes me. Being the perfect child is easy. At least she makes it seem easy.

Grandma looks like Ella Fitzgerald. She doesn't sing like her, but she is as graceful and commanding. She is always kind, yet sweetly snide. She doesn't wait for anyone to do anything for her. She is a friendly leader. There is a level of comfort I feel with her that I don't feel with my mom, aunt, or uncle.

Grandma told me that she had my mother at nineteen and my mom had me at nineteen too. Despite the double age gap between my grandma and me, I don't see her as a grandma. That's just what I call her. Family role names don't really mean much to me. All I know is that she is the coolest forty-six-year-old in my life.

The first time I understood how I felt about her was when she looked me in the eyes with a deep stare and said, "You and your sister are the best things that has happened in my life, my dear. Because you are you and that's all you ever have to be." Her voice had broken with emotion, and I knew she loved us deeply for being ourselves, whatever that means.

When we leave the restaurant, Grandma pulls my cream knit hat over my ears and buttons Shelly's coat. I am relieved because I have one hand stuffed in my pocket and the other cradled in her leather-gloved hand. Even though I have gloves on, I still feel the warmth of her firm and protective hold. It is Christmas, 1981, and I turned eight years old in October. I feel like a little woman. We walk the short distance to Broadway and 145th street. We turn north and our excitement grows as we see the red, blue, green, and golden balls hanging in the windows of Woolworths along with wrapped boxes, glass bowls of candy canes, and statues of Mr. and Mrs. Santa Clause.

"Can we go in and get peppermint candy canes, pleeease?" We ask in unison as I pull Grandma along.

"Well, you know we can't pass Woolworths and not get candy canes for our tree. And yes, you may have one," she says, patting me on the shoulder, and Shelly on her head. Grandma's cheeks are rosy from the chill, her smile creating creases around her eyes.

The dancing combination of blinking and steady light strings hanging from fire escapes gives off a show of laughter and joy. We had wrapped the big bulbs around each pole of our fire escape, so they lit up the second and first floors and shined a bit upward toward Mrs. Smith's apartment on the third floor. Any night when Grandma isn't working, we sit at the window and sip hot chocolate while watching people stroll past with shopping bags and skipping kids in tow. We sing along to the holiday music on the radio and from cars passing by, filling the streets with jazz version of Old Saint Nick. I pull Shelly up to dance with me and Grandma breaks out in peals of tinkly laughter. The night is magical, and I think how lucky I am that every time with Grandma feels just like this.

One of my favorite pastimes is writing stories to share with my grandma. My desire to always make her happy causes me to not only read as much as I can but also to write her the sweetest notes. She taught me how to lick a stamp and address an envelope. "What a fun, grown-up thing to do," I think every time I skip next to her to the small post office, which is only two buildings up the street from our apartment.

Today, I put the learning into practice. "I already wrote my first letter to you, Grandma!" I say while waving the crayon-marked envelope in front of her face.

She is in bed during the day, and I am surprised. I thought she was home to spend time with Shelly and me since we will soon be taking our summer trip to North Carolina, to be with Grandpa James's family. Grandpa takes us every summer and Grandma stays home in New York to take care of everything else.

"What are you doing home? Are you spending the day with us?" I ask, excited to have her to myself.

"I'm just a little tired today, sweetie pie."

Her eyes, usually glistening and watching, are droopy and dull. Her head is wrapped in a hair scarf, and the same old can of beer from the night before sits on the floor next to her ashtray.

"I want you to hold on to that letter until you get a chance to mail it to me. It's not the same to give it to me before you leave," she says.

"Okay, I'm going to squirt scents on it before I mail it. Will you send your letter for me as soon as you get mine, so it gets there fast?"

She whispers a laugh and reaches out to me. I climb onto the bed and settle into her arm.

"What would I do without you and your sister?" she whispers.

As I lie there, I inhale her perfume mixed with the smell of cigarettes and think I will have her forever.

The home of NASCAR, the most delicious apples you could taste, and country singing at its best are found in North Carolina. It is a world covered in grass that hugs the feet. Endless fields that are inviting and warm. Trees that bear fruit and serve as homes for singing birds, and streams move water clear as glass.

It is our third time spending the summer in North Carolina. I already know what to expect. The first time almost made my grandpa turn around and take me back home. We had left at night with fried chicken, ham and cheese sandwiches, soda cans wrapped in foil, and Grandpa's stash of beer. Traveling at night excited me so much that I had been wide awake. Then we got to the George Washington Bridge. It looked like it was just floating in the air and would fall at any minute. The bridge went on forever, light after light. Highlights and lowlights and more lights in the sky on what looked like ropes. How could cars not make it fall? I didn't want to go across and let out a wail that surely half the country could hear.

"Girl, you better not cry like this the whole time, goddammit!" Grandpa snapped, his cigarette dangling from the side of his mouth. He assured me that the bridge was supported by concrete. I didn't believe him because I only saw lights, rope, and sky.

"Just put your head down. Why are you looking at it anyway?" he asked.

"Yes, just stop looking. It doesn't bother me at all," Shelly had said.

I couldn't look away; it was fascinating and scary at the same time. How could it be so big? A single hanging light show that lit up the dark. I loved the lights and the other cars driving along the bridge. I thought that if those cars weren't falling, then we surely wouldn't either. Maybe it was a magic bridge that God put there for people who were driving to the other side of darkness.

"What's on the other side? It's just dark there… Will the bridge end and we'll crash into something?" I was feeling braver, but still unsure.

"It's New Jersey, girl. We aren't going to crash into nothin'. Just close your eyes," he reassured me.

"What's New Jersey?"

"For Christ's sake, go to sleep!"

New Jersey must be someone who holds the other end of the bridge up, I thought. *Hopefully Grandpa can see better than I can.* I started to feel tired and closed my eyes without knowing what happened to those lights in the sky.

Once I woke up and looked out the window, the sight was airy, free, and gorgeous. Vicksboro Road ran down the middle of endless lawns with houses that played peek-a-boo with each other and seemed to be expecting me with their surrounding corn fields, farms doll house churches, and sky-high trees. There were no tall apartment buildings, no sidewalks, no cars lining the streets. Birds danced in and out of clouds, using wind as music. The smells of daffodils, lilies, and fruit trees pushed the leather scent of the car out of my nose and made themselves at home.

"Are we there yet?" I asked, staring out of that window like I'd just seen the pyramids in person.

"Look who's awake. Not yet, Little Bit, but almost."

The tobacco fields, hills, cows, and occasional horses were right out of my picture books. There was so much grass, so many big trees and animals.

I smile as I remember my first journey, and here I am again, three years later. Grandpa reminds me we've only got forty miles to go until we reach the tiny town of Henderson.

Grandpa starts slowing down and stops at the dirt path entrance to a big white house in the middle of a green lawn. The house gets bigger as we get closer. It looks like Cinderella lives there. A big white house, lace curtains, and a lawn as green as the inside of a music box. I smile at the attached porch that stretches across the entire back of the house with a swing and single chair— I've spent lovely summers in that swing.

Knowing that Shelly and I always try to race to the swing first, Grandpa says, "Your great-grandma will want to see you first, before you go running off to play!"

My great-grandmother Fannie and my grandpa's brother, Uncle Milton, live together in the white house. I call her Gram. Gram is stocky and hunched over, hands worn from years of hard work. She is feminine and lots of fun but has an authority about her that causes everybody to listen when she speaks. Uncle Milton, who is my grandfather's brother, and his best friend Wilbert who lives across the road are like the real-life version of the Dukes of Hazard, always creating havoc in town.

During the week Shelly and I have chores to do. And we have to do them before we are allowed to play outside. I'd never even heard the word "chores" until Gram used it. "Chores means taking care of what God gave you," she says, handing me a peeler and setting down several long carrots on the table. "A home won't take care of itself, clothes don't get washed by ghosts, and food isn't prepared by fairies."

I held the peeler, uncertain. Gram took pity on me and showed me how to use it on the first carrot. "You may not do much of this kind of thing in the city, but especially now that you're eight, you have to help around here, young lady," she said.

I help with the vegetable garden, which I love, and also with the cooking, ironing, and cleaning. There is a washing machine in the back foyer. It is so small that only about ten items of clothing can fit into the narrow cylinder. On top, what looks like two rolling pins are joined together on a metal clamp. She says that is how we will wring out the clothes.

"Child, don't you dare put your fingers close to the rollers. I'll start the clothes, and you pull from the other side," she says.

"Yes ma'am."

After we do the clothes, it is my job to hang them on the line outside. Our other chores include dusting all the wood with a cloth and lemon oil, learning how to use a metal iron and salt to make the clothes straight as an arrow, and polishing silverware. She has huge mahogany cabinets with glass doors and inside were what she called antique dishes that are so beautiful, I don't know why she makes me clean them.

Gram shows me once and has a tone that puts the fear of heck into me. No way would I break anything. I treat those antiques like they are the last in the world and non-replaceable.

No one gives me a bath; I have to wash myself. Gram lets Shelly and me take baths in a big tin tub next to the porch swing. She heats up water in her tea kettle and pours it in so we will be warm. I love washing in that tin tub and watching her back lawn sparkle like the stars in a southern night sky—country life feels natural to me.

Grandma is back at home, working to take care of all of us, and while I miss her, I write her often about what I'm doing and how much I love being here.

Uncle Milton has a stutter. I don't think anything of it. I find it to be cool. He always keeps his salt and pepper beard short and smells of oil, gas, and aftershave lotion. He has a bow-legged walk and wears his pants too short, always in a plaid shirt with a white t-shirt under it. He lets me follow him around when I finish making mud pies. He also lets me bring him some of the pies and pile them up on his table where he fixes cars. I love the smell of the place where he fixes cars. It smells like magic markers.

One time, Shelly and I are riding in the back of his yellow pick-up truck, getting smacked with flying dust and sand, when he pulls over and gets out of his truck, stands by the door, and puts his hand over his heart. Slowly coming down the other side of the road is a funeral procession. The hearse looks like a massive head of a slow-moving worm, leading the rest of the cars, all moving as one. The farmer in the corn fields holds his heart, the gas station attendant makes the sign of the cross, and the woman on the side of the road holding a basket bows her head.

I am amazed and feel like we are all paying attention to God. Paying attention to life as it ends and how we respect still being here. The dust in the air seems to settle to the ground in rhythm. The birds fly high, the sun is bright, and the trees sway. The apples glisten like red rubies hanging from bright green leaves, and the smell of grass floats past my nose with joy. There goes the procession, creating a pause in the movement of life, a pause that makes me feel good inside.

The woman with the basket looks up and then picks up her stride down the road. The farmer picks his corn, and the gas station attendant greets a new customer. My uncle turns up the country music on his truck radio.

Country music snatches me into its world, like a grown-up who hurries a child along when in a rush. I am working *9 to 5* with Dolly Parton, cheering Johnny on for beating the devil in a fiddle battle, and wondering how Charlie Daniels could tell such a story. I feel lightheaded and sad when Bill Withers sings "Ain't no Sunshine," and thank the Heavens when John Denver sings "Sunshine on my Shoulders."

Country music is to people in the south what disco and rock are to people up north: religious. I watch my uncle tap his fingers to the beat of Johnny Cash on his beer. Move his feet back and forth while sitting when a line dance song blares through the rickety radio.

When my uncle goes to the porch after dinner, I love going with him. I am scared to sit out there at night alone, but with him I don't notice my fears. Tonight, there seems to be fewer fireflies. The sky is darker at dusk, and there are more crows circling the sky than usual. The wind is picking up, which is nice, but I've heard of tornados and hope one isn't coming.

"Where do fireflies come from? Where are they during the day? Are there bears here at night? Dogs? Snakes?" I ask as he drinks his beer and stutters an answer here and there. Mostly, he just shakes his head yes or no.

It is a struggle for me to spot a glimmer of a lightning bug in the deep night. I can usually see far-away stars as if they are sitting right on the lawn, but I can't see any tonight. The moths, in small groups, surround the porch light, so much that it dims its glow.

The swing squeaks as it moves back and forth, swaying like the people at church. I cross my arms and squint my eyes up toward the sky, feeling heavy and sad, yet I don't know why. I say my prayers, thinking of Grandma back home, and go to bed.

The bedroom is warmer than usual, and I spend a little extra time preparing a letter I want to send to Grandma in New York. I write her once or twice a week, and she keeps up the pace, so it almost seems as though she is here with me.

I give the letter a squirt of the purple perfume from Gram's vanity. I always lick the stamp twice because I like the taste of the glue. *Another masterpiece*, I think as I stare at the envelope. I hear Gram's voice calling from downstairs. "Come down here. I have something to tell you both."

Gram doesn't usually call up for me, so I am downstairs before she can stir her biscuit batter twice. Her voice is calm yet solemn. There is a lump in my throat and knots in my stomach because I can feel there is something wrong. Gram sits at the kitchen table, where she stares at the cup of coffee, she makes every morning. She gives me a little cup of it every morning too, and while I can't say how she made it, I love that little taste of grown-up fun in a teacup.

She gets up and picks up the mixed batter for biscuits, places a cast iron pan on the wood-burning stove, fixes the wire clothes hanger on the small black and white television, and waves a fly from a plate of fried fish that Grandpa brought in last night. I watch, all the while feeling annoyed at the way my trip to the mailbox was interrupted. At the very least, some coffee would be nice.

"The Price Is Right" is on the screen; I hate Bob Barker at that moment, and I wonder where the people come from who cheer from the audience. Gram stops mixing her batter, walks up to Shelly and me, and cradles my head with one hand and pulls Shelly in closer to her with the other.

"Your grandmother passed away last night. The funeral will be here at the local funeral home. She will even be buried at the cemetery next to the church."

Shelly starts whimpering while holding her hand over her mouth. I look at her and feel a mix of anger and fear that her crying is making something real, something I am scared to know.

Before I can breathe, Gram pulls us in, squeezing the both of us against her stained apron.

"What?" Something inside me stills.

"She is in Heaven now, child," she says, still not letting go.

"I have a letter for her. Is she coming back?"

Shelly is crying louder now.

"No child, she died."

The letter, clenched in my hand, is as smothered as I feel. I suck air through that apron and let out a wail-like sound, muffled by the apron, suddenly wet with saliva and tears.

Shelly pushes herself back, and yells, "Why would she die while we are here, here in this house? She didn't tell us anything about that when we left her in New York. What happened to God being so good?" Shelly turns and runs out of the kitchen.

"She said she wasn't going to Heaven any time soon!" Grandma told me about Heaven, but she never said that once you go there, you don't come back. Could that really be true? I am choked up, speaking through my tears, and gulping remnants of air.

"God bless you, child, it's alright; it's alright."

The breath in my lungs turns into a hard lump in my throat, a lump as big as my body. Will it consume me and take me to Heaven too? I feel the urge to stomp my feet and throw that coffee straight out the window.

"What makes people go to Heaven?" I muffle through the apron.

"God took her home. We all have to go home, child."

"I live with her. That's home. Why would God do that? What about me?!"

"Oh my…" she says while stroking my head. I've never seen or felt her so physically tender. "God takes everyone home, just at different times, nothing we can do about that child."

"I HATE GOD! I HATE GOD FOR DOING THAT! WHOEVER GOD IS, I HATE HIM!" I yell.

"Don't say those things, child. I know you are hurt and sad, but God does not want us to be angry. Your grandma was sick, and he took her pain away. He needed her with him. And they both will always be with you."

I am getting angrier by the second. I don't understand any of what she's just said. How can she know how good God is and, at the same time, not notice or care that I don't know what sickness my grandma had that made him want to fix it by taking her away altogether?

"Couldn't she take the medicine we have to take for our asthma?" I asked.

"It wasn't that kind of sickness, dear. Sometimes there are sicknesses that medicine can't fix. And so, some people have to go home before others."

"I want to go home and see for myself. Are my mom and uncle Allan and Aunt Kim still there?"

"Yes. And I'm talking about home in Heaven. God's home," Gram says, stroking my hair.

"Can I put her letter in the mailbox, please?" *Maybe she will get it before she gets to Heaven, and she will have to come back.*

Gram looks at me with such compassion. Her lip trembles, and she takes my hand that is holding the letter. While she looks up at her low ceiling, her gaze appears to go beyond that. To what, I don't know.

"Of course, you should mail your letter. Be careful crossing the road. You can sit in here with me when you come back. Be careful, child."

"Thank you," I say, in my lowest voice. The heaviness of my heart and the fear in my body are too much for me.

Gram cries in front of me, but only little tears. Her restraint is painfully more visible. I walk up the dirt path, toward the mailbox, not smelling the berry bushes or counting the butterflies, not even picking a couple of grapes from the vine as I usually do.

The road is steamy. The dirt is motionless. The heat under my small feet is hotter than usual, the pavement slightly giving way like molding clay. A passing car kicks up the heat waves, and the dust that follows makes a ribbon-like wave along the road. It is the mail carrier. I just missed him. He is already past my friend's house, and I can't run to catch up.

That lump in my throat comes back with a vengeance, and with a painful swallow, I think, *I will be home with those grapes soon; love you, Grandma.* I sit against the wooden mail post, wanting to figure out a way to get back home to New York.

As I kick the dirt on the path while walking back toward the house, the silence is pelted by the growing volume on the television. It seems as if I am getting screamed at, and each clap from the audience is a smack in the face. I look back at the mailbox that appears hazy. I leave my letter in there and put the old bent flag up.

My mom walks next to me and Shelly, looking down and sliding her feet along the dirt path. I want to grab her hand, but she is gripping a paper flyer that has my grandmother's picture on it.

Shelly and I glance at each other. Shelly looks down and wipes her eyes. I walk closer to her, my eyes already drowning.

My family is gathered by the church entrance, dabbing their faces and hugging each other. *What kind of church is this? Where is Grandma?* Maybe she would visit us from Heaven and take me with her. Or better yet, stay.

I see Uncle Allan and he snaps into a jolly mood. He claps his hands, picks me up, and says, "Hey, Little Bit, how are we today?" How 'bout you sis?" he bellows as he hugs Shelly with his other arm. Shelly looks up and says, "Ah, we are doing okay thank you."

His voice starts to crack as my eyes search his sad expression for genuine joy.

He hands me back to my mom and I ask her. I look around, feeling confused and at the same time surprised. Not the good surprised like when someone gets a party they didn't know about. Shelly is looking at our family as puzzled as I feel.

We have never seen Uncle Allan, Aunt Kim or our other older cousins and family members come down here from New York. "Why are we here?" I ask Mom as she stands to the side with her head down.

"Because Grandma has gone on to Heaven, and we all miss her," she solemnly replies.

"Why didn't we get to see her first. Didn't she want to see us?"

My mother nudges me, rolls her eyes, and inhales through her teeth. I have to move along without getting an answer, the sounds of muffled sniffles floating behind us. The smell inside the church reminds me of the moth balls Gram keeps in her closets. I love that smell, but not in this place. It is cold, too.

We walk into a little room where women dressed in peach, black, and pink dresses with big matching hats line the room. They sit on both sides of a long burgundy rug that leads all the way to the front of the room. An older man with white hair is playing the piano. My music teacher back home plays happier music, and the music at Convent Avenue Baptist church is not like this either. This music has deeper chords, calling for comfort and direction from the Lord. It is the music of pain. Sorrow. Grief. And that is exactly what I start to feel, except these feelings are new and painful, and I don't know what they mean.

I try to ignore the music and the hanging faces looking at me— the faces of people who need to say something, but the words get tied up and strangled in their throat. The verses are written on their faces, faces of agony.

Holding Shelly's arm, we both gasp at grandma lying in a wooden box at the front of the room. The box has a top made of beautiful oak and mahogany, and it is lined with brass trim, golden flowers scrolled along the side. Her head rests on a white satin pillow, and the entire box is surrounded by flowers.

I try to run up to her, but my mother puts a vice grip on my hand and jerks me back. Rage fills me when I look at her, her stony expression overshadowing any words she could say. The room is so quiet, but I can't understand the silence combined with my physical pain. I snatch my hand away and scream, "Why is Grandma lying like that? Is she getting up?"

"Stop yelling or we will get in trouble." Shelly's shaky voice sounds like a gurgle while she desperately tries to hold in her sobs.

"Get in trouble… why, why, why?" I say and I notice the people with grim faces begin to transform into distorted clowns, and their huge, curved mouths let out louder wails.

"She isn't getting up. She is in Heaven," my mother says while shaking my arm, forcing me into a seat. I start to hate her in this moment.

"She isn't in Heaven; she is right there!" I declare, growing more panic-stricken.

Shelly scoots closer into the corner of the pew, shaking her head and crying into her hands. *I am not sitting next to her or in that trap of a velvet seat at all*, I think as mom is still pulling me.

"I'm not going to tell you again to sit…" Those clenched teeth are now growling at me. Breaking away, I run up to the fancy bed Grandma is resting in, and I want to tell that man to stop playing the piano. Maybe his sad music is making Grandma stay asleep.

"Grandma, wake up, it's me, wake up!"

But she doesn't move. Why won't she move and open her eyes? An overwhelming feeling of fear comes over me. Fear and confusion. I reach for her face and, upon touching it, snatch my hand back as if I had been burned. It is so cold and hard. How in the world could Grandma's face be this way? The make-up is painted on; she would never do this. Is she not listening to me? Does she want this cold, hard, painted skin? As always, she is dressed beautifully in a white silk shirt and pants with pearls on her wrist and earrings to compliment her golden ears. She looks like she is smiling. Covering her head is a wig, but I don't notice it is not attached to her head until I clench her shirt and hair, at which point it moves a bit. I tilt my head and narrow my eyes to try to figure out what that means but am quickly jolted back to reality.

Having joined me at the front of the church, my mother digs her nails into my shoulder. "Get to the seat. This is Grandma's body; her spirit is in Heaven."

I grab the box, and the man either stops playing the dreadful piano or my crying takes over his miserable chords. My uncle stands on one side of me and my mother on the other, working together to pull me away. I grip my grandmother's arm as tightly as possible. My screaming and crying breaks out and through that little house of horrors stronger than a southern hurricane.

"She is not in Heaven! Wake up, wake up!" I am screaming, wailing, and choking, choking so hard I can't get a word to make sense. Would God even understand me? My Grandma's silk shirt is riding up and exposing the shell of a woman I can't bear to imagine being soulless. Cold. Hard. Not really here.

They keep pulling me, peeling my fingers one by one from the box. The box rocks back and forth, and the wailing turns to screams of terror.

"Please get up! Why didn't you write to me, why didn't you say you were leaving? Please don't leave me. I wrote you a letter. Tell God to let you stay!"

Shelly is beside me, and I don't know what she is saying. We are holding each other while I am holding the box at the same time. I want Shelly to do something; I want anyone to do something to end my horrible feelings.

My fingers are aching and smudging the shirt with stains. My last attempt to reach her leads me into a frenzy of grabbing and snatching everything I can. Don't take me away from her! I am trying to stay with Grandma, fighting to hold her, pushing and punching that box, gripping her hands, her face, that icy face.

"Get up!" My breath comes short and fast. "Did you get my letter?"

They break me free from the box while ushers stand in front of it and hold the top to keep it from slamming down over Grandma. They re-fold her hands on her stomach in a cup-like position, as if she were carefully holding something delicate. Everyone is screaming, crying, bent over in pain or shame. I don't know which one.

I faintly hear the music that awful man had been playing, the chords of a broken heart, as I collapse and am carried out of the church.

CHAPTER 2

The busy streets of Harlem are a shock when Shelly and I arrive home from North Carolina. I feel like nothing is the same. Our apartment that used to feel warm and happy, is now sad and empty. My mom spends more time alone in her room, and she doesn't smile like Grandma did. She looks at me with vacant eyes sometimes, and I feel more distant from her each day.

Grandma always shopped for our school clothes at Saks Fifth Avenue. The smell of new shoes and brand-new cotton filled the massive floors along with whiffs of perfume. With bags in tow, we had also stopped at Woolworths for school supplies. I got high off the smell of new books, magic markers, and crayons. We organized my books, and I wrote my name in all of them. I read my library books in a flash and loved taking neat notes. I always had a crisp new school bag that I picked out, Little Miss Muffin or blue for the Smurfs. The cartoon world in school gear was mine for the taking. I want my mother to pick up where my grandma left off. Between Shelly and I, we asked her every day after returning from North Carolina to take us shopping. She always replied, "I don't have time. Maybe tomorrow."

A week before school starts, me and Shelly are watching "Scooby Doo" in the living room. Uncle Allan comes home, shuffling several bags between his hands. He hands us two bags of clothes he picked out for us, along with our school supplies and shoes.

"Thank you!" We yell as we jump up and hug him. He spins us around as he always does and lets us slide down his leg.

As I dig into the first bag, he looks toward the bedroom. "Where is your mother?" he bellows with his deep voice.

"I don't know, she said she would be back soon," Shelly says.

I am unsure how he will react to her leaving us alone again. We don't tell him that she does it all the time.

I distract him by holding up my new book bag, pink and purple with yellow and orange flowers.

"I love it, it's perfect!" he says, as his shadow moves from hovering over me.

"Tell your mother I am looking for her when she gets back."

"Okay and thank you for our school clothes," Shelly says as she mimics trying on her clothes.

"Okay, love you, thank you for my school supplies."

He did well for a burly uncle. He picked out clothes in the right size and our favorite colors. Blue, green, and pink for me, and purple, orange and yellow for Shelly, with colorful decorative school supplies to match.

How did he know that Grandma always did that for us? I'm so grateful he noticed the routine we had with her and tried to make us feel better by doing the same this year. I can't help wondering why my mom doesn't take us shopping.

"Does she not even care what we wear to school or if we have colorful paper or pens to write with?" Shelly asks. I wanted to say something, but she said it first.

"I don't know. It seems those things grandma did are not fun to her or something."

We sit quietly for a few moments. Shelly picks up her bag.

"I'm happy with my new supplies."

"Me too," I add. But I decide that instead of using what my uncle gave me, I will save it and use what I had last year. Just my way of keeping a part of Grandma with me in school.

My mother walks into the apartment as my uncle is heading toward the door. He points to the bedroom once occupied by Grandma and she follows him in with a lowered head. I know she

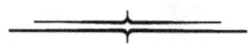

isn't praying. I hear raised voices, my mother whining and sobbing.

"What do you think he is saying?" Shelly asks.

"I don't know but it sounds bad. Let's go in the room." I say as I gather my things and head toward our room with Shelly close behind.

A few minutes later he storms out, slamming the door to the apartment. Mom goes into the kitchen, and I hear her opening and closing cabinets, the sound of tinkling cutlery and utensils alerting me to the fact she is preparing dinner.

"I'm so hungry," I say to Shelly. She is organizing her school supplies, the Smurfs keeping us company on TV, when Mom tells us to come eat.

She pushes small piles of paper and envelopes to the side, clearing a space on the overrun table.

"Thank you," we say in unison. Shelly's face is blank, dim. I sigh as I look at the canned French cut green beans that resemble green playdough, and the burger that looks like it doesn't know its place sitting on one piece of soggy bread.

Grandma had always put food on the table and made sure the fridge was full of snacks. She worked hard and didn't spend long cooking, but always made sure we were full of good food and taken care of. There is no more real home cooking, no food from Reliable or McDonalds. Things are so different now.

"Look what I got for school!" I say as I hold up my pencil case, a distraction from the sad-looking dinner in front of me.

"That's nice," she says, blowing past me and into her room. She closes the door but briefly opens it again to call out, "Make sure you both clean up after you're finished!"

On the first day of fourth grade, we are walking up the street next to Mom.

"Make sure you walk straight home. Don't stop to talk to anyone. See you after school," she says, nudging us forward without so much as a hug. She turns back a few seconds after walking away and waves her hand, as if scooting a sheep back toward its flock, and says, "Go on, don't just stand there."

The halls are dim and bare. They don't seem colorful like last year. The sound of laughing kids pierces and rips through my ears. They sound like mocking hyenas. Everyone goes about their business normally, having no idea how my life has changed. Changed in a way that even I don't fully understand. And I want the whole school to stop acting like nothing has happened.

School used to excite me, even though I wasn't the kid that had playdates and sleepovers, I had a few friends, usually befriending the girl who looked lonely in the back of the classroom or standing alone in the school yard during recess.

Out in the yard during break, I get up the courage to make a new friend. I don't want to depend on my sister all the time. "Wanna play hopscotch?" I ask a girl standing against the fence. I never used to fear rejection. If a kid said no, I would start playing alone, or eventually join up with other kids. This time, I am nervous. I feel like my loneliness and sadness is tattooed all over me and that other kids look at me like I were a sickness.

"Sure, what's your name?" she says.

"I'm Margarette. Are you new here?" I am surely relieved she didn't ignore me.

I'm Denise. I come to this school already. I was in a different class in third grade. I sit behind you in class." She throws a paper-covered rock onto the first square and hops on to it with one foot.

I pick up the rock and toss it.

"Oh, I didn't know. I usually know all the names of the kids in my class by the end of the first day."

"Why would you want to do that? I don't speak to many kids. I don't have many friends." She tosses the rock to the fourth square and hops along.

"I don't know why I do it. I like to know who everyone is." Everyone knew who my grandma was; it feels good when people know who you are. People liked and respected my grandma, and I want to take after her. I like to be seen as kind and helpful, just like Grandma was.

"I hope you're not one of those nerdy kids who always does their homework," she says, hopping down the squares.

I don't want to tell her that I am, because more than anything, I want to fit in. Besides, Shelly is the real book worm in our family. "Nah, course not," I say, then take my turn. True to my word, I stop doing my homework. Denise isn't the only one who doesn't do it—nobody does, apart from Shelly. So why should I? Like me, she doesn't have anyone at home who really cares about what she does anyway. I quickly develop a reputation of being likeable, but not focused on my work. Plus, what I care most about right now is music.

Michael Jackson, Diana Ross, Lionel Richie, Wham, The Police, Steven Tyler, and other voices of their generation are all frequent musical stars in our apartment. At night when I am in bed, I tuck a small radio under my covers, imagine making up dance steps to the songs, and dream of dancing with the musicians on stage. Shelly complains about my music because she says she can hear it across the room, and it stops her getting to sleep.

Music and movement send a feeling through me, make me feel like I am flying; I am nowhere but everywhere all at once. Even church music has a comfort to it that makes me feel the world is joyous and calm, belying the chaos now inside my own life. The visitors to our apartment are very different from our friends at church. Watching people lose themselves in drink and song is still mesmerizing, and I want to know what they are feeling and thinking. I watch people more often now, especially since I am not in constant conversation with my grandma. I miss our shared love of music and performance, and how excited she was for me to learn the piano.

"The piano is one of the most beautiful instruments in the world. There are many ways to play music on it, and many of the wonderful musicians you listen to play the piano," she once said when we were listening to her records.

She decided to take me to piano lessons with Mrs. Dawson when I was six. I loved the stacks of sheet music that lined the bookshelves and the top of the glistening, baby grand piano, which seemed quite big. I sat next to her on the piano seat, and she pulled out a book and leaned it against the music stand above the keys. I remember staring at those keys in amazement. She played Twinkle Twinkle Little Star, and I thought she was magical. How lovely it sounded.

"Start with middle C. Then we go up the scale, you should know this by now; C, D, E, F, G, A, B, and we end at the next octave, C. Which is the next eighth C note." The piano was so astonishing to me, the keys look like soldiers waiting for the order to march separately or together. Each beat and note sounded lovely on its own and amazing when played together. I felt butterflies in my stomach when it was my turn to try. I wanted to sound perfect. As perfect as the piano looked, I didn't feel worthy enough to play like my teacher. But Grandma took us to lessons, and especially as Shelly doesn't seem to love music in the same way that I do, I wanted to be great at anything I did for Grandma's sake.

Sitting up straight and sticking my bony chest out, I took a deep breath and imagined I was my teacher. The notes would sound just right when she played the piano. Grandma was smiling at me over her book, and my feet swung a little faster under the piano bench.

C-D-E-F-G- "That's it, nice and smooth," my teacher said in a voice that sang with the note. The next note sliced into my trance and stride. I pressed a sharp note and my legs stiffened up.

When Mrs. Dawson started talking about eighth notes and octaves, it sounded like another language. I felt lost, like it was all some part of a fancy potion. But she said not to worry and finally let me press each key with the fingers of my right hand, which had to be slightly bent. Also, all professional musicians had to sit up straight; there was absolutely no slouching. Another mistake I made.

While she gave me corrections, I also heard people talking loudly in another apartment, the horns on the street amplified, and the pigeons flying angrily over the Henry Hudson River.

Grandma peeped at me with her kind eyes as Mrs. Dawson said, "That's alright. There are no mistakes in trying. There is failure in giving up. All music can be one note or several strung together. This is what practice is for."

When she touched the keys, the music flowed throughout the room, under the door jambs and out the windows. She made it look effortless, and I wondered why I couldn't play just like her.

As soon as I felt like I had to be good, I messed up. But when I was alone, imagining myself dancing in front of people or playing the piano like a maestro, I was a genius.

Grandma never said anything negative. "Trying is always the gift. The gift of choice is God given. Never feel bad about trying," she'd say, squeezing my hand as we walked up the hill from Riverside Drive to Broadway, where I could faintly hear the music coming from her apartment window. The same music we dance to in ballet class.

In addition to piano, ballet, and more classical training, Grandma enrolled us into the African dance class at Harlem School of the Arts in the same year. The school was started by Dorothy Maynor, a concert soprano who loved the arts so much that she started teaching classes in the basement of a Presbyterian church. It grew into a performing arts school on Saint Nicholas Avenue between 141st and 125th streets. Just one avenue east of the Convent Avenue Baptist church we attended.

The school is now managed by a man named Mr. Burtrum. We called him the school father, and there was never a time when he was not shining his smile at us as we walked through the front door.

I loved it from the moment I took my first class, African dance with Mrs. Rhymes, that was followed by a tap class. There is ballet class two times a week, and a drama class on Saturdays. Shelly could take it or leave it, but I loved being there. Since Grandma died, Harlem School had become more like my home than the apartment we lived in with our mom.

There are older girls in my classes who have been here longer and have more experience. They lead the class warmup for Mrs. Rhymes as she sits in her chair, holding her gold, green, and red African cane, banging it to the beat and shouting on the fourth and eighth counts. She treats us like we belong to her through dance. When she pushes herself up with her cane, the room, lights, drummer, and people watching from the balcony all get brighter and taller and louder. I absolutely love her and this class.

"Come on, you are in the center. Show some love, everyone!" she shouts. No one has a chance to shy away, and with everyone cheering, no one *wants* to shy away. Even the drummer makes us feel like we are stars. I feel overwhelmingly embraced in the middle of that studio.

The older girls are mentors and friends to the younger girls, and I can feel my addiction to the stage taking on a life of its own. The last note, last hit of the drum, and screams from the dancers and audience take me to another place, another world. One that I never want to leave.

When the house lights come up and the stage lights are dimmed, it's a reminder that reality awaits. The stage is a world of make believe that comes from truth, and it seems easier to be on stage as a character than to be a caricature of myself in real life.

Grandma was always front and center when we had a show, whereas my mom has been different. When we come home from shows and I tell her about my experience, her reaction is slow and muted, and I feel blocked in some way. She's never shown the excitement Grandma did. Even my aunt and uncle are anxious to hear how things are going when I tell them about the dance shows.

"Did you hear me, Mom?" I often ask, continuing to talk before noticing she is staring off into the distance, looking at her nails or tapping her fingers with boredom—anything but looking interested in what I am saying.

She nods her head and says, "Yes that's nice." My grandma used to make up for all the attention I didn't get from my mom—all the attention that, at the time, I didn't even notice I wanted or needed. Now that Grandma has passed, my piano lessons have stopped. My mother still lets me take the free dance lessons because I beg her as if it were oxygen and she oversees the air supply.

I have my dance lessons, but I don't have what I most need and crave—her love.

The first summer after Grandma's death, my grandpa isn't able to pick us up for our trip to North Carolina, so my mom, Shelly and me take the Greyhound bus at Port Authority. She won't stay with us there; she'll return home the following day, so this bus trip is our only time together this summer. My mother is nowhere near as fun as my grandpa, and I am certain there will be no music on the bus, no fun, no conversation. I barely speak to her for fear she will snap at me or pinch me or something similarly unpleasant. Shelly nabs the seat on its own, while I am sitting with Mom. Spending over nine hours on a bus is not my idea of fun.

The lights go off in the bus, and the driver announces we are leaving. Everyone settles into their seats with blankets, books, and food.

I sit by the window and shiver a little. Partially because of the air conditioning shooting out of the side window vent and partially because of the loud whoosh of air the bus let out before the driver hit the gas.

"Put this on," my mother says as she hands me a balled-up sweater. I recognize it from my kindergarten graduation. She wore a green dress along with it and she looked like an ebony statue in crisp sharp clothing. Almost as if she were a paper mâché doll. Long lashes, glistening teeth, and a floating air about her.

I put the dull, worn garment on and take out a book *Are You There, God? It's Me, Margaret.* I chose it from the school library because Margaret is close to my name, although spelled differently. I don't want to admit that I am always asking if God is there myself. Maybe this Margaret found him, and I'll know what to do when I finish the book. I look at my mother. She is dozing off. I want to ask her about breasts, just like Margaret does in the book. I'm not sure if I should wake her, but I yearn to talk to her.

"What are breasts?" I ask, shaking her shoulder.

"These," she says, quickly pointing her finger back and forth at her chest, not opening her eyes. "Why?" she adds.

"Because this girl in the book is asking God for them."

"You get them naturally. God created women that way so they can feed their babies."

"What? Food comes out of those things?" It seems a ridiculous notion.

"No, milk. Babies drink it until they are big enough for real food."

"Did you do that with me and Shelly?" I ask in utter horror.

"Nope," she mutters while waving her hand once in the air as if she were excused from such actions. "Both of you were bottle fed; it was hard for my body to make milk." Her eyes are halfway open. She can tell this conversation is not going away.

"Well why does she want them?"

"Who?"

"The girl in the book. Margaret."

"Because she is being a sass, too much for her own age. Girls grow them when it's time. When they get older."

I look over at her in the seat next to me on that cold dark bus. Her breasts lie flat under her wrinkled sweatshirt. Tired and used. Not like anything that would feed babies. I remember once seeing my grandmother putting on a bra with only one pad and wondered if she asked God for one or two.

"Why did Grandma have only one?" I whisper so no one else will hear me.

"Have one what? Here, eat this," she says while handing me a ham and cheese sandwich she bought from the corner store before we got on the train in our neighborhood.

"One breast, like in my book."

"No, your grandmother had two breasts, like all women. She got sick. She had what's called breast cancer. It's a disease. And the doctors had to take one to help her get better. But she got sick again and they couldn't do anything more for her after all the medication. After a long time in the hospital, she died." Her voice starts to crack and she turns to look out the window to darkness.

This is the first time she has ever talked to me about how and why Grandma passed away.

"Is that why I didn't see her much before I went to North Carolina that summer?"

"Yes, she was very sick, and she didn't want you and your sister to see her that way," she says, not turning from the window.

I would have loved more time with her, regardless. "I wouldn't have minded at all," I say.

"Yes, we know. She loved you and Shelly very much, and she was afraid you would be too sad to see her so sick."

"Ma, can you pass me my sandwich please?" Shelly says through the slim space between me and Mom's chair. Mom passes her sandwich and her drink over my head. Shelly's hand appears and disappears like a turtle snatching food and retreating into its shell.

"Are you going to get cancer?" I ask tentatively, fearing she will say the same thing my grandmother used to say, which turned out to be untrue—that she would be here forever. We have no one else. And I'll truly feel like we would be orphans if we have no mother.

"Of course not! Don't be silly, now read your book." She reaches up and holds onto the chair in front of her to get on her tip toes to reach the overhead light.

This is the first time Mom has talked about Grandma without changing the subject or being able to leave the room. She can't yell or snap on the bus because she hates embarrassing herself.

My breath softens and I smile at her with my eyes. I picture her at my kindergarten graduation, clapping and waving at me while my grandmother snapped pictures. As much as I am saddened by God giving Grandma a cancerous breast, I like to think that my mother is telling me something I have wondered about since the day it happened. Talking to me without making me feel like I am this energy that hinders her existence.

The bus is driving toward the George Washington Bridge. I am not scared of it anymore. I know it connects New York and New Jersey. I colored both states when I drew the map for an assignment Mrs. Henderson gave us in school. But that bridge connects way more than just two states. It also connects me to my grandmother at the little church. It leads me to the garden and the cornfields where I help my great-grandmother with chores because she is not as mobile as she used to be. It also holds the bus that just gave me a glimpse of hope about happiness with my mother.

CHAPTER 3

The summer passes quickly, as does my hope that things with Mom will improve. Grandma would call and write me often while we were in North Carolina, so in comparison, my mother's lack of communication is loud and meaningful.

Once back home, my mother stops attending our recitals. She is a constant no-show at the fifth-grade parent-teacher meetings and seems to pawn us off to anyone who feels sorry for her. Worse than the favors are the one-shot deals. We are hauled off to school by person after person, until we eventually walk to school alone. The more I want her to be different, the more she disappoints me.

It is even worse having a sister who seems to do the right thing in every situation. "You should be more like your sister," Mom says so often that I constantly feel like she likes Shelly more than me. I grow to hate her with every fiber of my small being. When we are home alone for what seems like a bottomless pit of hours, I look through old bags, clothes, worn boxes, and the kitchen. Always the kitchen.

"What are you looking for?" Shelly asks one day as she sits by the window looking out, searching for Mom or whatever.

"I don't know, anything, I guess. I don't know how you act like you are not mad that Mom leaves us here and does nothing for us."

"How do you know I don't care. I just don't really know what we can do." Shelly wraps her arms around her knees.

"I heard you crying last night. You miss grandma too, right?" I ask as I dig my hands under the flattened sofa cushion.

"I miss her, I miss how things were and I hate feeling lost and lonely."

I look up, frozen. "You feel lost and lonely?" I ask, not moving my arm from under the sofa cushion. Shelly always seemed to handle things better than I did. She usually didn't show or speak much about feelings. I am surprised she is telling me this.

"I hear you crying at times too." Shelly says. She walks over and sits on the side of the sofa I already searched.

I pull my hand out, turn and lean against the sofa to sit on the floor. I think of how I purposely hold my feelings in now. I used to show my sadness to Shelly all the time. Even though my sadness came from an emotional cartoon or movie. And when I cried when leaving for North Carolina and leaving North Carolina to come back to New York.

My crying now is heavier, more painful. I don't cry as much. And I am surprised at that. I truly thought I was the only one who missed grandma so much.

I open my hand and stare at the dollar bill I grabbed under the sofa seat. I turn, grab my school bag and pull out the two cupcakes I took from another kid's lunch tray. I hand one to Shelly.

"I found a dollar under the seat. One of Mom's friends may have lost it last night. I will give you half when we go to school tomorrow. I can get change from the corner store."

Shelly opens the cupcake wrapper, "Where did you get these from?"

"Who cares where I got them from. Never question the pleasure. Just enjoy it," I say as I take a big bite of mine.

We sit in the now dusk filled living room looking at a dull wall. The sounds of rustling cupcake wrappers floating above our heads.

Why is it that when I feel sad, things that seem like they are bad to do, make me feel so good?

One day, I find a bottle of Smirnoff under the kitchen sink. I have never seen anyone drink it, but I know it is liquor. I take a giant swig. Holy burning. I feel like my throat is torched. It takes what seems like forever to stop stinging. When it does, I forget I am angry, lonely, and especially sad. I feel so sad at only ten years old.

The little me, the girl in me, is quieted by the liquor. A new me is born from that drink. A girl with sharper edges, who doesn't need people and who doesn't feel sad. Yet the thought of hating her makes me sick to my stomach. I feel I'll be punished by God and Grandma in some way for hating her. I take a few more swigs and the feeling fades away, along with the stinging in my throat.

I could get used to this feeling.

My mother and uncle both work in hospital administration and he has arranged to dress up as Santa and hand out toys to the kids. They clap and wave at Santa as he arrives. My uncle and the nurses and doctors are dancing to the Christmas music, singing along. "Santa Claus is coming to town, yea yea!" Looking at the joyous scene in front of me, I remember Grandma's words: "Christmas is about our Lord and savior, Jesus. Not about asking for things. The way life gives us miracles is when we give; not just give but give with love and no expectations," she used to say.

Seeing the kids in wheelchairs, walkers, or jumping up and down outside of their rooms is so exciting. We go into the common playroom, and everyone comes in to get gifts. As we help hand them out, the happiness I feel is inexplicable. Watching my uncle belt out "Ho Ho Ho" sends a lovely shiver through my body. For the children who can't make it out of bed to the playroom, we get a list of room numbers and deliver the toys.

"This is from Santa," I say. "He will be by to say 'hello' soon."

"Really? Will he come to my room?" they ask.

"Yes," I promise. "He wants to see all the children."

One of the kids hugs me, and I almost start crying. I wonder where his parents are and if Santa has ever come to his house.

As I leave the hospital after the event, I feel lighter. Giving to others feels so good. Seeing the happiness on their faces when Santa remembers them makes me temporarily forget that since Grandma died, Santa and Jesus both seem to have forgotten me.

And they aren't the only people who seem to be overlooking my existence. I've also noticed a noticeable decline in visitors to our apartment. Even when I do make friends, Mom ensures they don't get too close and doesn't allow Shelly or me to have our friends over. Still, I keep trying to make them.

"Hi, Patti." I hug my old friend in front of our gym class.

"Hi, Margarette. I haven't seen you in a while. Do you want to play tag with those girls across the gym? I played with them last week. They were nice."

"Sure," I say as we drop our bags on the floor against the wall of the gym and join the game.

Patti, short for Patricia, is a little taller than me, which is why I initially noticed her while standing in line for the lunchroom last year. She was in the same grade, but taller.

"That girl is a giraffe!" Brian said while the other kids snickered. "I bet she got left back and is older than we are!"

Patti turned around, barreled through the line, and pushed Brian so hard that he fell to the floor.

"Say that again and I'll do worse!" she said, turning like a graceful dancer and reclaimed her place in the line. Brian scrambled to his feet, lowering his head while the kids, including me, laughed at him.

"Patti, you have detention!" Mrs. Fletcher, the hall monitor, heckled like a strained bird from the back of the line.

"Hmmf," Patti grunted and shrugged her shoulders. "Here," she said as she slid her apple sauce to me, clearly noticing I had already polished mine off.

"I'm sorry you got detention. He deserved to get knocked on the floor," I said.

"I don't care about detention. I hate smart-mouth kids. He won't say anything to me from now on. I will only have detention today. He will look stupid forever."

I laughed like I was being tickled inside and immediately knew I liked her. She was a sweetheart and a stand-up-for-yourself girl in the same body. She wasn't scared of punishment, and I figured I could learn a lot from her.

We met at the lunchroom for breakfast most mornings. Sometimes she walked to my building and called up to my window or rang the bell.

But over the last year, we drifted apart, and seeing her at gym class brings back the memories of the fun we used to have. I want to invite her over and bring some light into the darkness that has formed in our apartment.

"Can Patti come upstairs?" I ask my mom one morning.

Without opening her eyes, buried under the clothing on the bed, she blew out, "NO!"

Back at school, I don't want to admit the truth. "I asked my mom if you could come up. She said one day after school; she will tell me when," I say.

I feel angry lying for my mother when I don't know why she won't let her, or anyone else come up. Doesn't she want me to have friends? I'm persistent, so I ask for after-school time with her or to go to her apartment. Again, Mom says no, and when I ask why, her infamous reply is, "Because I said so. Ask me again and you will regret it."

I don't know what that means, but I don't want to find out. The idea of what might come worries me. Who would have thought someone could have so much sadness and worry at only ten years old?

At home I worry, and at school I worry. "You are not as interested in class, young lady," Mrs. Harrison says one day, as she takes her glasses off.

"I don't know why, Mrs. Harrison. But I don't find school fun anymore."

"Well, why is that?" She is holding a test paper I took earlier today.

I watch the kids file out of class for lunch and recess, anxious to get to lunch myself. That has been my one certain meal other than the school breakfast.

"I guess I'm sad. I miss my grandma."

"Yes, my dear. Your uncle stopped by at the beginning of the school year and told me that your grandma is in Heaven. I know that must be very sad for you."

I want to leave. Why had my uncle come to school and told Mrs. Harrison about Grandma? *Why wouldn't my mom do that?* I don't want to talk to Mrs. Harrison; she can't possibly understand what it's like to lose the one person who made me feel good all the time. Plus, I'm missing lunch!

"You didn't do well on your spelling test. You also didn't do well on your math test."

"My grandma used to help me. I don't understand the work as much now."

"Isn't your mother helping you?" she asks, as she puts my test under a pile of other papers. I notice the first paper has 100 written on it.

"Ah, she ah…"

"Don't say ahhh, young lady. Ahh means you looking for something to say other than what you feel. What is it? Does she help you or not?" She gently squeezes my hand.

My stomach starts to grumble. I'm tapping my foot and biting my lip. I don't want to tell her that my mother sleeps all day and spends time with grownups in the apartment at night, or that some days she isn't home at all. It feels wrong to tell her the truth. Even though Grandma always said that the truth is always the right thing to say.

"Yes, all the time. My sister helps too. I guess I just don't remember when we take a test."

"Okay, well maybe if I talk to her, we can come up with a plan to help you with your sadness. I'm sure that's what's wrong, you sweet child." She hands me a small envelope and a peppermint, and I'm reminded of the way Grandma gave me peppermints. I loved them.

"Give this to your mother, okay?" she says, handing me a small envelope. "Remember you can always talk to your grandma in Heaven. She is watching over you. I want you to know that. God also has people here to look after you. Now run along to lunch before recess is over."

I spend the rest of recess chucking down lunch and even eating someone's leftovers that were abandoned on the table. I'm too hungry to worry about the letter until I meet Shelly to walk home. On our way home from school I'm feeling nervous, knowing that Mrs Harrison wants a meeting with my mother, and I don't know how Mom will react.

The note from my teacher moves to the back of my mind when we arrive home and there is a huge padlock on the door with a sticker that says, "City Marshal Eviction Notice". What does that mean?

There is another note on the door affixed with the same tape, the two notices now politely sharing space. The note is written in my mother's beautiful, scrolling handwriting.

Go upstairs to Mrs. Jones' place.

That's all it says. We don't move. We only keep staring at the words on the papers. Eviction, Mrs. Jones, Notice, Premise sealed by Marshall Sheriff. The chain—the big, chipped silver chain—protruding through the door lock.

We go upstairs and knock on Mrs. Jones' door. "Come in!" she calls from inside. Mrs. Jones is an older, heavy woman. She is my friend Tonya's grandmother, and Tonya stays with her on weekends, and sometimes during the week when her mother works odd hours.

Mr. Jones is much shorter with a big voice, and he loves to go jogging. He often says, "People should always exercise when they got the chance. It's good for the heart!" They have a big German Shepherd named Duke, and Mr. Jones takes him to run at Riverside Park. Duke is nice and is in the living room when we walk down the hallway of the apartment. He runs up to us and I bend down and let him lick my face. I start to giggle.

"Duke, let that girl alone, no jumping!"

"Hello, Mrs. Jones. I like when Duke jumps on me. It's fun."

Without missing a beat or looking away from the television, she says,

"You girls want something to eat? There's sandwiches and juice in the kitchen for you both. Wash your hands."

"Thank you. Come on, Duke," I say, and he trots behind me.

I sit in the kitchen and look out the window toward the courtyard. Everything is quiet, the courtyard is gloomy; the sun doesn't seem to spill over the roof into the space anymore. Her kitchen looks like my Gram's kitchen in North Carolina. Dining table with metal trim and chairs with plush plastic worn cushions, ripped in some places and sharp in others. Her kitchen smells good, like food was always visiting and didn't want to leave. The ham and cheese sandwich is delicious, and the cherry Kool Aid is like juice from Heaven. I reach down and give Duke a couple pieces of my bread. He is so happy when I give him snacks. Since Grandma died, Shelly and I haven't liked the food at home much, and I feel like a pig in mud eating this sandwich.

Shelly wipes her eyes. I pet Duke to distract myself. I don't want to ask her why she is crying. I want to cry too. I have no idea what happened with our apartment. As much as I hate living there, all of a sudden, I miss it.

I clean up and go into the living room. Mrs. Jones is still sitting in her recliner chair, staring at the television.

The living room is covered in carpet and plastic. There are big sofas and a clunky coffee table. A huge floor model TV framed in shiny burgundy wood sits on the smallest wall. I think they must be rich. Our apartment has no carpet or plastic on the worn sofa. No plushy over-stuffed recliners. And the TV is tiny compared to theirs.

"Thank you again for the sandwich. Do you know where my mom is?" I ask as I sit on the floor next to Duke.

"Hopefully somewhere working on getting you back into your apartment," she says sharply.

"Why is that chain on our door?"

Her eyes narrow to a thin slit, like an almost sleeping cat that is secretly watching everything. "Don't know, child, I'm sure you have homework to do. Then you can watch TV until your mom gets back."

I open my notebook, the cover and pages held together by scraps of masking tape and pretend to read and do work. The letter Mrs. Harrison gave me for my mother falls out. I hold it and remember the letters I wrote to grandma. I wonder what my teacher wrote. I want to open it, but it's sealed as tight as Fort Knox. Mrs. Harrison must have licked that envelope a million times to get it to stick like that.

I feel a lump in my throat, like I am standing backstage waiting for a part in a show, but the creator, dancers, and stage crew have no idea I exist. I feel tears welling up in my eyes. I hold back, refusing to cry in front of Mrs. Jones because I don't know what she would do. I don't know whether she'd yell at me or hug me. I want to know what's going on, but this is adult business. I'm not allowed to ask questions of grown-ups, so I don't ask Mrs. Jones anything else. I look around for Shelly, who is hunkered down in the other corner of the room. She isn't saying a word.

I shove the letter back into the notebook and scribble gibberish on a blank page to make it seem like I am doing something. "Can I go to Dave's room?" Dave is Tonya's older brother, and he lives here with his grandparents.

His room has everything in it: a record player, TV, radio, and Henry the turtle! Henry thumps across his glass case so slowly, and I wonder if he ever gets frustrated about his travel time. He even eats his lettuce slowly. Good thing turtles know how to store food. As I watch him inch his way toward his destination, I marvel at his thick shell, a great shield from things that want to eat or otherwise hurt him.

Flipping through Dave's records, I glance at Ella Fitzgerald, Etta James, Louis Armstrong, and Nina Simone, then stop because I love how she looks. Kind of like a Star Trek character, glaring out from the record cover's tan background, like she can see everything inside of me. I don't remember ever hearing her, so I put the record on and turn the volume low, so Mrs. Jones doesn't stop me from using the player.

I Put a Spell on You starts to play. The first bar of the music is as slow as Henry, but it's carrying me to another place. Her voice is not very feminine, but it's strong and definite. She isn't joking around at all. I am spellbound by the different tones in her voice. I wonder if she is ever sad, like me. She sounds and looks different to the other female singers I like, and I feel drawn to her for that. I don't know if she ever feels lost, but she takes control of the black hole I felt inside before I played the song. I forget that I am not in my own apartment. I am with Nina and her spells, making life right again.

The trance is broken when Shelly comes into the room. She plonks herself down on the bed and starts to cry. "What does this mean?" she says through her tears. "Do we have to live with the Jones' now?"

I walk over and put my arms around her, but before I can say anything, Mr. Jones comes in. He gives us both a hug and says, "Hey, kiddos, what ya up to?"

"Oh, nothing... Just listening to music and watching Henry," I say.

"Your mom is here so you can get your bag. Did you eat something and do a little exercise today?" His voice commanding and yet kind as he quizzes us both.

"Yes, sir!" we say, and he gives us each a high five.

I head out first and walk toward the kitchen, then hear my mother's low voice. Mrs. Jones is responding, and I can only hear snatches of their conversation. "You can do better... those children ... Sarah."

They stop when they see me walk past. I grab my bag.

"Thank you for the food and for letting us hang with Henry, Mrs. Jones."

My mother is already at the door, and we scurry behind her. We walk down the stairs to our apartment. She doesn't look back at us or say a word.

"The stickers are gone. Who put that chain there and why couldn't we go in? What is a Marshall? Was there something wrong with the house, Mom?"

Slamming the door behind her, she storms into the apartment. She is under five feet tall, so at this point, I am almost her height. She doesn't have to bend down anymore as her finger pokes and jabs me on my forehead.

"Keep asking questions like that and watch what will happen to you." She is almost growling, clenching her teeth.

My lip starts trembling. "But I..." I hold back tears and my voice is cracking.

"I said stop being grown and fresh. It's no one's business either. Don't you let me hear that you opened your mouth. You hear me?" She jabs me two more times, harder.

I let the tears fall, flowing down my cheeks, lips, and chin, then dripping down my neck and onto my dingy shirt.

"Yea." My confusion turns to anger, and I can't understand her reaction to what I feel are simple questions. Why is she like this and why isn't Shelly defending me? I can hear her whimpering in the bathroom.

Her hand turns into a frog's tongue with a fist, and she whips that fist at me so fast and punches me square in the head, so hard I feel dizzy. Her hitting me with such abrupt force feels like being stung by the snake that was right under my nose. She would never have thought of doing that to me if Grandma was here. My stomach is tight, from, fear, and madness.

"Don't you ever say 'Yea' to me. Who do you think you are talking to?!"

I can't get an answer out from beyond my uncontrollable weeping. I look her in the eyes. I don't know what possesses me to do that. The anger is almost numbing me.

"Yesssss…" I say with what sounds like a hiss.

Her face and mouth soften. Her eyes lower. She turns slowly and walks into the kitchen while I stand there, dumbfounded. *What the heck just happened?* I've seen her back down against adults, but never me. I am the only person she is normally angry towards, not Shelly. But this time I cry, and she retreats. Her clenched teeth and short patience are normal to me, but not this.

I walk into the bedroom and sit on the cold, wrinkled bed. *The letter,* I think. *I want her to read it.* I want her to sit with Mrs. Harrison and tell her why I'm not happy in school. I want Mrs. Harrison to see that she isn't my grandma. Mom is something else. Something my grandma would not like. I don't like her anymore either. And if Mrs. Harrison saw for herself, Mom would feel bad, say she was sorry for what she'd done, and change.

While mom is slamming pots into the sink, Shelly and I are eating another sad and very small looking meal. I walk into the kitchen and say, "My teacher wanted me to give this to you." I say, not looking at her. I just hand it to her and sit back in my chair. I am welcomed again by the three chunks of cheese struggling to look appropriate on a plastic plate. Three chunks—not cut but gouged off and jagged edged as if an animal got to them before they were smashed between two pieces of stale, sorry-looking bread.

"What does it say? What did you do?" she says with her

automatic clenched teeth. I take a deep breath. She takes the letter and walks into her room. I hear her door slam shut.

I lie in my cold bed, hoping or wishing something or someone would take me away from her. The little radio on station WBLS is playing a song by Gladys Knight, "Midnight Train to Georgia." I want to be on that train with Gladys and her band. It sounds fun. Then again, anything sounds more fun than lying in this bed feeling lost and lonely.

I think about what Mrs. Harrison said about talking to Grandma; that she is watching over me. I don't truly believe that, because if it were true, my mother wouldn't be so mean. Mom can't believe that God or Grandma is watching over us, so why should I? I decide in this moment not to talk to Grandma or God anymore.

The door opens a crack, and my mom pokes her head in. "Your teacher wants to see me. I don't have time for that, so whatever the problem is, you better start gettin' yourself together," she says, and closes the door without giving me the opportunity to reply.

All day I've been dreading her reading that letter, but now I can't decide what's worse getting into trouble, or her thinking that I'm not even worth a trip in to see my teacher to find out why I'm not doing very well in school. At least if I got into trouble, I'd know it's because she expects better.

No, I decide the latter is much, much worse.

Why doesn't she care?! What did I do wrong?! The heat rises up in my body, and I clench my fists, as though it will stop the tears which are threatening to spill out my eyes and onto the pillow. I will not cry because of her right now.

I turn and look at Shelly in bed. She is snoring a little so I know she is sleeping. I jump out of bed to find the Bible I threw into the closet a few weeks ago—I want to rip it to pieces, just like my heart.

When I pull the closet door open, a bottle of clear liquid falls out. It looks just like the drink that made me feel better last time. Forgetting about the Bible, I lie back in bed and sip out of the bottle. A warmth comes over me, and I welcome the sensation as the angry feelings start to fade away. I feel sleepy listening to the low conversations on the street, a few car horns, and the radio. Slow music is playing. Drifting off into a slumber feels nice, and the bed finally feels warm.

CHAPTER 4

Jacques d'Amboise gazes around the room, looking at us with deep intent, curiosity, and light in his eyes. He touches our heads, shakes our hands, hugs us, and bows to us while helping us learn to curtsey. He walks tall and has the skill of being able to look us right in the eyes. When he smiles, the room blooms and lets in the calmness I love in dance studios. My 12-year-old body immediately wants to hug him.

"I own a company named National Dance Institute," he says. "And I visit schools around this country and other countries, and we all study dance in a fun way. We believe that a child fully embraces themselves when there are no tight rules and definitions of expression."

He told us he attended Julliard; was a principal dancer with the New York City Ballet, and Balanchine was his mentor. He inspires me to embrace dance without having any fears. He looks brutish, rough, and wild, yet his tenderness is overwhelming. He doesn't look like anyone I've seen in my neighborhood, and he cares about us as if we are his own children.

They came to our middle school to choose children to be a part of the company. They perform all over the country, and at the end of the school year, they have a massive performance at Madison Square Garden. *Wow, what a way to see and meet other kids.* Plus, to be on stage at Madison Square Garden is a dream. The concerts I hear my mom and family talk about are things I've believed I'll never see, let alone be on the same stage that has been shared by world-famous athletes and musicians.

We are in a trance. We all stare at him, hanging onto his every word.

The young lady with him, Ellen, wears a purple t-shirt that says NDI. She smiles at us, waves, and giggles and tells us to all stand behind Jacques.

Then, they attach a speaker to the class radio, put on a tape, and ask us to follow along with them. The beat is that of a hip hop/jazz combination. We all bop our heads and tap our feet.

"Slap your thigh with your hands, to the rhythm. Then shout whatever you want: FREE, LOVE, KITE—anything you want—on the fourth beat."

We all laugh while we shout out words. I choose "cry" because that's what I want to do. I don't know if I want to cry because I am so happy or because this class is going to end soon, and I'll have to go home, where there are no Jacques or Mr. Garcias or Ellens.

Jacques has us jump around and flail our arms like we are funky monkeys. We are all being silly and having so much fun. He weaves in and out of us and takes our hands, spinning us around like we are line dancing in a cowboy country scene. I guess we impress them, because a week later a letter will arrive, inviting us to join them at the National Dance Institute.

We run home, excited to tell Mom that we got in. "We got accepted to the National Dance Institute! Can you believe they practice at the same school as *Fame* on the weekends?" I say, beaming towards her as she sits watching the football. Shelly is bouncing beside me.

Without looking over her shoulder, Mom replies, "Good job!" reacting better than I had expected. I make a mental note to always talk about important things while she is glued to football.

I am a huge fan of the TV show *Fame*. I am glued to the television every week to watch the show and am immersed in the lives of the dancers. *That's going to be my life,* I think. *I'm going to have my dance family around me at school every day. Debbie Allen is going to be like my mother.* The idea of dancing every day is intoxicating to me;

it is all I want. I am disappointed to learn that the NDI classes held at LaGuardia on weekends are not even in the same building as the show. Nonetheless, I am still excited about having a new family at school, just like at Harlem School of the Arts, and just like the kids of Fame. Of course I have a family, but since Grandma died, I feel like we've become disconnected and ill-fitting, much like a rogue leftover piece in a jigsaw puzzle.

Taking the train down there seems like going through a force field and emerging into another world altogether. The fountain, the Metropolitan Opera, and Avery Fisher Hall are all astounding to see in person. The school doesn't look like the actual school in the TV show, but it is the school the show was based on, and I am so proud to be able to go there.

Our first meeting with the company is the following weekend, and I ask my mom for the money we'll need for travel and food. "Here," she says, sliding four dollars across the table. What happened to the happy woman who congratulated us when we were accepted? What changed? I look at the four singles and my heart sinks. It's just enough for train fare, so we have to choose between eating lunch and walking eighty blocks home.

Still, my excitement is bigger than my trepidation. I am going to see inside Lincoln Center for the first time. As the train goes through the dark tunnels, I feel a jolt and my heart races. We are in another world, a world that is not Harlem. The performance is in Avery Fisher Hall, and we have rehearsals there for two days before the show. The red carpets seem to scold me for being out of my normal environment, and I push the lack of support from my mother to the back of my mind. I can't help feeling special for being here. It is one of the most beautiful places I have ever seen, aside from church.

The staff and Jacque choreograph a dance called "We Real Cool" based on a poem by Gwendolyn Brooks, and the piece is going to be part of the show. The music is slow jazz, instrumental, and the story is about a group of kids who feel they are too cool for school and live a street life of hustle, prostitution, drugs, theft, and eventually death. The words are limited; the music and dance steps say it all.

"We real cool… We left school… We lurk late… We strike straight… We sing sin… We thin gin… We jazz June… We…die…soon…"

As the dancers tell the story, they mirror each phase, and by the end they fade into a graffiti wall, their silhouettes traced within a mosaic of beautiful chaos. The chaos swallows them up, and they disappear from the world, the piano, trumpet, bass, and horn fading with them. I always cry while watching that creation, from the beginning rehearsals to the full-fledged performances. As a new, young dancer, I am part of the rehearsals for this piece, but not part of the final number. I love being there so much that I work hard every day. We both make friends there, but I barely even notice my sister in the classes with me. This feels like *my* thing. NDI has become my family, and a home away from the home that saddens me so much.

There are times we are invited to rehearse at Jacque's home on the west side. He lives in a brownstone near Riverside Drive. The group of us meet there, and he has lunch for us set up in a dance studio he has created on the top floor. The wood and lighting look like that of an old marquee theater, one filled with warmth and love. We can make as much noise as we want to because the whole house belongs to him.

I have too much fun and want to stay forever. He always tells us that the arts are God's gift to humans and that everyone has a path in them. That we must appreciate our uniqueness and never let anyone take that away from us. I wish my mother felt the same. With significant effort, I am able to get the necessary train and bus fare from her, but nothing else. No dance clothes, no lunch money, nothing extra that would help us get by more easily. But I'm surprised she allows us to go at all, so I keep quiet and figure out how to stay involved despite her lack of support.

The chilly December air cracks against the window, and although my bedroom is warm and dry, I feel cold inside. My beloved *The Nutcracker* is playing on the small TV in my room, and I know every movement, every step. I used to perform parts of it in the living room for Shelly and Grandma, but Grandma is no longer here, and the emptiness I feel inside is palpable.

I hear the sounds of my mother's friends in the living room, laughing, swearing, teasing. They sit around a square table, playing cards and drinking, paying no attention to me. I listen to their voices and the disco music mixing with the music from the television. I haven't cried much since being back in New York, but my eyes water while watching Clara run around her living room on the TV screen. Why does she get to play in the living room and have a great time? My eyelids feel heavy, and my mother's laugh fades away. After the heaviness of the day, I welcome the reprieve of sleep.

However, my slumber doesn't bring the relief I was hoping for. My dream turns into a nightmare when I start by dancing the nutcracker and soon it morphs into a hallucination from Harlem hell, including a devilish Uncle Drosselmeyer with a maniacal laugh, an evil, broken nutcracker, and my grandma in the audience fading away. I toss and turn, sweat drenching my sheets, and just as a snake wraps itself around my neck, I scream out in my sleep and wake myself up.

I almost jump out of my bed, gripping the thin sheet and panting like a thirsty dog. Across the room is Shelly in the other bed, the sunlight spotlighting the dingy wrinkled sheets, a reminder that I am home.

I have always loved The Nutcracker, as it was special to my grandma and me, so why am I seeing it in a nightmare? I draw my knees to my chest and try to slow my rapid breathing, relieved that the nightmare isn't real and sad that my reality isn't much different.

Grandpa must have arrived while I was sleeping. I hear his voice, like a low thunder, saying something to my mother in the living room. I want to run out and hug him. I haven't seen him since he brought us back from North Carolina in August. We spoke on the phone when he called. I made sure I spoke to Gram, and she talked about how much she enjoyed my letters. Writing to her more became something I felt I had to do. I needed another kind of grandmother.

She couldn't replace my grandma, but she cared and loved me. The letter connection felt like a way to ease the pain of never getting a letter from Grandma again. Gram couldn't write letters because of her ailing hands, but she received my letters, and then she'd call and we'd talk. I realize that I haven't heard from them in a while and wonder why they don't call anymore.

The sound of my grandpa's voice getting louder brings me back to the moment. "Did you have your phone cut off, Stephanie?" he asks. I'm not sure what he means. What is wrong with the phone? I hear Mom stuttering and responding with short answers. Grandpa snaps back. The air in our room seems to tremble. Just when I want to hop up and go see him, the sound of the apartment door slamming tells me that Grandpa left. And I didn't get to see him.

I sleep in Grandma's bed. I try to imagine Grandma there and I am lying next to her like before. If I try hard enough, maybe she will appear and prove that this was all a long-drawn-out horrible dream.

The heavy feeling in the apartment isn't the only place there is a gaping hole. Every weekend before dance practice, I search for something I can take with me that will resemble the homemade meals the other girls bring to class. But the kitchen cabinets once stuffed with treats, snacks, and food are replaced with white and black boxes of food that are handed out at the church line. Nothing I can take and go.

I feel like a scavenger, hunting in the woods—except, instead of acorns and pinecones, I find a molded piece of cheese and bread. The once clean apartment has turned into piles of clothes, paper, dust, and roaches. There is an all-out war between me and those thoughtless, relentless creatures. I scramble to put what I can into plastic bags to keep the roaches and mice out. Not being allowed to use the stove, the most eaten commodities are cereal and powdered milk. Thank goodness for peanut butter and jelly, although the roaches did get into the jar of jelly, despite it being in the fridge. They died from suffocation, and I realize that my breathing doesn't feel any freer than theirs; it is as though I am being swallowed up by the quicksand of my life.

There are a few cans of beer and a half empty bottle of liquor squeezed into the corner behind the dishrack, remnants of the gathering Mom had last night. I look around quickly to make sure I'm alone and drink the beers. Apart from the warm feeling it gives me, I notice that I'm not so hungry anymore. I take the liquor bottle and stash it in my room to save for later.

The kitchen isn't the only place my mom falls short. Gram had taught Shelly and me how to wash clothes by hand and mend holes. I start digging out whatever I can find to wash, sick of going to school and dance class wearing mended but dirty, stinky clothes.

I feel so far away from my mother and am nervous, if not outright scared, to speak to her. I often wonder while staring at her through a crack in the door to her room, *What happened to her? Why is she so sad? Why won't she have anything to do with us?* I start to feel like I am the reason she never laughs and dances anymore. Even though Shelly says that isn't true; Mom isn't that much different with her.

One day, I come home from school and my uncle is gone, along with my little cousin. He used to take us to the circus, parades, and the museum. I have a feeling all that is over. I hate that my grandma was the first to go. Did she go because my mother was mean? Did everyone else follow just to get away from her? I start to say something to Shelly, but she is already down the hall, banging on Mom's bedroom door, asking where he is. Mom doesn't respond or even open the door. Maybe that's my answer.

I feel like I don't mean anything to anyone. Why are Shelly and I the only ones left? Left with the one person who is supposed to love me like Grandma did but doesn't? My hatred for my mother is biting, and I wish she'd gone to Heaven instead.

CHAPTER 5

I shift my focus to winning my mother's love by attempting to be great at everything. Everyone in seventh grade is given a catalog and order form to sell Girl Scout cookies. My bed creeks as I scoot back to lean on the wall and open the catalog.

Someone is walking by outside with a boombox playing It's the *End of the World as We Know It*. I know that song because Uncle Allan likes groups like REM and U2. He was blasting it on the radio when it first aired. "You are too young to understand real music kiddo," he had said as I watched him mimicking drum sounds to the band.

"Just because I am twelve doesn't mean I don't understand good music."

He stopped his drumming, looked at me and said, "You know, you may be right." We giggled together while REM filled the room with their voices.

I am annoyed now because my song was getting drowned out by the boombox interruption outside. As I close the window, I bob my head to *Faith* by George Michael playing on my little radio on my bed.

I carefully look through the pages to see how many cookies we have to sell to win each of the different prizes. I want us to be the best sellers and get the best prize.

There, on the last page, is a pink and white bicycle with shiny silver streaks, and I convince Shelly that we can share it. I figure we can always split the work, with Shelly going around one part of the apartment building and the other buildings on the street, and me going around the other half, getting as many sales as we can.

Right after school, I wait on the stoop of the building and make a few sales to people I know before they go inside. I keep at it until it starts to get dark, and my mother surprisingly lets us go to as many apartments as we can over the next week.

I keep the money with me the whole time. The last night of selling, we count the money in our room. We've made $333, and everyone paid us right there on the spot. That bicycle is all ours, and we even have a little left over for a tin bucket of variety popcorn! My mother will be proud that she no longer has to listen to me bug her about getting a bike.

I put the money in the bottom drawer of the dresser, which is on the landing outside our bedroom doors. We use it for odds and ends, and it's the perfect place to hide my money. I slip the money under a bunch of old clothes and dream of riding that bike with my tin of popcorn nestled in my backpack.

The next morning, I hop out of bed and, after grabbing my book bag and coat, go to get the money. But it isn't there. I throw everything out of that drawer, even look in all the other drawers. I ask Shelly if she took it, but she says no. My stomach sinks. There is no way I didn't put that envelope into that specific drawer. What is even more strange is the fact that the order form and catalog are there, the coveted bicycle still circled, and the envelope is there. But it is empty.

The door to my mother's room is closed as always, and I bang on it. Hard. I couldn't care less if she hits me for being rude.

"Where is the money for the Girl Scout sale?!" I scream, already holding in the cry that makes my chest feel like it will explode. She jerks open the door and looks at me through slitted eyes and a tight mouth.

"Who do you think you are yelling at?" she demands.

"Where is the money? We worked hard to sell those cookies, and we have to turn it in today."

"I don't know what you're talking about. You probably lost it," she flatly states, her finger jabbing me in the chest with every word. As she pushes me back with each stinging poke, I edge out the door and trip over the open drawer, falling onto my back. Every inch of anger comes out, the crying, screaming, rage, and hatred.

Shelly has come out of our room and is gaping helplessly at the scene unfolding before her.

"I didn't lose it, and why are you pushing me?" I scream at my mother. "You took it like you took everything else in this house. That was not yours to take, and what about everyone who bought cookies from us? Should we tell them that you stole it? What about our bike? *You* can't buy us one! We worked for that. I'll tell everyone that you stole it, and I'll tell my teacher too, because you did, you did, I hate you!" I can barely get it all out between breaths. My crying is so heavy it seems as assaulting as she is.

She punches me on my head twice, stopping my rant. I hold my head. Usually, I would have been scared to go farther, but not on this day.

"I will always hate you anyway, no matter what," I snarl, as I snatch my bag and leave. Shelly runs after me and doesn't even look back to see what Mom is doing.

Walking to school I am finally able to speak. "I can't believe Mom would take the money," I say.

"I know," Shelly says. "What are we going to do?"

"I wish she would die," is the only thing I can think of to say.

"That is a horrible thing to say. But I am so embarrassed and sad that she took the money that I can't blame you for feeling that way," Shelly says as I just stare straight ahead.

At school, Shelly hugs me and says, "Don't cry. It'll be okay." She disappears to the library, and I smell the breakfast from the cafeteria door as I stand outside. "Maybe everyone will know that she took the money," I think. My stomach is in knots. I am shaking with fear and anger. I don't want to admit that she took the money we worked so hard for. No wonder she let us visit all those people. She knew she was going to take it when she had the chance. I don't want to think of my mother as a thief. "Thou shall not steal" is one of the commandments I remember the most.

I knew that Mom has stolen other things. We used to play dress up with my grandma's beautiful leather bags, her fox fur that scared me half to death, and my favorite owl necklace she gave me on Christmas. I haven't seen them for a while and have the gut-wrenching realization that she has become a heartless thief with no limit to hurting or lying to us.

Does she even care that Grandma and God know what she has done? What hurts the most is her taking something I earned. I truly believe she hates us, and she can show it now that Grandma isn't around to protect us. The people who made home fun and full of love left because my mother is the devil. Stories in the Bible about hell and sin become my reality, and the major culprit is the woman I once had so much respect for.

A few kids run past me into the cafeteria, and I am reminded that I came to school early just to get breakfast. Yet another thing my mother took from us. Food. Sitting alone at the table, I cry into my french toast. Not from having lost the bike but from hatred, embarrassment, and sadness for all the people who trusted me with their future box of cookies.

My focus is blurry and clouded in class as my sixth-grade teacher, Mrs. Olive, is speaking. She wears glasses around her neck and has big dark curls and brown skin. The classroom always smells like flowers, but I never see any.

"Hello, young people," she greets us every morning.

"Hello, Mrs. Olive," we reply in unison.

She never yells or looks angry. When we are all talking at once, all she has to do is put her glasses on the tip of her nose, and we know to cut the chatter and listen up. I make sure to complete my assignments early because she always notices my work. Ever since our first eviction, the lights and phone have often been cut off in our apartment, so Shelly and I have spent many afternoons in the library, a neighbor's home, or the hallway doing homework. Whenever we are back in our apartment, but the lights are off, I use whatever candles I can find. My mother won't let us use candles in our bedroom, so I sit in the kitchen with the candles burning on the stove. This kind of existence, while frightening at first, has become normal.

I am terrified of Mrs. Olive asking us to turn in our Girl Scout envelopes.

I haven't been to a Girl Scout meeting since Grandma died.

Having the fundraiser through the school used to be fun. Dread comes over me for having to tell her what happened.

"Today is the day you all turn in your envelopes. I hope you all were able to sell enough to get the prizes you want. And the cookies are delicious for all your friends and family who bought them!"

She giggles, which is a rare sight. As kind as I feel she is, she's also quite stoic, so that giggle makes her more admirable.

Why doesn't she ever worry? Does she have children? Are they happy? I wonder. I don't want to disappoint her. I can't imagine what she will think of my mother. I figure I will slip out of class when it is time for recess, and she won't notice that I never gave her anything.

She gets up from her desk and starts collecting the packets from each kid, moving from desk to desk. *Oh my God... Can't she just let everyone pile them on top of her desk when we leave for lunch?*

This is grueling. Then I notice another kid who doesn't have anything. *Did his mother steal his money also?* I don't feel so alone now, but the embarrassment still feels stifling. Another kid asks to go to the bathroom and doesn't wait for permission to run out. *Maybe I should do that.* I have the feeling Mrs. Olive is smarter than that though and will ask me when she has the chance anyway.

She is two desks away. My eyes start to water, and my stomach feels like someone is kicking me repeatedly. Her scent is right under my nose as I hang my head down. "I don't have my package, Mrs. Olive." I can't lift my head; it is being held down by blocks of shame.

"Okay, dear, just see me after class, okay?"

"Yes, Mrs. Olive."

She places all the packets neatly on her desk, puts her silver glasses on, and looks around at the class.

"I want to congratulate everyone who did their best with the fundraiser.

There are no losers in the world. Only people who feel like they are losers. This whole fundraiser was for the benefit of the Girl Scouts and to help the school keep activates we all love like music and the arts."

I tried so hard to get my mother to pay attention to me and be proud, that I didn't anticipate this horrible failure of her doing. I barely went to dance class because of her, my piano lessons were in the wind, and now this. Defeat is an emotion not even close to how bad I feel.

The love I had of God has changed to anger, because he allowed this to happen to me. I don't care if he or my grandma know how much I hate them. My mother always seems to escape punishment, but I have never seen her read the Bible or attend church, so I shouldn't be surprised.

I'm starting to make a habit out of lying.

When class ends, I stand at Mrs. Olive's desk. "Ah," I start, and falter. I am choked up and panic. *Say something quick and get it over with...* "I didn't sell anything because I lost the packet, and I didn't know If I would be able to replace it. I'm sorry, Mrs. Olive."

The room is empty. Silence has never sounded so horrid. Two minutes could have passed, but it feels like an hour. I stare at the desk. I can't even look her in the eye. Part of me feels horrible. The thought of defending my mother is making me sick. I want to tell so badly but I can't bring myself to do it. On the other hand, I feel good lying to protect my mother, but not to Mrs. Olive. If she knew, I would feel awful because I respect her.

"I know you, young lady. You try your best at everything. I can't imagine you lost the packet and didn't say anything for two weeks."

I glance down at the well-worn hole in my sneaker and notice a new hole has appeared in the other. I bite my lip.

"Yes, I must have been too nervous. I didn't want to tell you I lost it."

She gets up and comes around to the front of her desk. She takes a deep breath and gives me a hug. There is no way I am going to cry. I am done crying. My mother has turned my sadness into anger, and I refuse to let Mrs. Olive know why I am so angry. While she hugs me, I wish she was my mother. I let my arms hug her back. That hug is the first time I've felt safe and loved in a long time.

"Well, no harm done except for your keeping quiet when you didn't have to. But I have some good news. You did so well on the

American States drawing that you earned a trip to my house. Isn't that great?"

We'd had to draw America and name all the states. I had made a colorful illustration of the country using what was left of my crayons. As I drew little people and families dotted around the country, I wondered if anyone else in that colorful illustration was as sad, angry, and lonely as I was.

When she gave us the assignment, some of the kids had groaned. The perfectly packaged girl in the front asked a million questions and I knew she would win. I wanted to win because staying anywhere was better than staying with my mother.

Staring into the darkness of the room, except for the streetlights cutting through the windows, I wonder why things have become so sad, why everyone has left the apartment. Why am I the only one here? The sounds of music and laughter startle me. I'm not alone after all. The streetlights illuminate the other side of the room and part of the floor. I am hungry as usual and only have half of a cupcake hidden under my bed. As I walk toward the kitchen for water, I notice a light coming through the cracked door of my mother's room. I tiptoe over to get a look through the crack.

There is a plain wooden table with an old lamp on it. The lampshade has a slit in it, and the slits are curling inward, like a wound confused about which way to heal. The shade is wearing thin from the heat of the lightbulb. A rectangular mirror hangs over the bed, lengthwise. I look into the mirror to see who is talking with my mother, but can only see a stream of smoke rising like a dancing Genie, circling up toward the ceiling. It is a man drinking a beer and smoking a slim cigarette. They are sitting on the bed next to each other. The nightstand is covered with cigarette ashes. My mother picks up a white straw and blows some of the ashes away.

What are they doing? Are they about to drink something? I wonder, my feet glued to the floor.

She takes the straw out of the paper wrapper, which she tosses to the floor. It floats like a falling leaf, landing on several empty cans of beer and cigarette boxes, which are mixed into and on top of clothes. I take a deep breath and let it out slowly. I don't want her to hear me.

She uses a small pair of scissors to cut the straw at a bit over the halfway mark, but on a diagonal, ignoring the longer piece that falls onto the bed. Holding the short part of the straw with her left hand and a folded bill in her right, she keeps the sharp diagonal side pointed down and bends her head toward it. She puts her nose over the uncut end of the straw and deeply inhales. She then drops the straw into the dollar bill and pinches her nose shut.

The man then takes the straw and dollar bill from her and takes a breath through each side of his nose. They both wipe the white stuff off their noses. My eyes are watery, and I have to pee, but I can't move and squint my eyes to try and get a better look.

My neck feels tight. My eyes are seething and my is heart on fire. I don't know what they are doing, but I know in my gut that it's not something good. What kind of life is this? Why am I attached to it and her? The loneliness I feel on the other side of that door in the dark is many miles away from them, yet right in my hand. Hungry, hurt, and light years from any saving.

He drinks another beer and grabs his jacket. Walking toward the door, he says coldly, "I'll see you later." I run back into my room and pretend to be sleeping. I hear him walk past my room and out through the apartment door.

After lying awake for what feels like hours, I get up and go to my mother's room. The door is slightly open, and I watch her sleep. I go in, holding my nose against the stench of burning metal, and turn the lamp off, open the window, and close the door.

There is a half of can of peanut butter, a bag of bread, and three slices of molded cheese in the fridge. I don't feel like picking the mold off. There is also a box of powdered milk and a generic brand of cereal called Puffed Rice. I pour the cereal into a bowl, mix the powered milk with water in a separate cup, and pour the mixture onto the cereal. I cry while I eat, hating the metallic, sweat-mixed-with-beer smell that wafts in from my mother's room.

I wonder if that man is our father.

Standing in the kitchen, looking around at the mess, I get a garbage bag from under the sink and start to pick up any rubbish I see. My mother seems comfortable with the strewn about papers, piles of random clothing, ripped and worn furniture, a dark and dreary apartment, and an empty kitchen. We have no stable home, no food, no friends. She's lying to me, and everyone who I thought loved me is gone. Doesn't she care that I am still her daughter?

The answer is obvious. The reasons are not.

CHAPTER 6

"Hi, Gram, how are you doing?!" I say with excitement while standing in the dreary kitchen.

"Hello, child. I am doing as well as God intended me to do. I'm so happy to talk to you. What's doing over there? You know, I tried calling last week and it didn't connect…"

Shelly is standing next to me, listening.

She leans in closer and is moving her hand like she is making a sock puppet talk.

"Tell her what's going on," She says in a whisper that isn't all that quiet.

I swat my hand at her as if a fly is buzzing in front of me and shake my head.

I cover the receiver and say, "I can't. What if Mom gets mad for telling?"

"She will never get mad at us if Gram has anything to do with it," Shelly says while pointing sharply toward Mom's bedroom.

I want to tell her how much I miss her and the country. The flowers, her food, and Duke. I also want to tell her that the phone was shut off from time to time so calling her was difficult. I feel I would ruin our talk and decide on keeping things light.

"Everything is good." I close the refrigerator door. I feel foolish for even looking in it. Shelly is trying to take the receiver so she can talk to Gram. I pull my body around so that she can't grasp it and she storms out of the kitchen.

Gram is still talking. "I read your letter. I'm happy you are still dancing. You must keep it up this summer since you both are not visiting this time, you know?"

My head snaps back from staring at Shelly's retreating figure. "I'm not?"

"Oh, I thought your mother told you. As much as I love your visits, I am getting older, child. I can't look after you as much so we decided you would both stay with your mom during the summer. Your grandpa will try and bring me up if I can make the trip. Make sure you write and call me, Stephanie."

"Gram, you called me Stephanie," I say, holding back the lump in my throat. There is silence on the other end. I am getting mad and sad at the same time. "Gram, are you there? It's me, Margarette!" I feel like I am calling for something in the room that really isn't there. I look around the kitchen as if I am in an unfamiliar place.

"Oh, oh, that Bob Barker is something," Gram says, laughing, as I stare at the receiver. My breathing is faster, and I grip my chest, wanting to go through the phone to see why she is speaking this way.

"Gram, its eight o'clock at night. He isn't on TV"

"Yes, okay, keep dancing, I…" The phone disconnects.

I press the phone buttons. *Beep beep beep,* silence. I slam the phone onto the receiver and look up. I can't think. There are so many questions going through my head. My mother is walking down the hallway. I meet her halfway.

"Why didn't you tell me I'm not going to see Gram this summer?"

"What?" my mother says as she clenches her mouth and stares at me with the 'you better move out of my way' stare. I move over just an inch without giving her a chance to answer.

She is carrying a pile of sheets and pillowcases. *Wow, finally new sheets,* I think as she walks over to the ironing board that is set up by the living room window, reaches down, and plugs in the iron.

"The phone cut off when we were still talking."

"Well, she is getting too old, and her memory is going; she may not know what she is talking about. The phone is working fine."

"I tried using it after the disconnection. It isn't working."

She picks up the pile of sheets and drops it on the ironing board. She grabs the iron and turns toward me.

"I think the cord is broken. It's too long. I must get another one—that's what the problem is." She licks her finger and taps the plate of the iron.

I narrow my eyes. I don't believe most of what she says anymore. I can't help but ask her questions, hoping she will say something that makes me feel better. Even if what she says is hurtful, it's better than being hurtful *and* a lie.

"What am I going to do here this summer?"

I am grasping at ideas of how to fill my time. I have spent the last six summers in North Carolina. It is my safe place, my respite. I had a routine that Gram let me develop. After church, I would sit with Grandma at her grave and talk to her. The first time I cried until Gram came back from the after-church lunch to get me. After that, I used that time to talk about all my fears. I had told Grandma everything while sitting under the North Carolina heat in my sundress. The things I always wanted to say to my mother, the questions I always wanted to ask, and the nerves I always felt had flowed out with ease when I sat on the red hard dirt in the small cemetery. The birds would sing along with me as I went on and on with my tales. Now that's being taken away from me, too.

Looking at my mom ironing sheets, calm as a maiden bathing in a lake, I grow furious.

"Why couldn't you have just told me that I wasn't going to North Carolina? I talk to Grandma when I am there. I can't do that now. I felt the same way when she died. I was just told. No chance to say anything. No one spoke to me before things happened."

"If Gram can't take care of you, then you can't go. You can find something to keep you busy." She folds the sheet in half.

"Are those our sheets?"

"No, why would I iron sheets for us? These are for Mrs. Jones;

she can't do it anymore because she has arthritis in her hands. I'm helping her out."

My stomach drops. My eyes are on fire. *Why would she iron sheets for someone else, and not even wash my clothes for school?!*

I've been washing my clothes, or what's left of them, by hand for what seems like forever. I even sew buttons on what needs mending. She has no problem with that, and she sits here ironing someone else's sheets? I can't get a word out, my throat is so tight.

The decision is made. Just like any other decision. Without my input. My mind races with images of North Carolina and New York. From dance class to the Victorian home in the middle of the great green lawn.

I start to panic. I hear a sharp *snap* that brings me back to the moment. The iron stops hissing, the dancing steam fading away before reaching the ceiling.

The electricity is off. Again.

"I hate being here!" I scream while sobbing, walking to my room.

I turn to look at my mother, who is also sobbing and banging her hand on the edge of the ironing board.

My heart hurts so bad I feel like it's going to rip right out of my chest. It seems as though my mom and I are suffering continuous punishment for a crime we have no idea we committed.

I still believe in something, and that is I truly hate God and I know my grandma is not visiting New York from Heaven.

Hours after our argument I'm trying to get some sleep, but Mom's friends are noisy in the living room, and I get up to see what they're doing. Everyone snatches items off the table in a mad dash as if they are human versions of Hungry Hungry Hippo. They are shoving things into their shirt and pants pockets while wiping their noses as if they are being tickled by dust bunnies, invisible to the eye. I ignore their movements; I know they're up to no good, but I am focused on my plan.

My mother's friends, the people who took the place of the

cousins and friends who frequented the apartment before Grandma died, are Jake and Troy, ambulance drivers. Their uniforms give this away. There's Sharon, a neighbor who has fancy furniture and clothes I admire when I stay with her during the times mom is not home or we get evicted, and Celeste, my mother's long-time friend who lives in a townhouse in the Bronx.

"Hey, kiddo!" Jake says as he gets up and play punches me in the arm. I hug him. I like him and Troy.

"Hello, sweetie pie," Celeste says as she takes a sip of her whiskey. I am a pro at identifying smells by now. I've started taking what they leave lying around and drinking it after they leave and Mom falls asleep.

Troy gives me a high five and Sharon gets up to go to the bathroom. I fold my arms across my chest and turn to my mother, who is staring at me with disapproval.

"Mom, I wanted to remind you that you said I can go to the school trip tomorrow to the Bronx Zoo." She places her hands in her lap and balls up her hands into a fist. She is looking past Jake, seemingly out the window. "Remember, you said you would give me money for lunch and games. You forgot when I had trips before, and I couldn't get lunch. I didn't have much fun."

I smirk a bit, staring at her. Her jaw clenches.

"Oh no worries about that, kiddo!" Jake belts out while standing up. Troy follows, and they both start pulling out bills from their junk-filled pockets.

"Here you go, kiddo; have a great time. Make sure you get me something like a lollipop or a stuffed bear!" Jake laughs at himself while handing me ten dollars.

Wow! I thought, *this is amazing!*

"Same here, young lady." Troy also gives me ten dollars. I'm staring at the two bills, swishing them in-between my fingers, feeling them as though they were fine silk.

"I will. Thank you both so much!" I walk around the table and hug Jake first and kiss him on the cheek. I peer over at my mother who looks like she is about to cry and scream at the same time.

"You are very welcome. Your mama tells us you are doing great in school. You deserve it," Troy says as we break from our hug.

I'm not about to tell him that it seems to take all my energy to find any interest in school at all, let alone do very well. But since my mom has a problem telling the truth, even when it hurts me, I have no problem letting them think I am a brainiac.

"Yes, I am. School is certainly fun," I say while walking away, gleaming at mom. She chuckles, reminiscent of the green witch in the Wizard of Oz. Hunched over, her back and feet swing back and forth under her seat. She is wise to what I'm doing but doesn't want to show that she's mad or embarrassed.

Celeste is back in her seat. "Oh, I heard the ending; take this, girl, come here," she says, wiping her nose again and digging into her purse.

She grabs a few coins and shakes them back and forth in her hand.

I don't want to take them because she's giving them to me with her nose-rubbing hand. But that's a fleeting thought. I hold out my hand and let the coins drop into it like a slow anvil. The weight causes my small fist to drop a little. I hug her and say goodnight to everyone.

Wrapping five dollars' worth of coins in a sock was a first for me. Then I stuff the two ten-dollar bills in the sock and put it in my underwear. I lay in bed with my hands behind my head as if I am on a beach. I remember Gram taking me to Virginia Beach one year. I was in awe of the endless sight of water, the seagulls, the salt smell, and the sky that felt more powerful than it looked. That is how I feel lying in bed. Except I am looking up at the chipped, dingy ceiling. I can't imagine heights past that anymore.

I decide that the way I am going to get things from my mother from now on is to do it in front of her friends. I can lie with no guilt. She can thank herself for being a great teacher.

When summer starts, I'm so angry with my mom's behavior that I do what I like as often as I can get away with it. I still can't have friends over, and I still have a curfew, but now that I'm a teenager, I push the limits as often as possible. Shelly is a straight A student and a book worm, and it starts becoming obvious to everybody how very different we are.

Staying in the city for the summer has its benefits though. I run into some girls I know from middle school, and it's good to hang out with somebody other than my sister. I see them at a block party and they welcome me into the fold.

With Harlem School of the Arts holding a limited summer timetable, and NDI on weekends as my only outlet for dance, the weeks crawl by. At least when we were in North Carolina, I spent my days with Gram, helping at home, playing in the garden, spending time with family who love me. The warm sun lights up the fields and trees in vibrant color. I feel alive there.

Summer in New York is a whole new experience. Days are long, hot, and empty, meeting up with the same people, talking about the same things. It's stale, suffocating almost.

When we are bored at night, one of the guys opens the fire hydrant and sprays us while we run around in the street. It's nice to still play like a kid, even though I feel less like one with each passing day. We all grow restless and often entertain ourselves with beer, liquor, and the marijuana I recently tried for the first time. I don't think this is much of a problem. It will be busy enough when school starts and being alone in my mother's apartment while she and Shelly are out, or walking around looking for things to do alone seems a much worse alternative.

Soon, I start drinking and smoking marijuana every day. I actually hate the feeling that smoking gives me. I hate feeling like I am drifting up into the sky where something could swallow me up at any moment. When I want to come back down, the sky won't let me because I made a deal... and lost.

The lessons in school or on the TV are always the same. "Say no to drugs. Tell a grown-up if anyone offers it to you. Just say no." But there are no lessons on what to do if your parent is the holder of this forbidden substance. No one taught me how to have a drug-addicted mother. There were no lessons on what to do if you had a parent you wanted to love but couldn't. There were no lessons on how to get a parent to love you. Why is it my job to get her to love me anyway? I can't understand why we have to be taught about the ancestors of all kinds of people, yet no one teaches me how to love or be loved by a mother who seems to hate that I exist. How to feel good about myself when I am hungry and eating out of the garbage. The lessons I am learning in life and those I am learning in school don't seem like good dance partners.

There are also no lessons on what happens when a kid decides to try cocaine. I remember that she used a straw, and I find one in the kitchen. The wrapper on the straw is old and cracked. I lightly scrape it off with my index finger and thumb. I inspect the inside of the straw for any dirt or bugs before I cut it on a diagonal, just like Mom did.

Dip in into the powder and scoop some in. Then lift the straw and sniff it quickly. Just like Mom does. You have watched her plenty of times. You know what to do.

It feels like someone is coaching me. A beautiful voice. Like Glinda the Good Witch is standing right next to me. When I stick the straw into my nose, it scratches the skin. I feel a sting and a few drops of blood fall out of my nose. *Sniff quick!* The sting is stronger and makes my eyes tear up.

I grab a tissue and dab the inside of my nose, shaking my head back and forth a couple of times before I decide to try the other nostril. *Maybe there is a good side and bad side.* I feel a bit brilliant. Determined to do it right, I scoop a lot of the powder into the straw, now stained with bits of dried blood. I push the straw further back into my nose and inhale deeply. I pinch my nose and eyes closed as tight as I can. I am tiny yet magnificent. Everything is in slow motion, but my imagination is fast. The inside of my eyelids are red. Like they are bleeding, too.

I move my mouth from side to side and open it as if trying to stretch my face. It feels like melted hot metal sliding down my throat. My neck and mouth feel tight, like my skin is being pulled from down and behind. My head feels like it's in a vice grip. I shake my head to get my focus, and realize my heart is beating hard and fast.

The tingling and tightness ease up. I don't feel like a little girl anymore. I can't if I'm doing what I watched my mother do for so long. I certainly don't like it as much as drinking and smoking, but I feel a sense of disconnect that separates me from confusion and sadness. I almost don't care about anything. It's like the drug smashes some part of my emotions, the part of my emotions that need too much attention and love.

I manage to feel a little relief for being rid of that annoying person—the girl who wants her mother's love. I feel a little more grown up and in control.

What if she catches me? I would normally have an emotional reaction to my thoughts about my mother and what she thinks of me. I am drawing from an empty bucket while the drug eliminates any care I may have had.

I shove another scoop into my nose. This one goes down much easier. I am getting back at her. I think I am petrified, but don't feel the slightest bit afraid.

There is not much powder left in the plastic paper, and I don't know if I should just put it back. *What the hell?* I think. *Is she gonna ask me about it? Is she gonna ask me if I stole it?*

I shrug my shoulders, fill up the straw with the rest of the powder, and take the deepest inhale I can. I lie in bed, my mind racing, trying to outpace my heart. I start to regret trying cocaine. After all, I can't take it out of my body once I don't like it anymore. The moon is strikingly bright, illuminating the courtyard that looks like a Roman center stage.

My eyes wide and stark, my pupils dart back and forth. The door lock is turning, but it can't be Shelly because she's at a sleepover. Is it my imagination? I shut my eyes and turn on my side, facing the window.

"Are you up?" Mom says, pushing me as if trying to tip me over a cliff. I can't move. I can't let her see me acting like a frantic bat. I squeeze my eyes tighter and fake a snore. She leaves the room and closes the door.

I don't want to care anymore about what she thinks, but I still do. I wish there were an after-school special that would cover what to do now. Instead, I'm on my own.

CHAPTER 7

Sitting in the balcony of Convent Avenue Church, it is dark. Not many people sit here when there isn't a holiday service. I don't listen to the sermon. Instead, I look through the women in their dull colored outfits, swaying back and forth, in a hypnotic trance. I'm thirteen now, and my mother has been sending us to church alone for a long time, but Shelly and I don't even sit together anymore. She is down on the ground floor with her friends while I am up in the balcony. No doubt she feels all pious about the different paths we are taking in life, and it's not only at church that we're apart.

I have no one to look forward to when I am there, and no one to look forward to when I return home.

The choir starts singing *Trust and Obey*, and the congregation starts with the foot stomping. People are standing, waving their hands. The collection basket is being passed down the row. I have nothing to put into the basket, and my stomach is as tight as the chords inside the piano. People add a dollar here and five dollars there, and I watch it move toward me like a snake—a snake with hopes of biting me.

I lean over toward the man holding the basket and set it down on the other side of me, opening my bag and pretending I'm looking for change. I take out a piece of paper, stick my hand into the basket, ball up a few bills into my hand, and pass it along. The song ends, and I leave the church. I hate myself for doing that. But I hate God more. Not only did He give me a mother who stole my happiness, but He also took the only person who made me feel worthy. God doesn't care, so why should I continue to be good when it gets me crap in return? Going to church on Sunday to steal from the collection basket becomes a routine. I even attend the lunch after service to fill up before heading to the store, where I buy snacks and then hide them.

Every Sunday, I sit in the same pew until the basket passes. I even drop in a quarter at times to make up for what I've taken with me. After a while, I don't even feel bad anymore. God didn't give me a mother who would take care of me, so I'll just have to take care of myself.

A couple of months into eighth grade, we are given a list of high schools and applications to look over. When I see LaGuardia on the list, I am excited, but I never imagined I would be able to attend the Fame school and live out my dream of having a dance family led by Debbie Allen, my new mom. I fill out that application first. The choices I have for auditions are dance and drama. I love both and think I have a chance at either. The thing is, I can only choose one, so dance it is.

I tell my mother that I am applying for the school. "Oh, that's really nice. I'm sure you will do okay," she says, blankly staring at the television.

"You know, Debbie Allen visited the school when I am there with NDI. I was in the elevator with her, and I was so happy to meet her. She watched us dance and said I should apply."

I thought my mom would be all over this news, and I long to be part of something she's excited about. But when she's not as enthused as I thought she'd be, sadness creeps in. Maybe she knows that Ms. Allen is going to replace her if I go there. Or maybe she's more excited about the graphic arts school Shelly wants to go to.

The letter comes in the mail, explaining that I have an

appointment for an audition. I don't even bother showing my mom the letter, because I don't want to be let down again. At least I know my dance teachers will be happy for me. After African dance class, Mrs. Rhymes gathers everyone around.

"Everyone let's congratulate Margarette on her huge accomplishment of getting an audition with LaGuardia High School! This is not something we see often!" Everyone is clapping and cheering. Mrs. Rhymes gives me a hug and says, "You will be just fine. Believe in yourself; you belong where your heart takes you."

It feels good to have her support, but secretly, I feel like a fraud. I'm using drugs, I'm drinking, I'm stealing. I'm not the girl I was when I started dance. I don't know who I am, but I'm not proud of myself anymore. I've reached the age limit for both Harlem School of the Arts and NDI, so they won't want me soon either. I'm getting nervous—I don't know if getting to know a new group of dancers will feel the same as it did before.

I'm already familiar with the school and studios. We all sit in one room with numbers pinned to our backs. A short woman comes into the room and says that the ballet auditions will be first. I know my strongest styles: modern, jazz, and African. I am not bad at ballet, and practice in my pointe shoes as often as I can. As a result, the shoes are worn out, and there is no way I can get another pair before this audition. We start at the barre, and I keep looking at the judge's table. Mrs. McDermott, along with two other women, glance up and make notes throughout the audition.

Are they looking at me? Am I in the correct position? I am trying to copy the girl in front of me who looks like a music box ballerina, her body lean, strong, and straight. She has no problem performing the steps; it seems so easy to her. I am sweating profusely, and we are only doing a few of the routines at the barre.

Most of the other dancers are great. They seem to have way more ballet training than I do, and their parents are all downstairs waiting for them.

No one is waiting for me, but I want to tell my teachers good news. I really want to get in. That way, I will have a place to go every day outside of the apartment and my neighborhood. The Lincoln Center area is so pretty and quiet. The trees are greener, the sidewalks are brighter, the school has statues and art in the lobby, and I feel like I'll be a part of the TV show. I believe I'll have a family there (and Debbie Allen to look after me).

We move to the center of the room, and that's when I notice that the other girls have way more control over the adagio than I do. I start to feel like a panicked chicken. I want to give up. But I know I will hate myself if I stop trying right in front of everyone.

After the first group of us have finished at the barre, we go to another room for center work, which is a modern variation. I feel a little better because I do not have to focus so much on the strictness of ballet technique. However, my mind is preoccupied with whether I could have done better at the barre. The way the other girls moves is connected, fluent, and confident. When I watched ballet with Grandma and saw how graceful and beautiful the dancers were, I didn't feel worthy of such beauty. Other forms of dance felt more natural. Nevertheless, I had become obsessed with trying to be pretty by getting better with the one form of dance that felt unattainable: the modern variation.

At LaGuardia, they studied the Martha Graham technique. She was all about abstract movement and movement based on emotion, about sharing the human condition through dance and arriving at a solution. The solution may not always be happy or joyful, but the journey is life itself. The arrival at the solution was the means to knowing that life has many turns, twists, ups, and downs, just like movement. The key is moving through life and one's emotions without being destroyed by them, and music is the vehicle that carries one through it all.

We take a break for lunch. Most people leave the building to get food. I see a few of the girls with their parents in a pizza shop nearby and decide to go in and try talking to them. I order a slice of pizza and ask for a cup of water. The root beer I love costs way more than I have, but at least I am able to get the pizza. I look over at the table where the girls and their parents are sitting. One girl is looking at me but quickly turns away when our eyes meet. Her mother looks my way and then back at her food. The other girl waves at me and points at a seat next to them.

"Hi, I'm Kendra. This is my mom and dad."

"Hi," I say while brutally trying not to eat my whole slice of pizza in one bite.

The first girl decides to introduce herself when her mother nudges her, after first staring out the window.

"I'm Nichole. Where are your parents?"

I feel crappy being alone. If my mom or Shelly were with me, maybe I wouldn't have looked so desperate and alone.

"She had to work; she couldn't make it."

"Oh well, what about your dad?"

For a moment I'm unsure what to say, but I am used to making up stories about the parents I wish I had. I don't even mention my sister.

"He died when I was younger; he was sick."

"Oh, I'm so sorry," Nichole's mother says. "That must have been hard on you and your mother. Well, good luck, and be proud of yourself for being able to audition for this school. It's the best performing arts school in the city. My Nichole will get in; she has been training since she was three years old."

Nichole rolls her eyes and looks away, nibbling at her salad. Kendra offers me a napkin. "Where do you study now?"

"I dance with Harlem School of the Arts and National Dance Institute."

Kendra's mom interrupts. "Oh, you live in Harlem, near Strivers Row? I once had a doctor friend who lived there. I've only been once. Shame that that's the only nice part of Harlem. The Apollo Theatre was amazing as well, but that area has turned into some kind of war zone. We live in New Jersey; city life just wasn't for us anymore."

"No, I don't live near Strivers Row. I live further up north of the Apollo Theater. I watch the talent shows and often imagine being on that stage—any stage for that matter. I just love performing."

Kendra's mom looks at me and touches my hand. She has kind eyes and a warm smile. She reminds me of my mother's friend, Sharon. Sharon let me stay in her house when we got evicted and made sure I was fed. She has a distant, lost look in her eyes, a look I've grown used to seeing in my mother's eyes as well as through my reflection in the mirror. Kendra's mom has that same look.

"Well, you are going places, young lady."

"Thank you," I say and eat the last of my pizza wishing I could put some in my bag for later.

After lunch, we have one more round of dance. Jazz is the last part. The piece is short, and I imagine that all the kids I am dancing with are my friends, and I channel the feeling I had back in our jazz piece at NDI. I am floating through the routine, remembering the reverence of the room when we performed that piece. I am relaxed, in flow, and my imagination takes off into the world of story through the stage and the music.

They split us into two groups across two rooms. The sea of girls and two boys in the room are murmuring, wondering what this means. I look at the girl in front of me—no. 268—the perfect ballerina with the flaming red hair. She was so good in her audition and being next to her gives me hope. *Maybe I have a chance?*

Despite my attempts to stay relaxed, I am biting my fingers and looking around the room, tapping my foot. My breath is shallow, and I am repeating, *I hope I get in, I hope I get in* ad nauseum in my mind.

The dance director, Mrs. McDermott, walks into the room with an expressionless face. My stomach drops. Then she breaks into a smile and says, "Congratulations, everyone. We would like to invite you back for a second audition." I am so happy I think I might burst. The other kids are in the lobby hugging their parents. Some are weeping, while others walk out with their parents, cursing the world. I ride the train home alone, silently thanking my grandma for introducing me to dance.

The second audition comes up quickly, and despite my nerves, I feel good about my performance. Waiting for the letter to arrive, which will determine my fate, is excruciating.

I spend most of my free time outside looking for my local school friends. I usually see a girl named Sammy sitting by her window when I visit my friend who lives in her building. Sammy never says much to us, but after a while she starts speaking to me a little more. Sitting on the inside ledge of her window, I think she is one of the prettiest girls I know with her droopy, hazel eyes. Her mom is Spanish, and her dad is Indian. Not the version of Indian I imagined from the books I've read. She has dull, golden hair that falls to the middle of her back. It is perfectly straight, not a curl to be found.

"What school are you going to?" she asks, looking down from her windowsill.

"I auditioned for LaGuardia School for Performing Arts and I'm waiting to find out if I got in." I think that adding that little tidbit might impress her.

"Isn't that the Fame School?" she asks, leaning out a little further. That is the moment she and I become friends. I am so happy she knows about the school. We never go anywhere except the front steps of her building, but we always have the nicest talks until her boyfriend picks her up. He is a pretty boy of the streets. Light skin, clean cut, and always dressed in the best clothes. Always new, always in a different car. He is the head drug dealer from the neighborhood. He is quiet and always gives me a pat on the head before saying, "Stay in school, kid, this street shit ain't cute."

I start to admire Sammy for reasons outside her beauty. She doesn't have to work or go to school, and she has this boyfriend who takes care of her.

My problem is, I look nothing like her. The girls who look like me are usually dirty and have no boyfriends. Or, they have boyfriends who are just as dirty. We have no mentors, and I feel like I'm just floating though life.

I have to figure out a way to make money and look better. I'm tired of the more frequent evictions and lack of food. I feel so out of place, and at thirteen I am too young to get a job. I start braiding hair for the girls in the neighborhood whose mothers pay me ten to twenty dollars each. Enticed by my ability to make money, my mother lets them come over to our place. I'm embarrassed by how it looks, but once I make enough money to buy food, I start buying cleaning supplies for the apartment to make it look a little better. All the skills I learned in North Carolina kick in.

I also start buying beer and liquor when I'm hanging out with my friends. Getting anything is easy; we just pay an addict to get us what we want. I feel guilty at first, but not long after I feel the fear melting inside of me, the dissipating sadness and ugliness I feel toward myself drowning in alcohol. I know I have found something to help me deal with life during the hours I'm not at dance practice.

My mother leaves the letter on the kitchen table on top of the piles of old papers, unopened envelopes, and dusty trinkets that remind me of happier times. That table has always been surrounded by family and friends. Now it holds junk.

Dear Ms. Allyn,
We are pleased to inform you…

I keep staring at the letter, thinking of the happy faces on the TV, reading the boards that I will soon be on. Debbie Allen is my idol and now I'll be following in her footsteps.

It's been months since my audition, and I've been waiting for this day—the happiest day of my life so far.

"I got in; can you believe it? I actually got into LaGuardia!" I wave the letter like a flag in front of Sammy's face. Sitting on her front steps, she covers her mouth with one of her frail fists while coughing and reaches for my letter with the other. I sit down next to her, and we hug.

"This is so nice. Wow, you should really be proud of yourself. What did your mom say? I'm sure she was happy."

"She wasn't home. Did you see her?"

She shakes her head and coughs again.

"Are you okay? Your face looks dull. Do you have a cold in the summer?"

"I don't know what it is. Maybe allergies or something."

Her boyfriend pulls up. She puts her hand on my leg. "Listen girl, take care of yourself. Stay in that school. Not many people get that chance."

I rub her back and smile. She waves as the car pulls off. I'm lucky to have a friend like Sammy. She's the only person who seems to be excited about me getting into LaGuardia. Nobody else seems to care, or know, the significance of what this school means to me. But the people around me are also the ones I see every day, and I need to fit in. I feel comfortable around them too, they are also my people. They might not be like my dance people, but these are the people who get me. I'm not a frequent flyer in the Lincoln Center neighborhood, and I know my place in the world.

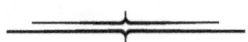

Middle school graduation is bittersweet. I hug my friends closely; we're all going our separate ways for high school and I know most of us won't see each other again. At the same time, I'm dizzy with anticipation at my next move. At LaGuardia, I'll be surrounded by other dancers and performers, who will be my ticket out of this neighborhood.

Summer can't finish fast enough. My friends have boyfriends and disappear for days at a time. I'm alone and don't like hanging out in our dreary apartment. I don't have dance to keep me busy and my feet are itching to grace the stage at my new school.

I'm buying cigarettes at the corner store and a deep voice whispers in my ear. "I know your ass ain't got nobody. I be snatchin' you up soon," he says and the strong smell of Fahrenheit from the 125th Street African vendors fills my nostrils. I look over my shoulder to see a guy I recognize from the neighborhood. I have never spoken to him before, but I know his name is Ron and he works for Sammy's boyfriend, which means he's a drug dealer, too. "Don't think I haven't noticed you on the stoop wit' your friends. I know nobody picked you up, but you're wit' me now."

No man has ever noticed me before, and especially no one like him. He is at least ten years older than I am, and his well-fitting jeans and red and white Jordan sneakers compliment his bright white smile. He looks so good, and he is clear that he wants me.

Who needs a middle school or even a high school boyfriend, when a real man is interested in you? Shelly isn't even interested in boys, but it's just another way her and I are so different.

Over the coming weeks, we hang out on the street and

occasionally visit the Lennox Lounge and Oasis bars, where nobody notices I'm underage. If they do, they don't care.

I feel tired when I start at LaGuardia; I've been smoking, drinking, and hanging out with adults for months. I'm ready to be shiny and new with my Fame family at my new school. But the first day I walk in, the lobby is cold and desolate, despite the droves of students checking noticeboards for their new homeroom and first classes. I smile tentatively at a few girls, dressed in leotards, jackets, and leg warmers; they look through me and run to the nearest corridor, giggling.

Maybe they knew each other from before, and we'll become friends soon.

After my first few days, I complain to Ron that I feel left out and shabbily dressed. I want to tell him that I don't fit in. My lazy summer left me inflexible and unprepared for the onslaught of fast paced dance classes. The teachers float through their movements with ease, but I'm out of practice and can't pick up the combinations like the other girls do. The students in different majors are separate and aloof, rarely speaking to each other, and the teachers don't pull us together into conversation circles, like they do on the small screen version of the school.

I want to tell him that I don't belong, that I'm struggling more each day, that I am sick of wearing my faded leotard and washing my tights every night so that I always had a pair to wear. But he isn't interested. "Here," he says, blowing smoke over his shoulder, and hands me twenty dollars. "Buy something new."

That marks the end of the conversation.

A few weeks later I'm waiting on the stoop for Ron to pick me up. He missed my fourteenth birthday and to make up for that, he is finally taking me on an official date, instead of the usual fast food and bar hopping. I can't even believe I have a boyfriend now. My friends have talked about being taken to restaurants downtown and amusement parks, and their boyfriends are always buying them clothes and giving them spending money. They are all sexually active, and again, I feel like the odd one out.

Last night we'd been fooling around in the hallway of my building, and when I wanted him to stop, he'd said, "Don't move my hand away. I'm sick of waiting."

At least this time we're going on a real date and I can join the ranks of my mature girlfriends who have already lost their virginity. I know what will happen and I love that he wants our first time to be romantic.

Ron arrives in the back of a cab and motions for me to get in. The cab ride goes by in silence as I see the crack houses and abandoned buildings on the upper east side of 116th Street.

"Right, we're here," he says, jumping out of the cab in front of a cheap-looking Chinese restaurant. This is it? The graffiti on the windows, hard wooden seating, and harsh fluorescent lighting aren't giving me a romantic vibe. He walks up to the window to order and asks me what I want to eat. I don't want to look ungrateful, so I ask for chicken wings, french fries, and a root beer. The date crawls past with lots of stilted conversation and awkward silences, and eventually I pour some of the Jack Daniels from his inside jacket pocket into my root beer. That will settle my nerves.

After dinner we catch a cab to the apartment he shares with his mother, whom I can hear snoring in the next room. The faint light coming from the TV is all I have to make out the surroundings. He sits me on top of a hard surface in the kitchen and starts kissing me, licking my cheek, breathing hard, and yanking my pants down.

I have no time to feel much discomfort and frankly wouldn't have noticed it given the surface I was on, the pressure he was putting on my neck, and the swiftness of his movements.

The minute it is over, I think, *This is not what I would have imagined.* The walk home is heavy, slow, and dreadful.

A week later, I am supposed to be in school for a dance exam and can't imagine making it through. I tear through the Yellow Pages and find the information for a free clinic a few train stops away. Traveling to another country would have been faster, as I exit the train right into a downpour. I walk, buckle-kneed, for a few blocks. When I reach the clinic, soaked through to my skin, I explain to the receptionist that I need to see a doctor because I got my period along with another issue that seems to need treatment.

Never looking up at me, she hands me a clipboard and tells me to sign in and wait in the seating area. The water from the rain disguises the water in my eyes. I wait and watch the other people in the office, people of all ages, go in and out as they are handed paperwork and medicine. I wonder what the doctor will say is the matter. I can barely sit still; I feel like there are hot coals in my pants. My breathing is shallow as I dread the feeling of fire on every breath. Holding it and passing out seems like a nice option.

"You have gonorrhea," the doctor barks, like I'm one of a thousand dirty women in an assembly line. In exchange for my virginity, I was given The Clap.

My so-called boyfriend becomes hard to pin down, as I look for him to tell him about the condition, he gave me. I finally meet up with him on the corner of his street while I'm standing in a payphone booth. The slap comes out of nowhere and stings me hard across the cheek. "Bitch, you got that from someone else," he grunts. He grabs my neck and slams my head back against the phone, making the receiver jump out of its cradle. "I should make sure you didn't give me anything, you black bitch," he says, then turns around and storms back up the street.

As I watch him walk away, he looks back and laughs at me. Nursing the back of my head, which already feels bruised, I wonder, *how did I get here?*

Sammy soon gets very sick and is in the hospital for a long time. I visit every chance I get. No one, not even her parents, knows what is wrong with her. Or, if the grown-ups know, they don't tell us.

I think about going to church to pray for her, but I haven't been to church for a long time and suspect I won't be welcome there after nearly being caught for stealing a couple of years ago. Instead, I just bring her flowers.

"I'm doing it, Sammy. I'm at the Fame School. If you can hear me, squeeze my hand." I might not love my experience at LaGuardia so far, but I love seeing her being excited for me, and maybe her seeing me on stage will be the boost that I need. Neither Ron nor my mother show any enthusiasm, and I need somebody to be in my corner. At least Sammy has always been that person for me.

I plead with her closed eyes, the hiss of the ventilator searing through the cold hospital room. I am sure she squeezes my hand, and my heart is brave enough to have a moment of hope.

I kiss her pallid, cold cheek and whisper, "You will be well enough to see me dance in no time."

Sammy never gets to see me dance. She passes away soon after. She hadn't even reached her eighteenth birthday.

CHAPTER 8

I end up being a regular at the free clinic and an equal regular at receiving beatings. I am getting high and drunk almost every day, and the abuse from Ron is becoming more frequent. I am used to being hit by my mother, and although his blows are harder, I am learning to hit back and defend myself.

One afternoon while resting in my room, my mom comes in holding a bottle of my antibiotics. "What are you taking these for?" she asks, her eyebrows raised. Mom has worked in hospitals for years, so I am confident she will know and don't risk lying to her.

"I have an infection and had to take them," I say, wishing the bed would swallow me whole.

"Someone told me you've been hanging out with Ron," she says. "I'm sure you know you have no business hanging out with him, so I better not catch you with him, you hear me?" She throws the pills on the bed and walks out of the room. I silently decide to never confide in her any further about what's happening, because I know I won't have her support.

Later, Ron and I are sitting on a bench at Amsterdam and 144th Street. It's getting dark, and the evening air is cool on my shoulders. I pull my jacket tightly around me and observe the street movement. My friends have gone to pick up their vices for the evening, and we are alone.

"You know, my mother doesn't like me hanging out with you," I say, taking a drag of my cigarette. I look away, secretly hopeful that, if he knows I'm defying her to be with him, it will soften his behavior towards me.

He removes a flask from his pocket and takes a big swig. "She doesn't act that way when I'm giving her those drugs," he says. "You ain't nothin' but a bastard nigga with a junkie mom; you wanna act like you a fancy dancer with respect? Bitch please!" I go to stand up, and he grabs my neck and says through clenched teeth, "Don't think everybody doesn't know." He pinches a fold of skin from my cheek and wiggles it in between his fingers. "Remember that." He chuckles, gets up from the bench, and walks away, his swagger telling me that he's proud of the bombshell he's just dropped on me. My friends are walking toward me, laughing, and joking with each other. I watch them, the heat of shame burning my cheeks. I feel like I have made a deal with the devil, and I am losing, big time.

My days melt into weeks and then into months, and life continues the same path. At school I feel invisible, like the homeless guy I ignore begging for money outside the train station every morning. Sitting alone in the morning, waiting for class to start, a group of girls run into the room. Their buns are high and smooth, their tights perfect, pink, clean. "What time do we need to be at the showcase? I don't know if we got enough practice in," says Kendra, who I met at the audition and probably hasn't smoked a cigarette or swigged a beer in her life. I didn't even know there *was* a showcase. It shows how far out of the loop I am.

Feeling left out becomes normal. Kids spending Mondays gushing about their weekend family outings, planning, and practicing dance projects that I'm never invited to be part of and spending my lunch breaks with voice or acting majors, because the dance girls are nowhere to be seen.

The expectation of the school being like Fame had started deflating from the start. The last time I saw Debbie Allen was when I was with NDI. I wanted the dancing in the hallways and lunchroom. I wanted the group of best friends I always hung out with in and out of school. Instead, I've felt lost from day one.

My music changes from Nina Simone and Janet Jackson to Snoop Dog and Lil Kim; from beautiful composers of my dance music like Tchaikovsky and Wynton Marsalis to rap groups that call people niggers, bitches, and hoes.

"What's the matter with you? Why are you acting like this?" Shelly says to me when I skulk through the door one night.

"Shut up; I'm sick of you and Mom acting like I'm the problem and you guys know everything," I say, putting on my headphones and turning up the volume to drown out her self-righteous dribble.

The façade of a hard-core street chick is brutal to keep up, and drugs and alcohol become my way to ignore how I really feel inside. The true feelings never go away but trying to act like a robot is easier than trying to trust people again. I want to celebrate my fifteenth birthday with a Friday night party at the apartment while my mom is at work. I haven't invited Ron, because I am tired of the way he is treating me and going to the clinic every second week is exhausting and embarrassing. He doesn't recognize me as a girlfriend anyway, so I don't imagine he will want to come. I've never had a boyfriend before, so I have nothing to compare him to, but looking at my friends with their boyfriends, I know I have gotten the short end of the stick.

Shelly doesn't want any part of the party, but she has nowhere to go. She is hiding away in our room, doing homework. "They better be out of here by midnight," she'd warned me before everyone arrived.

My friends are drinking, smoking, laughing, and yelling at each other over the sounds of Ice Cube through the speakers. I faintly hear the doorbell and turn down the music to be sure. It rings again, and one of my girlfriends leans out the window to see who is there. "Oh shit, it's Ron," she says.

"Come back in the window," I say, "so, he doesn't know we're here."

"It's too late, he just followed someone into the building."

The sound of thumping at the door tells me he's already here.

"If you don't open this door, you know what will happen when I see you!" he yells.

"When the hell are you going to cut that asshole off?" Emily says to me, shaking her head. "You deserve better." I shrug, but inside I know she is right. It's time to end this once and for all.

I open the door with trepidation. I don't want to let him in, but I don't want him to be angry either. As soon as I see him, I can tell he's high. His mouth is twitching, and his eyes are darting back and forth over his shoulder, as though he's running from someone. He doesn't wait for me to invite him in and pushes past me into the apartment. He walks into the living room and the party atmosphere of a few moments ago is immediately gone. Everybody turns to look at him, a sense of apprehension heavy in the air. LL Cool J's "I Need Love" is bursting through the speakers, its semi-romantic lyrics and slow music stark against the tension.

Emily looks at Ron, rolls her eyes, and turns around to talk to her boyfriend Jake. Ron greets a few people in the room, slapping fives to each other, and hands a little bag to one of the guys. *Really? He has the nerve to sell drugs in my home?*

He skulks over to me and clutches my arm. "Come on," he says. I don't know where he wants to take me, but wherever it is, I'm not going. I snatch my arm away and his face tells me I've made a grave error by defying him in front of a crowd. He'll never let me get away with this.

The first slap comes as no surprise. I back up because I don't want to fight in front of my friends. He lunges forward and tries to grab me again. "That's right, into the bedroom," he says, jerking his head sideways to indicate where I should go.

I yank my arm away from him again and head straight to the front door, opening it with purpose. "Get out," I say, calm and controlled. I don't want to cause a scene in case the neighbors tell my mother we were having a party.

Instinctively, I know he isn't going to leave. He lunges forward, grabs my hair, and punches me in the stomach. I gag, gasping for breath as I double over in pain. I fall a few steps outside the apartment door, and it slams behind me. Standing up straight as I can, I draw my hand back, ready to hit him, but he grabs it to prevent the flow. I kick him between his legs and race down the hall towards the stairs.

Before I can make it out the lobby, he comes thundering behind me and grabs my hair, snapping my head back. Then he pushes it forward and smashes my face straight into the glass lobby door, which cracks like a series of spider legs, and I see stars exploding in front of my eyes. I stumble out the door and down the short flight of stairs toward the street.

I see an empty beer bottle on the ground and lurch forward to swipe it up and throw it at him. He avoids the impact by jumping sideways like a wide receiver and laughs that I've missed him. "You missed, bitch," he snarls.

I run a few steps towards the street corner, wheezing and out of breath, my lungs on fire. "I don't know why you keep tryna fight me," he says, then draws back his fist and punches me so hard in the face I lose my footing and tumble into a pile of garbage bags that are piled on the corner. "If this isn't what you wanted, you shoulda stayed at your party like I told you to," he says, walking away, as police sirens scream in the distance.

I slowly open my eyes and look up at the moon. For the first time in a long time, I think about Heaven and whether Grandma is watching over me. I lie in that pile of garbage, reflecting on how I got here. *What happened to my life?*

Two days later, Ron is shot several times in the street by another drug dealer, and while he survives, it seems a fitting punctuation to the end of our relationship.

CHAPTER 9

I t's the summer before my junior year. I'm working for the second summer in a row at the Department of Parks and Recreation in New York City, cleaning up what was known to us as 7th Avenue down to 110th Street and 5th Avenue and further south to 103rd Street.

While cleaning Central Park 110th Street, all the needles, beer cans, and liquor bottles that filled my garbage bags remind me of the dead weight my life feels like. There are motels and rundown apartment buildings lining the opposite side of Central Park, from 5th Avenue to Central Park West. It is a grungy area; jobless drunks litter the benches. Music from passing cars combined with the stench of marijuana and stale crack are security blankets for the people who live there.

Shelly told me about the summer youth program, and she was also hired by Parks and Recreation to work in the main office downtown—in air conditioning and around nice restaurants. How that happened I will never know.

I hate this job; I hate the long hours for the crap money we are paid. I hate feeling just as shitty on the inside as the dirty job conditions I have on the outside.

In elementary school, we took a trip to Central Park to hike small hills and rocks, but I never saw this part of the area. At murky Mere Lake, gray and brown water pigeons have taken up occupancy. The grass is as dry as North Carolina in the fall. As I'm shoving cans into my garbage bag, a homeless man sitting up against the stone-lined wall holding a paper bag looks up at me and says, "Stay right, kid. You startin' off good; just stay right."

"What happened to your path?" I ask, wishing I had a drink myself.

"Well, I used to believe, but I just don't no more…" He starts mumbling and takes a drink from his paper bag. "Damn, young people are so stupid," he snaps.

As I stare at him, we quickly became the only two people there, the bench holding him up and the earth holding me up. *He was a boy once*, I think. And I was a girl once. *He started off just like me*, I think, scooping the rest of the needles and broken glass into my bag.

As I walk away to continue with my job, I hear him singing behind me. I'm surprised by his beautiful voice and turn around to see him swigging from the unseen bottle in its paper bag. I wonder why he didn't pursue a career in singing with that voice of his. It seems talent wasn't enough to save him from living on a park bench.

I might hate dance right now, because I hate LaGuardia, but at least I'm still trying to dance. Besides, Julliard will save me, so I still have that to look forward to. Everything will change once I get there. So really, he and I are nothing alike. I'll never end up on a park bench.

At the start of my junior year, I spend my spare time practicing dance alone at home. The academic side of school is of no interest to me, and my grades are abysmal. I have to practice dance to even keep my head above water at school. I feel so tired every day, and at times my lethargy feels insurmountable. Why am I so damn tired all the time? And why hasn't Debbie Allen come to visit, even once?

At night I want to get out of the apartment and lose myself in the neighborhood, in the things that make me feel like I actually fit in somewhere, the things that make me believe that what I truly want really doesn't matter. Dance is slipping away from me; I can feel it. The streets are taking over, and I feel like that's where I belong.

At least I have a better job now at Woolworth's on 145th Street and Broadway. It is certainly a step up from cleaning up drug paraphernalia and empty liquor bottles from Central Park. One day while I am stocking shelves, I suddenly feel like someone shot me with a tranquilizer. I sit on the bottom shelf, attempting to gain some kind of composure. I feel several hard pokes on my shoulder, and when I open my eyes, my manager is standing over me.

"What's wrong with you? Wake up! The customers can't see you sleeping here. If you do this again, you're fired!"

Only last week he raved about how quickly I learned my job and went above and beyond. Now, I feel shards of his disappointment and frustration spilling over me. Instead of asking if I am okay, he has gone from "You're great" to "Customers are more important than your health… loser." I go to the suffocating room called The Lounge and cry like I've just been sentenced to Attica.

Over the next few weeks, I have the same trouble staying awake. After work, I grab a few drinks and hang out at home with a friend or with my mom. She has actually become somebody I get along with. When things ended with Ron so dramatically, she seemed to soften. Maybe in a funny and unexpected way, he brought us together. "Marg, I know I didn't make it seem like you could talk to me in the past, and I could have done things better, but I want you to know you can tell me anything," she'd said shortly after what happened with Ron. "No matter what it is." She's not a different person and I'm still wary, but we talk now and at least she doesn't completely ignore me the way she did when I was younger.

One evening, I'm awakened by the ringing phone. "Get up, the doctor is on the phone for you," my mother says while walking away. She sits next to the phone, staring at the TV while rocking back and forth, the way she did when she was worried or knew I'd found something out that she didn't want me to know.

I pick up the phone and let out a huge breath.

"Hi, dear, it's Doctor Waldman. I have the results of your test. Sweetie, you are pregnant. Almost three months. I thought you were taking the birth control pills I gave you. What happened? Did you stop?"

I have been taking them—at least when I remember to. Days, nights, and mornings often blend into one long blur. The whole time I am listening, I am also watching my mother. Her movements are peripatetic, as is my mind. "You have to come in tomorrow so we can talk about your options."

Options? What options do I have? I don't even know who the father is. It's either Steve, the married man who's almost forty; or Frankie, the guy from my neighborhood who I only slept with out of pity a few times. Neither is a good option for my future.

Tears well up in my eyes as I focus on my mother. My mind is swimming with thoughts and images of my life, my struggles, my history, this baby. The colors and sounds flash through my head like an out-of-control movie wheel. A haze of light and noise mesh into one big nightmarish headache.

On the outside I remain somewhat composed. "Yes, I'll be there. Thank you, doctor, goodnight."

Motionless on the arm of the sofa, my mother says, "You're pregnant, right?"

"How did you know?"

"How can I not? I'm your mother."

The fall of Goliath is nothing compared to the defeat I feel. The wrath of Noah's Ark's flood wasn't enough to drown me. The dread of emptiness and shame is enough to send the worst thought of disappointment through every inch of my body and soul. *What does she think of me?* It's one thing for my hatred toward her to made me feel a little empowered, but this—this makes me feel like I broke her heart. The heart I never thought she had.

"Well, I'm not going to tell you what to do. You have to figure that out on your own," she says.

When I get to the door of my room, I look down the dark hallway at the soft yellow light shining on her from one side. The muted TV shows the Giants game illuminated her front. Back and forth she rocks, never looking back.

Shelly is lying on her bed, reading. "Is that phone call what I think it was?" she asks.

"Yeah," I say, unable to even look at her.

"What the hell are you doing? You're such a mess..."

"Shut up. I don't need your opinion," I say, turning away from her.

I am sixteen—three years younger than my mother was when I was born. Lying in my bed, staring at the ceiling, I ponder my situation. I'm soon going to be in senior year. I'm planning my future at Julliard, and my dance career relies upon me being fit and available. I know the decision I have to make, and it weighs heavily upon me, like the load of a thousand boulders.

I can't have this baby.

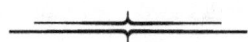

I feel a sharp poke and someone shaking my arm. Before I can crack one eye open, I feel the stabbing pain in my stomach. The kind of cramps that I have never felt before. I groan and force my eyes to open and focus on the recovery room of the hospital. I am gripping my stomach with both hands. The feeling of regret is drowning me.

"It's time to wake up," the nurse says in a slow, sultry Jamaican accent.

"My stomach hurts. It hurts bad..." My voice trails off and I close my eyes. The nurse shakes me again. I grunt and shrug her hand off my shoulder.

"Well, dear, abortions are not painless. Might as well have had the baby."

All my knowledge of manners dissipates into the thick foul air of that recovery room. I am half crying and furious.

"Mind your business. No one asked you anything about what I am doing. Just help me with this pain!"

The room is filled with stretchers carrying of women of all ages. A few other nurses glance over, and I turn my head toward the wall like a bad kid standing in the corner of the classroom of misery. What the heck have I done? I can't imagine praying or acknowledging Grandma or God. I feel like my cord to goodness has been permanently cut. Like I'm floating in an abyss. Like that dream where I'm falling into a hole with no bottom. The uproar in my stomach is unbearable.

The nurse returns with a small white cup. "Take these. You have to pee before we can remove the IV." She walks away before handing me the cup of water I need to down the pills. I reach over and feel another sharp pain in my stomach. *Jeez, I'm going to feel this decision for a long time.*

The nurse rolls a wheelchair toward my bed, and it takes what seems like forever for me to make it to the bathroom and pee. She waits for me to come out.

"Good job, young lady. Now I can remove this IV."

I sit there, staring into space, listening to the tape being peeled off my skin, smelling the alcohol pad that wipes it clean, seeing the IV-tube snapping off the supply bag then tossed into the garbage.

"I'm sorry I said that to you, child. It's… it's just that you are about my daughter's age. I don't know if I am heartbroken that you were pregnant or that you had an…" She is looking away, wiping her eyes.

I take my sneakers from her. My breath is short, afraid to fully release.

"Are you with the boyfriend?" She is rubbing my back. I haven't felt a woman's tenderness in so long I feel strange. Like it's wrong.

"No," I whisper.

"Why?"

I can't bring myself to admit to myself or to her that I have no idea who the boyfriend is. I have no idea who I am anymore. I don't think I ever did. I think for a moment about Steve and Frankie.

The first time I was with Steve, he had taken me to his apartment in the "fancy projects," as we called them. Not the projects with garbage replacing flower beds, but the ones with a bush or two on the front steps. All the elevators worked, and they didn't smell like a sewer. He led me right past the living room and illuminated kitchen where I noticed a pink sippy cup on the counter. The picture frames looked like moving shadows thanks to the darkness in the room.

While on my knees, face down on the bed, I craned my head to the side while he was behind me acting like a Marvel superhero. The streetlight was shining right on a photo of him, a woman, and a toddler. The little girl couldn't have been more than five years old.

"Are you with that woman?" I asked, as if I were having afternoon tea with a friend.

"Ah…" he stuttered, as he leaned over and slapped the frame face down on the table.

He flopped down next to me and kissed me on the cheek. *Isn't it strange,* I thought, *that that little girl has a father, and look at what he is doing.*

I was so deep in anger by then. Part of me loved the oblivion of my actions, and part of me felt rebellious. My thought process was along the lines of, *Well, I'm not the one who's married.* I barely knew what marriage meant.

Now, here I am being rolled down a hospital hallway. Not because I had an asthma attack. Because something was attacking me. And I was letting it. The feeling of defeat was rising like that ark of Noah's.

I see my mother sitting in a chair in the corner of the discharge room. She's wearing a red and black strap dress with flat flip flops. Her foot shakes one of the slippers off. She is at it again, picking her cuticles, her nervous tic.

I didn't know she was coming. I lied to my doctor when I said she would be there. I didn't even tell her what day it was. I am sure my doctor called and told her. All these emotions are boiling up inside of me. I feel like a gross failure. I can't look at her and see myself in her almond eyes. *What the heck is she thinking of me? Why would she even come?* My regret is growing.

The nurse rubs my shoulder. "I truly pray to God that you take care of yourself, young lady." She hands me my bag of belongings. It feels like it's filled with bricks.

"Thank you. And thank you for the pain pill." I have a feeling I am going to need more than a pain pill when I look at my mother.

She is looking out of the curtain. At what, I don't know. She turns her head, and we lock eyes. I want to run up to her and cuddle in her lap. I want to be a baby again. I hold back my tears. Slowly getting out of the chair, I grip the handles and she walks over to me.

"I'll push you over to the bed, don't walk yet," she softly says, her voice lyrical like Grandma's. "I got you something to eat from downstairs. How are you feeling?"

Ginger ale, a turkey sandwich, and Oreo cookies. Looks like a gourmet meal.

"My stomach hurts." She opens the sandwich and I start crying. I can't hold it in anymore. I don't care who hears. She lays the sandwich in my lap. I take a bite, still crying. She walks out of the room. I wipe my eyes with the shirt in my bag. When she comes back, her eyes are red, watery. She gives me the ginger ale and puts my sweater around my shoulders. She takes the leftover scraps of sandwich and places them on the table, and holds my pants so I can slip one leg in after the other. Then my socks. And she puts each sneaker on, taking care not to tie them tight.

I lean on her arm as I rise from the wheelchair. I don't stop crying the whole time. Why would she be here for me now? Wasn't I better when I was a clean, happy girl?

We don't say much in the taxi. The driver glances in the rear-view mirror, my mother stares out the window. The brown, red, ivory-stained buildings and people roll by on the film reel, the sky bright, the ground dim.

Mom strokes my back while I lay in bed staring at the wall. I hate that I did this to her. I hate myself for being in need and for her having to take care of me. I hate that I hated her for a long time. I hate that she is the only one here when I am in such pain. I want to know how to be anything but the person I am.

"You will be alright, baby. You will be alright," she sings as she rubs my back to a slow rhythm.

I start to doze off, thinking about the men in my life. I will cut Steve and Frankie off; I have no interest in either of them. I decide that I won't care for anyone because I end up more wrecked than before. From now on I'm choosing who to be with, and the condom companies will be rich off me. Sexually transmitted diseases scared me, but when I was drunk, I didn't care, even though Dr. Waldman said I may get something I couldn't get rid of. There is no getting rid of the hole inside of me.

Lying in the bed after having a doctor and nurses shred my insides is not what I ever imagined going through. I feel shame in the way of a merciless wrath. But in the midst of it all is a little feeling bouncing around my tired body like a furry bunny. It's a growing urge to drink.

CHAPTER 10

The spring of my senior year in high school, I am attending George Washington High School in Washington Heights at night, attempting to get my grades up so I can graduate on time. My drinking is at a steady rhythm well into the night on school nights. One of the reasons I even tolerate the miserable school is Trevor, the security guard I'd hooked up with. It wasn't long after my abortion that I searched for comfort in another person yet again.

Trevor would tell the teacher that I was present for class but had to help in the main office with administrative work. The teachers would mark me present, but I felt they could care less. I felt bad for them and the chaos they had to deal with. The students sat on desks, threw things at each other across the room, listened to their portable CD or tape players and never let the teacher speak a word. It was reminiscent of a scene out of the movie *Lean on Me*—except no one was getting a pick-me-up speech from Morgan Freeman.

Most of the teachers handed out packets and told us to read on our own while they disappeared for most of the class or read quietly at their desk. It was less painful to not sit in class at all. At least when I cut class at LaGuardia, it was to hang out and watch the drama students rehearse. LaGuardia was a mix of artistic disciplines and filled with character and personality. I didn't feel

96

like I fit in with any of them, but at least it was lively, colorful. Here, there is no color. The classrooms were painted a jail color grey, and they sported holes and graffiti. The bathrooms were mostly sex and drug gathering traps, and the horrific tube lighting in the classrooms and halls made even the smartest night school kids question their sanity.

Trevor was tall and had a little belly, which was strange to me, but he had the neatest, shiniest hair I ever saw other than on El Debarge.

"Where are you going, Chocolate?" he asked when I was cutting out of night school early one night. I liked that he called me Chocolate. It was a step up from the other names I had been called. It sounded sultry, sexy.

"Out of here. Why, are you going to write me up?"

"Depends on if I write my number and you use it."

It was cheesy, but he was letting me get away with leaving, so I bought his tacky come on. Next time I saw him we snuck into the security office. He spoiled me with liquor, cigarettes, and marijuana. And the fooling around was exciting. It was so easy being sexual while high. I let go of any cares I had when I was sober. Keeping my mind on thoughts of being wanted made it seem romantic. In the past, none of my engagements were anything close to romantic. I was so deeply uncomfortable that for years I couldn't grasp anything that felt true.

I had read *Looking for Mr. Goodbar* during my sophomore year, on recommendation from an older girl at school. I was scared shitless by the end of that book. I remember thinking, *don't ever pick up an ex-military dude!* Yet I was fascinated at how she got high off being two completely different people. I felt like I locked little Margarette up in a cement jail long ago. And the Margarette who got pregnant was in the cell right alongside her for being so stupid. The new Margarette has control over new matters. I am a new bitch. And the detachment that alcohol and drugs gives me feels good.

My night school experience is going well. If I have my liquor and Trevor, I am excited to go.

The bang on the door wakes me from my nap. I have school in a little while, and I'm irritated at my sleep being interrupted. I jump up and look at the time. Four o'clock. *The marshals can evict people until five*, I think. I take a chance and creep up to the door, looking through the peep hole.

He stands there holding a can of beer wrapped in a paper bag, tall and swimming in his clothes. His glasses overtake his face, and his slumped body brings my guard down considerably.

"Is your mother home?" he slurs in a surprisingly deep voice that doesn't fit his physique, moving as if he is listening to blues jazz.

"Ah, no, she isn't here," I say, rubbing my eyes while holding the door slightly open. "I don't know when she will be home; you can try later." *Must be one of her raggedy friends*, I think as I start to close the door.

He sticks his foot out to stop the door from closing. Perking up a little, he says, "You must be Margarette. Am I right?" He is trying to sound straightforward, but the beer isn't helping.

"Who are you? I snap.

"You sure do have... a... an attitude problem," he says, trying to hold his wobbly ground.

"Who are you? If you can't tell me, then wait downstairs for my mother."

"I'm you... your father." He burps.

My sass deserts me, and I feel like I have shrunk into a tiny person with a chipmunk voice. I am not prepared for this at all. For starters, his height is a shock. Mom only told me two things about him when I asked. His name – Michael, and his height – six feet, four inches. How he managed to get my four-foot eight-inch mother pregnant is disturbing to picture.

I want to ask so many questions, and I fear they'll sound like a run-on sentence. I am too nervous to say anything anyway. I wish Shelly was here, because she is always full of more mature questions. I look at his wrinkled hand holding a wrinkled paper bag and feel the resemblance.

"Ah..." I can't get any words to come out. I am so nervous my hands are clammy, and I am gripping the doorknob with my hand which is now cramping up. "As far as I know. We don't have one."

"I guess I deserve that," he says, squeezing out a grin on his crooked face. "Would you mind if I come in?"

We stand in the beginning of the long hall where I learned to ride a tricycle. The hall I ran through many times to meet Grandma. The hall that served as the gateway to the living room for all the people who took their version of refuge in the apartment. We look at each other. I want to hug him; I want him to hug me and say that everything before that moment never happened. That we can start from that day and begin a new life. A life with safe predictions, happy times, and what I've always thought a family should be.

"Where is your sister?" he asks as he looks around as if he is just as lost as I feel.

"She works after school," I say, relieved that I finally had a solid answer to something.

"I know this is uncomfortable for you. I sure am uncomfortable. But maybe we can talk a little and I can get to know something about you. If you let down that attitude a bit."

He sits on the sofa and places his bag on the chest that butts up against his towering knees. I feel obligated to help him feel less uncomfortable, yet I feel powerless and confused.

"I'm sure you have questions. I hope I can be of some decent company and help. I am not proud of not being part of you and your sister's life." He reaches into his pocket and pulls out a cigarette.

"You mind if I smoke?" he asks while he jiggles the pack and holds one in the corner of his mouth like my uncle in North Caroline used to do.

I grab the pack, take one and light it. He stares at me as if he's seen a ghost.

"This is one thing you can know about me," I say. "I smoke just like you."

"I guess I can't say anything about that. I wish you wouldn't, but you are a young lady now. A nice-looking young lady. Your mother says you are in dance school and your sister is in school for journalism." I didn't even know Mom kept in touch with him.

I suck that cigarette like it is oxygen. My throat is closing in on me. I can't tell him that I am a total mess and a failure. I can't tell him I feel worse than he looks, and I can't tell him that his little girl did all these bad things because she believed she didn't have good parents.

Instead, I say, while holding back tears, "Yes, school is going well. I am about to head off to night school to make up a few points for one of my classes."

"I hear you are going to college. I attended culinary college upstate, you know."

I can't believe I am sitting here talking to my father. There is a real person who is the other half of my existence. I never believed my mother when she said I had a father, but as it turns out, it wasn't a lie. I always thought he was maybe one of the men who breezed in and out of the apartment over the years. Or maybe a felon who was serving a life sentence, or maybe he died and she never knew. But here he is, in the flesh, and I can't have a conversation with him. It's not like an episode of "The Cosby show." TV really is a box of fairytale crap.

I want to say, *I don't have a clue about who or what I am.* Have I passed the point of wanting to get to know my father? *Where were you eight years ago when I needed you?* Should I be excited to finally have a father, like a princess being groomed her whole life for the prince that awaits her? Instead, I feel like the last kid left at the orphanage, and this sad, strange-looking man has shown up feeling sorry for me.

He blows smoke out of his nose—a nose that's identical to my own. Long, with a little bump at the end. I notice our similar long, lean, defined muscles. We both have long stopped working on our physique and taken up drinking as an alternative, it seems.

"There is no reason I would give you for not being here. You don't deserve ex...excuses. That's for sure. My choices were made by a young boy, not a man, and it resulted in me not being in you and your mother's life." He lowers his head then tilts it toward the window.

When he says "excuses," I feel a jolt inside, like something woke me up. I have been so busy making excuses for my anger and behavior. I can't remember when my sadness turned into something else, but that something else has been running me full speed ahead, and I don't want to be mad at him anymore. Finally being able to put a face to my missing father doesn't feel the way I imagined. It is not the storybook version by any means, but I don't have it in me to hate the man sitting on the sofa looking out of that window for something, anything.

I know that feeling. I don't know what to look for, but finally I feel I can stop looking for it through him or my mother. I can't understand his life as he lived it. I do know that if he wanted to be in my life, he would have been.

My choices were not attached to him or my mother, even though believing that they were has helped me at times.

My mother comes into the apartment and doesn't notice us until she is almost a few feet from the sofa. Michael stands up, and Mom looks at him. I am hoping she is feeling some kind of love and relief. She walks over to him, and they hug.

"Hi, um…how are…you doing?" She looks back at me.

"I am going to be late if I don't head out to school." I say, looking at Michael. "It was nice talking to you." I want to cry so badly. I turn and head to my room. I stuff my beer and liquor into my bag along with the assignment I have to turn in. Before I close the apartment door behind me, I look down the hall at his outline—tired, solemn, and lost as he sits next to Mom on the sofa, the sun reflecting its final rays of the day off the man I'd long wondered about. My mother's face is softened, like she is being tickled by a feather from the past. She has her hands in her lap and giggles at something he says. Maybe she is reminded of a time when she was young, vibrant, and happy.

I don't know why I should feel sorry for them, but I do. I try to have a joyous emotion and reaction, but it seems torture to fake. And in this moment, I kind of dislike him. Not for being absent in my life, but for dropping my mother like she was a nobody.

I want to hug her. What would that do? For the first time, I feel her loneliness. I feel her anguish. And I feel like I am a reminder of the mistakes she and my father made. I don't know if I will ever see my father again, but I want to be the one person who doesn't cause my mother to have a grim expression on her face. And I don't want to be her age years from now, wishing I made different choices. At least I still have a chance at Julliard.

"MARSHALL SHERIFF! EXECUTING EVICTION!"

I dash out of bed, grab a garbage bag from my closet, and start to throw a few clothes and schoolbooks inside. I hear scurrying from down the hall and kick a beer bottle that's up against the wall, left from the night before. "Shit!" I whisper, quickly rubbing my toe.

"Don't say anything; maybe they will go away!" Mom says as she suddenly appears next to me near the closet. My closet has a window. Many years ago, this apartment had servants, and this closet was a washroom for the people who had to live here. I smoked many cigarettes out of that window. My impulse is to jump out to avoid the embarrassment we are about to incur.

"MARSHAL SHERIFF, FINAL WARNING. WE WILL HAVE THE JANITOR OPEN THE DOOR!"

"They know we are in here; why bother acting like we are not?" I say as I grab my bottle of liquor, my keys that I am getting sick of, my cigarettes, and what is left of the money I made from braiding women's hair over the weekend.

"They will come in anyway," I continue. "What are we going to do, jump out of the window or have them drag us out? Move out of my way, I'm so sick of this; I so sick of you!"

"Shut up!" my mother says as she grabs my arm.

I break away and the apartment door swings open, slamming into the wall. Two mountain-tall men, one obnoxiously chewing gum, tower over me.

"You have ten minutes; you have to vacate due to…"

"I don't need your minutes, and I already know," I say as I nudge him to the side.

"Watch it, young lady."

"Fuck you!!" I snap. I never curse in front of my mother. Last time I tried, she smacked me. *Well, this is the perfect time.* I'm already in the habit of making bad situations worse. I look back at the abandoned, washed up, gray, dried-out figure behind the two men, swallow the rock in my throat, and drag my bag down the stairs.

We stand in front of our building. I am not a scared little girl anymore; I have grown used to the evictions. What I'm not used to is being here while it happens. Every time I believe my mother or give her the slightest bit of trust, my hopes are obliterated. Over and over.

My want for my mother to do more, however, is pointless. I look down at her. I am now taller than she is, and she seems so much smaller, so much weaker, so powerless. She is down to a few teeth, no half-decent attire, no half-decent pride. I can't help but wonder what kind of pain she must have endured to get her to this state.

"Hey, Steph, what's going on?" Sharon says as she comes out of the building. Her smile melts when she looks down at my half-filled garbage bag. "Oh... is everything...?" She stutters, grabs my mother's hand, and continues. "How did your procedure go at the hospital? Did the doctors tell you if it was cancer or not?"

I gasp. Mom snatches her hand away from Sharon and crosses her arms across her chest.

"I didn't have any procedure; what are you talking about?" Mom looks as horrified and angry as she used to right before she would hit me. I know she is lying. Sharon turns to me then back to Mom.

"Oh, you know, Stephanie, I... must be losing my mind. I was thinking about Celeste. You know how I get when I am... well, Margarette, you make sure you take care of your mom. I'm heading to the store. You want anything?"

I want to say, "Yea, a whole bag of food." But before I can fix my mouth to utter a word, mom belts out, "No! We will be fine. I'll just see you later."

Sharon gives my mother a hug, which Mom does not return. Mom is staring at our apartment window, like Medusa got a hold of her. I am already frozen. *Why didn't she tell me she may have had cancer? Why would she keep that in? Do her coworkers know? Does my uncle?* I look at her fading away, into the grey sidewalk. Two doofy giants walk out of the building, seemingly in slow motion, the one I pushed looking at my mother side eyed. They get into an unmarked brown car double parked in front of the fire hydrant we played in during hot summer days and drive away.

I have a horrible sinking feeling in my stomach. All the hatred I had for her was easy when I never thought she would die. I guess I always felt she was exempt from sickness since I pegged her as evil beyond human nature. Even when we started to get along, my comfort was short-lived. Now that Sharon let the cat out of the bag, I'm scared, and suddenly don't feel angry at her anymore. People who know us walk by, giving us the usual mechanical greetings, and I look into each of their eyes and, for the first time, feel their disgust, sorrow, and most of all, pity.

At that moment, I want to save my mother. Save her from embarrassment. Save her from feeling lost. Save her from herself. I feel so sorry for her, and I can't conjure up any more anger toward her. Her eyes, once giant orbs full of music, sparkle, and excitement, are now dull, brown rocks. I grab her arm and softly sob. "It's okay; I'm sure we will get back in." I squeeze her arm tightly while she keeps her other arm wrapped around herself. In this moment I realize how much pain she must be in from losing her own mother. The mother I know is buried somewhere under the drugs, misery, and despair. The mother I know can't find a way out. The mother standing on that sidewalk can't fathom a better way. And in this moment, I realize she can't love me any more than she loves herself.

)

CHAPTER 11

I hear high-pitched screeches in the locker room, like I'm at a Michael Jackson concert. I'm sitting on the ledge of the completely frosted window, where I sit every day after dance class. During the last year it has been my routine to leave after modern class and sit here smoking and drinking a beer that I store in my book bag. I'm here so often that I'm surprised I haven't left an imprint in the marble.

The dancers, some half or fully naked, are hugging each other while changing into dance clothes. Peony and cocoa butter scented lotion and body spray fill the air as the usual routine of body maintenance occurs before class.

"I'm going to San Francisco Ballet!" Janet says to Marie as she cinches on her tights. "That is amazing," Marie replies with her almost nonexistent Spanish accent; "I got into Boston. My parents were bummed that I didn't get NYC, but hey, it's better than nothing right?"

I want to jump out the window, but I'm only on the sixth floor and would probably only break my leg. Or my neck. My other option is to wring the necks of the overly confident dancers clucking about in the locker room.

"Hey, Margarette!" Rita, the dancer with legs forever and lovely banana feet which dancers swoon over, calls over the row of lockers.

"Yeah?" I answer, blowing smoke out of my mouth.

"McDermott wants to see you in her office."

The chatter calms to a simmer as I hear whispers from between the rows of lockers that hold more than dance clothes. A few girls peek their heads out and dart back in like startled turtles when I glance at them. I haven't made many friends in my four years here.

I spent so many breaks alone in this hallway, and now I'm taking the plank walk to see Mrs. McDermott. My stomach is in knots. I wave my hand around my face to get rid of any residual smell of smoke, I adjust my clothing, and tighten my hair.

Another dancer rushes past me into the locker room. After shoving me, blind to her actions, she yells, "Hey Shannon, I passed the audition, I made it!" The locker room door shuts so hard it hurts my ears. But I can still hear the laughs and cheers behind that heavy door.

The office is small. I've always wondered if it was a closet they made into an office to make a dance director feel important. Just glued a brass name tag on the door and, presto, it became a space fit for a queen. Dozens of folders are stacked on the desk. Pamphlets showcasing the senior performance I'm not in are scattered in piles to be sent to school sponsors and other patrons. I look through Mrs. McDermott's big wavy hair and the poster-covered walls to the half-open blinds partially blocking the sun I've come to detest.

Mrs. McDermott has shoulder length, dirty blonde hair. Her glasses frame her sharp face well. Her jaw line is defined and tinted with pink rouge that accents her lips, which are usually tight until she smiles. Her amazing green eyes are soft and land on me with kindness.

"Margarette, sweetie… I absolutely hate that we have to have this talk. We've had you in the office every year since you started at the school. You had such promise and talent, yet you never seemed to settle in. Your grades have not improved much and, as you know, both your dance performance and academic studies matter."

My anger is building along with an overwhelming urge to cry. *Of course I know that. I am the one who stopped going to class,* I think, as I adjust myself in the worn seat. Is there a biology formula for fixing one's home life? A history lesson on what happens when a kid finds the streets more comforting than home or school? No matter how pretty the school is, my life is ugly and savage enough to consume this school in one swallow.

I look down and rub my head which is still aching. "Yes, ma'am, I understand. I...I..."

"What dear? What happened? Why have you stopped working on your studies and dance? What has been troubling you? The last six months you've barely participated in anything." She is sitting on her desk, facing me, now holding my hand.

I start crying. I feel so embarrassed. And I'm furious that I am falling apart in front of her. How do I tell her that I can't take the wretched life at home anymore? Leaving school leaves me paralyzed with fear, wondering if we will have electricity or will have been evicted again. How do I tell the dance director that I had an abortion, and sexually transmitted diseases, and that I'm just as combative as my first horrific boyfriend? How do I eloquently tell her that I met a stranger who said he was my father, and my mother is lost in a mental and emotional jungle?

I feel like I'm running across an endless stage with no *exit left* cues, the script suddenly changed once again. Nothing I have done thus far made me feel as beautiful on the inside as the grace and joy of dance on the outside did. But dance alone will never beautify my insides.

"I thank you for always trying to help me." I wipe my nose and eyes with the tissue she hands me. "I had a hard time at home, and I just couldn't focus on school as much as I used to, I guess. I don't want to fail. I would love to graduate." The already tiny office grows smaller, and I feel my options caving in on me.

"Dear, you can still graduate. I truly wish you kept up your grades and that this conversation was going much differently. However, as much as it pains me to say this..."

I drop her hand and cover my face to hide my sobbing. "I'm so sorry, Margarette, I think we both know you are not going to Julliard or any other professional dance university. But you don't have to feel like this is the end."

What?! I thought. *Feel like this is the end? The end happened the day Grandma died. What happened to the girl who wanted to be as happy as*

Clara in the Nutcracker? The girl who stomped to the beat of her own drums and spoke from the drama stage in Harlem School of the Arts? And what happened to the girl who loved Jacque from National Dance Institute so much?

Where are all those people? What happened to my laughter and free spirit?

I nod my head frantically to signal that I understand her as she rubs my back.

"Sweetie, we are going to continue the assignments you have left so you can get your degree from LaGuardia. I can't imagine what you have been going through, but you can't blame yourself. We can still make it if you try. Don't give up now. No university will determine your success. Only you can do that, if you give yourself a bit of kindness and believe in yourself."

"Yes, Mrs. McDermott," I say, sucking in air like I have a plastic bag over my face.

I don't pay attention to much of what she's saying. Deep down I knew I no longer stood a chance at getting into Julliard. I've been trying to mold my experience into what I wanted it to be, rather than what it is. I've been fighting my reality like I'm in the middle of a Roman arena with a savage beast. The beast won.

I have become the beast.

I ride the train home, feeling like even Grandma might have been part of this nasty scheme to bring me into the world, let me be a happy kid for a few years, then change the game to make sure I lost.

The lives of some friends flash through my mind. The shelters, the fathers that left, the endless welfare, the lack of supportive family members. Some didn't make it past middle school. I tried so hard not to become like them, but my life, and all the things in it, feel like they are perched atop a dinghy full of holes. Nothing can save me.

I think about Shelly, when she used to tell me to stop hanging in the streets; she was trying to be the savior, but I know she was wasting her time trying to be what our mother should have been. I was just as mad at her as I was at our mother. And now we are all in the same sinking boat.

CHAPTER 12

W hy I studied computer programming in college, I will never know. The only class I love is public speaking, in which I will get an A. Every other class I struggle through as if I'm climbing a mountain barefoot in inclement weather with no safety equipment.

Borough of Manhattan Community College is shaped like a cube, halls, and corridors everywhere. I feel swallowed up in what seems like a college version of Grand Central Station. I hate the coldness of the building.

The last time I did coke was when I was in the Oasis bar on 148th Street and Broadway. It had become my hangout place. I'd sit there from early afternoon, alone, with Emily, or with anyone willing to buy me drinks. On weekends we go to the Shadow nightclub or some other overpriced, packed place in the city.

One night, I was in the sardine-tin-sized bathroom of the Oasis when Tara, one of the older women I hang out with, handed me a joint. I didn't even ask what it was; I assumed it was weed. I had already taken a few hits of coke in the stall, even though I was getting sick of it and only did it when someone else had it.

I took two long drags, and the last one made me feel like Mia Wallace from "Pulp Fiction". I jerked my head back as if being kicked by Ron, triggering a flashback, and then my eyes did an exorcist move and I blacked out, waking up later on my bedroom floor, covered in vomit.

Shelly was shaking me, "What the hell is wrong with you? This is disgusting! Get up before Mom gets home!"

After I showered and changed, Mom walked into the apartment from her midnight shift at the hospital. "Hey, are you off to school?" she asked, walking past me and into the kitchen. I had forgotten I had school. I didn't even know what day it was.

On the train ride in, I was still in shock at the outcome of the night. Mia never talked about her near-death experience again through the rest of "Pulp Fiction". As much as I wished my life was fiction, it wasn't. *What if I died from what was in that joint? Imagine my mother finding me covered in my own vomit.*

That day I made the decision to stop indulging in anything except alcohol. No one ever gets addicted to that.

I graduated without honors and buried my senior photo and degree somewhere at the bottom of my closet. I looked as shiny and new as a debutant in that picture. *All ready* for the world. Except I had no idea what door to walk through.

After two years at Borough of Manhattan Community College, drinking daily, and bumbling through countless crappy jobs, I ended up at a stock exchange firm. At just twenty-three, I'm junior and certainly not someone who makes money for the company. My position is part-time as a paper-pusher in the compliance department. I take the train to New Jersey every day. At what time varies, based on the severity of my hangover. When I arrive, I slide my ID card into the entrance gate, walk through the obnoxious marbled lobby lined with fresh flowers, and take the shiny elevator up to the fourteenth floor. I don't work in a formal office, of course, just a large room filled with cubicles. Some are decorated with barely-hanging-on plants and colorful calendars or plastic, faux mahogany clock radios.

Within a year, I start hearing about people being laid off, some of them full-time employees who make much more money than I do. If the company doesn't need *them*, it is surely just a matter of time before they hand me my walking papers. I'm standing in the cafeteria line waiting to pay way too much for onion-crusted bagels when I see my friend Diane and ask her, "Do you think they are going to start cutting the part-time employees?"

"I don't think so. There's such a high turnover rate with the part-timers that I don't see them doing that. Are you worried?" She doesn't seem perturbed, so maybe I shouldn't be. Still, I don't feel like I'm on solid ground. I'm constantly uncomfortable and anxious about what's going to happen next. My alcohol-fueled nights help sedate those feelings, but then I wake up and they kick in all over again. Of course, I'm worried. Good thing I don't love working here. I pick up my toasted bagel, grab two strawberry spread packets and butter, and move to the juice section.

"Well, what do you want to do? She asks. "You don't have to stay here, you know."

"I'm just wondering how all this isn't getting to you." I say, filling my coffee cup.

"Eight dollars," the cashier says, her long, red hair pulled into a low ponytail. *Is she happy?* I wonder. I bet she doesn't worry about getting laid off.

As we're riding up in the elevator, I can't help but notice the other people riding with us. There is a man wearing a green fleece jacket, tan slacks, and beat-up brown loafers. He has earphones in and occasionally chuckles to himself, stepping off the elevator on the tenth floor right before saying, "Good day, everyone." As the door closes, I hear a faint whistling, and agitation creeps into my stomach. I don't understand glee in others, so it infuriates me to witness it. I shake my head quickly and let out a puff of air. Why can't elevators go faster?

The woman standing in front of me is dressed so neatly she resembles a Macy's holiday window display with her lavender pencil skirt, white sheer stockings, silver short-sleeved silk blouse, and black pumps. Not a strand of her golden hair is out of place, and her face is framed with burgundy thin-rimmed glasses. I imagine the energy it must have taken to put her outfit together. I can barely take a shower with the pounding headache I have most days, let alone take time to turn myself into a career Barbie doll.

My head lowers a bit as I look down at my clothing—my costume, really—and wonder why I feel so invisible in such a tiny space. These elevator rides feel like a metaphor for my life; everyone else is going up while I feel trapped, suffocating.

Hours later, I'm taking a trip down to the trading floor to deliver the daily reports. The phones are ringing and being slammed down, computer keys being angrily punched. Papers and people are all over the place. It is organized chaos, and the center of attention is the full-circle view of the stock exchange monitor hanging from the middle of the ceiling.

"This is where the madness starts and ends," my coworker Dave says. He works alongside one of the managers of my department, and we've become friends.

"What would someone have to do to become a trader?" I ask.

"Lose their mind and soul, basically," he says cavalierly. "See that woman over there?" he says, gesturing. "She used to work with me. She organized parties for birthdays, decorated for the holidays, was always cheery, and gave great advice to people. Now she is stressed out of her mind."

Dave stops to shake hands with a man we pass on the trading floor. He then steps to the side and motions for me to go in front of him as we make our way through a narrow section of desks before he continues his story, much more loudly in order to be heard over the din of shouting, sweaty traders. "She must mirror an experienced trader to learn the ropes, the ropes that hang you after a while. The company pays for the training and certification. The payback is that she, just like any other trader, better make the right decisions for the company. Money is the bottom line in this business."

I listen to him and watch the woman he's speaking about. *The ropes that hang you after a while.* It sticks in my head like a spear. She's frantically scribbling notes on a pad while following her trading mentor around, wiping her forehead with her bare hand. She glances up, not at the monitor, but *all* the way up. Maybe asking God what the heck she's gotten herself into.

Everyone is in a zone. These are the same people who, at company parties, drink and talk their way into oblivion. Short sentences between shots of scotch and whiskey, obvious signs of snorting smeared on their cheeks and clothing after a few drinks. Ironically, it isn't that different from what we did in Harlem, listening to hip hop, R & B, and jazz in our living rooms and apartment stairwells, sputtering short sentences between drags of cigarettes and joints and shots of liquor before waking up to visit that working world again, waiting for the hour when we could again escape.

Up until now, I've acted and reacted based on what I needed. I've never thought about what I would do long-term. My dreams of dance are gone, and it's time I accept that. The stock exchange looks like it is bananas from start to finish, and I am learning firsthand that it's not a movie that ends well.

"Why didn't you become a trader?" I ask with a smirk.

"Why do that when I can get paid just as much for less misery?" he says, pointing to the bell above the chaos. As the bell goes off, the dark room is illuminated by dusty, high-hat lights. Everyone here could have just as easily been sitting at slot machines. The doors open, and the food delivery crew trails in. Food bags and trays are placed on some of the desks, while traders run out to grab food elsewhere. Some smoke at their desks while drinking hours-old cold coffee. The woman I've been observing doesn't even look up long enough to notice that her mentor has vanished and been replaced by a burger and fries. She takes some fries, stuffs them in her mouth, and flips through her notepad, looking for the answers to all her questions.

"What are you thinking about?" Dave asks, holding his elbow out for me as if we are about to waltz.

"I don't know, dear sir; I just don't know. Let's go eat."

We sit at a window table in a restaurant near the river. I look over at Manhattan. The sky is blue, the river is calm. Dirty, as usual, but calm.

"You know, I spent my whole life on that island and in that city," I say as I stuff a forkful of spaghetti in my mouth. "Isn't it crazy what life does to a person who grows up there?"

"Not as bad as growing up in some other places. Or in past times, times when we weren't even thought about," he said, taking a sip of his tea.

He's referring to his parents who immigrated to America from

Poland. I think back to a conversation we had a few weeks ago when he told me their story. They came to this country with a couple hundred dollars and a small bag of clothes, having left Poland for a better life. They lived with his father's sister and her three kids in a tiny apartment in Borough Park, Brooklyn. Dave was born there, along with his younger siblings. He said they'd been so poor that families took turns sharing dinner with other families in his building.

The waiter puts a coffee down in front of me, and I am brought back into the moment. "We were seldom encouraged to think past that place," he continues. "Our parents physically left Poland, but their minds were still there. They couldn't help but teach us to live like they did in Poland, like they were too traumatized to let themselves off the hook in America."

Listening to him, I think about my own situation and try to explain it to him. My mother and I did not grow up in poverty. She drove us there. I feel so much respect for Dave's parents, who did the best they could with a difficult situation, building a community to take care of each other. My mother made choices that impacted my life and limited the opportunities I had, as though she held onto me with a ball and chain, never letting me be truly free. But it didn't have to be that way. She could have started over.

"After my grandmother died, I no longer had a strong sense of self. So, I mimicked what I thought I should be," I say, watching the Macy's Barbie doll stroll out of the restaurant, giggling with the department president. "Some things or people never change," Dave says, wiping his mouth. "I'm glad you made it past that. It's not easy going against what you know. I couldn't follow my parents' advice. I know they meant well, but they were too afraid to understand that new life means building on the old one, not repeating it." He stuffs money into the check folder, and I hand him cash for my portion.

"Don't even think about it. Your part-time money is never welcome here," he says, holding up his iced tea. "Cheers to life."

I smile like the cat in *Alice in Wonderland*. "Cheers to you, Dave."

"By the way, have you heard anything about NYPD?"

Before I joined the Stock Exchange a year ago, I applied for the New York City Police Academy on a whim, after reading about a police officer who saved a six-year-old kid whose parents had both overdosed in their apartment. I felt that article in every bone of my body and knew there was something special and important about being a cop. I didn't think they would pick *me* to become a cop, but decided it was worth a try.

I've gone through the various steps of the application process and passed everything so far but still don't allow myself to expect anything will come of it. I'm too used to disappointment.

"Not yet, it's been almost a year. I'm just waiting to see if I got into the academy. Maybe risking getting shot is better than pursuing a career in finance." We both laugh so hard that some of the patrons look over at us.

"God, help us, right?" Dave says while we walk across the Maranda, the Manhattan skyline standing tall behind us.

There is a scene in the movie *Women of Brewster Place* that's stuck with me. The neighborhood was separated from the upscale area by a wall, and everyone who visited Brewster Place had horrid drama in their lives. After disaster upon disaster, the community wanted to be free and started chipping away at the wall with makeshift tools. They were crying and cheering while destroying the one thing that kept them hostage: the walls of victimhood and shame. I want to see what's on the other side of the wall I have lived behind for so long, even though part of me feels I don't deserve to be or have anything better than my crappy, aimless life.

The police department seems more down to earth, more like a family, which I have no real experience with but have always dreamed of. The Stock Exchange is like an elite level of society where they do all the same drugs and make all the same mistakes as the people down the block where I grew up, except they do it in Armani suits. I don't fit in here either and I know that one day they'll realize this too, and then I'll be out.

I want something in my life that will be there if I want it to be. I want something reliable, stable, and predictable. Somewhere I belong. And anything better than what I currently have.

As it turns out, I don't have to wait long. As though the universe has been listening, when I arrive home, there is a letter addressed to me lying on the kitchen table, almost unnoticeable, squashed between a phone book and the TV Guide.

The return address is New York City Police Department. I sit down at the table and open it with trepidation. *What if it's a rejection letter?* I don't think I can take another failure.

Dear Ms. Allyn, We are pleased to inform you…

No more jobs that don't mean anything, no more meaningless flings, no more worrying about my well-being or security. I am going to make it in the big leagues. I am on my way to freedom, to be on the biggest stage in the world, the NYPD. I am going to save people!

I run down the hall to Mom. "Look, I passed the NYPD exam! Can you believe that?!" I wave it in front of her face, which is glued to the TV, and then press the letter into her hand, willing her to read it.

"Oh my goodness, you were not kidding when you said you were going to apply. That's …" she trails off, engrossed in what she's watching, not looking at me or at the letter.

"Can't you be happy for one freaking thing I do?" I say, snatching the letter from her hand.

"Don't you snatch anything from me. If you want to be a cop, then go ahead. I'm not going to stop you." She turns toward the TV, and the crowd in the Giants Stadium roars.

"Are you scared? Is that it?" I ask.

"No, I'm not scared of anything. I know you will be alright. Leave me alone. I'm watching the game."

I hug her from behind. "I will be okay," I say. "I have no choice. I want something better; I can't keep bouncing from job to job, and I'm not happy with how things turned out so far for me. This is the least I can do."

She finally turns to face me. "Why are you not happy?"

"If I didn't lose my opportunity to dance, I would have been in show business by now, maybe dancing at Lincoln Center. But hey, we both know how that went."

She takes a quick breath, as if she hasn't been breathing this whole time. She opens her mouth, but nothing comes out. I stare at her and wait, but she just turns back to the TV and screams, "Go, Go, Go!" She picks up a cigarette and lights it, seemingly forgetting that I'm there. I turn around and walk down the hall, gently closing the apartment door behind me.

Do I believe that Muslims should be banned from the force? No. Is a five-cent piece of candy worth stealing? Of course not! Do I affiliate with any know criminals? Absolutely not. I am halfway through the fifteen hundred questions I am required to answer during the application process, shifting uncomfortably in a hard wooden chair in a room in Lefrak City Queens, my pencil almost breaking in half at this point. I grab my water bottle from the floor, wishing I'd filled it with liquor so I could drink the whole thing in one swallow. I loosen my sweater and wipe my head with my tissue that is slowly disintegrating.

Have I ever told a lie to avoid hurting someone's feelings? No. Do I believe in God? There's not a choice that says "not anymore" so I have to go with a feigned yes. I become mechanical, a tin man, halfway through, giving little to no thought to the answers after a while.

My next step is an appointment with the department psychologist. The waiting room is adorned with posters "Learn to cope with stress", "Join New York's Finest", "Drinking and driving is a crime." The fourth is a text-less picture of a yellow, green, and white flower.

Then come the physical tests. We have to run a mile and a half in thirteen minutes, complete thirty-six sit-ups in a minute, and bench-press eighty percent of our bodyweight. I am surprised that my dance experience serves no purpose during the run. I decide to start slow and build momentum. By the time I finish the twentieth lap, I feel like I've been dragged across the Henry Hudson River, backwards, by an alligator. But I finish. And I've officially completed all the tests necessary to be accepted into the academy.

Sitting in my cubicle at the stock exchange, I listen to the voicemail for the hundredth time. "Hello, this is Detective O'Malley. I am calling to inform you that you have passed your initial investigation. You are to report to the Police Academy to be sworn in on July 7 at 7am. Congratulations! See you there and be on time."

I call my mother to tell her the news. "Mom, guess what? I'm going into the academy! The investigator called and said I passed the investigation!"

I did it. I really did it. I achieved something so big, all on my own. I went through all the tests and the scrutiny, and they still wanted me. I might have left out a few details of my life, but still, they chose me.

"Mm-hm," she says, clearly not listening.

"What's wrong?" I ask.

"We got evicted again," she responds with a loud sigh. "They're not giving us another chance."

"Us? I didn't have anything to do with this, Mom. Don't tell me this again; not now. I'm going into the academy." She hangs up the phone and I stand up, staring at the receiver in my hand, mouth hanging open. Is she still so uninvested in my success? Even now? Even after I've just achieved something that nobody else in the history of my family has achieved? She just hung up on me, only after telling me that I—we have nowhere to live, of course.

Where will I live? Can I at least get my stuff? I can't even think straight. It's the end of the workday, and I'm ready to go home. It's a shame I don't actually have one to go to. I call Shelly at work to figure out what we should do. I tell her we've been evicted again and she sighs loudly.

"I can call Emily and ask if we can stay," I say, confident that it will be okay. Her mom said I'm always welcome to stay; they just have to make room because two of her brothers and her sister still live in the three-bedroom apartment.

"No, I'll call one of my own friends," Shelly says without hesitation.

I can feel the distance between us growing.

Later, at Emily's house, I find out that I can't get any of my clothing because the landlord won't let any of us into the apartment.

"We're going to get your shit," Emily says.

I look at her and protest, "But he said that—"

"We're going to get your shit."

Over the weekend we stop by and convince the neighbor above our apartment to let me go through the fire escape. I climb in through the window, which has been left open. Emily and her sister help me put my clothes into garbage bags. *Thank goodness for friends who will help me commit burglary.* While we are doing this, a couple of the local drug addicts come up to claim they are "helping" us and start stuffing my things into their pockets.

"Come on, girl, you don't need this; let me have it."

"Get your hands off of my clothes. Why are you in here anyway?"

"Everyone knows ya'll got evicted. Hey, we'll watch everything while you get a cab if you pay me ten dollars."

I push them out of the apartment, and Emily's sister watches over everything while I carry my television and a few bags of clothes plus pictures of me and my mother to the taxi waiting outside. I walk away from that apartment feeling like if I look back, that life will repeat itself. I feel like I finally broke through that wall around my life, or at the very least jumped over it.

Maybe now I'm free.

CHAPTER 13

"This is where we weed out the weak-minded. If you make it here, you will make it anywhere!" the sergeant standing on the gym stage yelled.

If I wasn't so scared, I'd think he was quoting Sinatra. We still have two weeks left of what they call D-Day Hell Weeks, and I'm already crapping my pants on day one.

I'm virtually homeless, I can't go back to the Stock Exchange, and I just walked into a military nightmare. This was supposed to be my saving grace. *If this is what my life is going to be like, I would rather get the firearm now and use it to kill myself.*

More than 300 of us are standing at attention in the academy gym. The smell is unbearable. We all wear whatever gym attire we could afford or found in our closets, and some of us are getting hammered for it. I had no choice but to wear the wrinkled shirt and shorts that look like parachutes because the official recruit uniforms are expensive, and I had to borrow the money from my cousin to purchase all the other equipment I need. I have to wait until I get my final check from the stock exchange to get the rest. The instructors wear blue shorts and shirts that read NYPD Physical Training and Tactics Unit. They are yelling at random recruits as they walk around the gym.

"Do you call yourself an officer? You look more like a stuffed teddy bear!" one of the instructors is screaming into the ear of a

120

guy who looks like he's about to pass out. I start to get nervous. I know they're going to say something about what I am wearing. What the heck will I say? That I'm homeless and barely hanging on by a thread? The other recruits say nothing. A few run out of the gym altogether, and someone else faints, right in the front row. A couple of instructors yell at other recruits to drag him off to the side as if he is roadkill getting in the way.

Before I can think up a lie, a female instructor is standing nose to nose with me. She is shorter than I am but manages to get her nose to touch mine. My eyes pop open so wide I think they might spring out and hit her.

"What are you looking at, recruit?"

"Nothing, ma'am," I whisper, terrified that I'm going to say the wrong thing or say the worse wrong thing. Three recruits are in the bear crawl position on my right side. The guy right in front of me is soaked, and he hasn't moved since we got in the gym. I want to die.

"I can't hear you, recruit. I said, what are you looking at?"

I think back to my piano lessons and feel going up an entire octave will be too much, so I raise my voice just a couple of notches. "I said, nothing, ma'am."

She starts yelling, and my knees buckle at the volume in her voice. "I saw you looking at those broken dirt bags on the side! You didn't think I was watching you, recruit? You have to know that you are always being watched, always. And you never know who will sneak up on you!"

I figure I better say something, or I may get kicked in the stomach. "Yes, Ma'am."

"Louder!"

"Yessssss, Ma'am!"

"The rest of you dirt bags better remember that!"

Someone behind me snickers.

Ohhh jeez, here it comes, I think

"What was that! Who laughed?"

I know she couldn't think it was me. I'm too busy holding my pee in.

"All of you bear crawl. Now!"

We drop to our hands. The floor is disgusting. It's rubber and wet with our sweat. I can't even tell what color it's supposed to be, but it seems a mixture of orange, yellow, torture, and blue. We groan while crawling around the gym's perimeter with Instructor Snap Trap giving us the business.

"You jerk, why did you have to laugh?" Mahoney says to the guy crawling next to her. She must be the class nerd. She is one of the few recruits who has a proper shirt with her name written on it.

"Loosen up, Mahoney. You better get used to this; they are going to do this to us for a month or more!" he retorts in between snickers.

"Fall back in formation!" the sergeant standing at the front stage yells.

"Thank goodness," I say under my breath as I slowly stand. I know I would never have been able to get away with this posture in ballet.

"It's not over yet, you rejects!" The sergeant yells from the gym stage.

I stop wondering when it's going to be over. It seems this is a long April Fool's joke.

"Push up position, move now!"

We make our way down to the position. Some of us look pathetic, including me. I can't get over the filth of the floor, the screaming and physical pain. *I have not done a push up my entire life!*

The sergeant drops to the floor, starts to do pushups, and screams, "One, up, two, up!"

He's going to get tired after ten.

My arm starts to hurt. I am only at three.

"15, 16, 16, 16, 16, 17!" He mechanically belts out, confusing us by repeating numbers.

This can't be real, I think, barely able to go down again. I am at six.

"Recruit! Are you kidding me? You can't make ten pushups and you want to be an officer?" A male instructor is kneeling next to me, screaming. Other instructors are making other recruits equally miserable, so at least I'm not in the spotlight alone.

"Can you hear me, recruit? Do you call yourself an officer?"

"Yes, sir," I say, drool slipping out of my mouth; my arms feel like they are going to break.

"Don't you touch that floor with your chest!"

My chest comes millimeters away from the gym floor before I manage to pull myself up for my final reps.

"You're not civilians anymore!" he roars. I wish I was one right now. "You're not allowed to have feelings!"

I have a thought to get up and leave. *Who the hell is he to make me do this?* Then I remember that I am homeless. *Where will I go? Back to Emily's house to tell her and her mother that I couldn't take getting yelled at while doing Hercules pushups?* My eyes are burning from the sweat, and I have a hellish cramp in my side from trying to hold myself up. I grip that tri-colored floor and dig my nails in, straightening my arms.

Before he started yelling at me, I thought he was cute. I can't think at all at this point, other than to lock my elbows and imagine living in a penthouse on Park Avenue, having the cast of Fame over for a party. That is the only thing that can keep my mind off my stomach knots and arms going numb. Over an hour of torture later, those who survived collapse onto the floor.

A wooden sign on the far wall catches my eye, black letters carved into its surface. "Integrity is who you are when no one is watching," it says. Something inside me stirs; they feel like words I need to remember.

The academic side of the academy is not my cup of tea either. I have always hated subjects other than dance, drama, and English. Statistics are rarely true, and it seems that we always have to agree with information because of the words of some intellect who never actually lived life. One of the classes at the academy is Police Science, taught by our main instructor, Instructor Gibbs, who was a former canine transit officer. He chose to teach in the academy after his German Shepherd was shot on the job.

"Why did you all decide to become police officers?" he asks.

Each of us has to answer. Some say "family tradition" while others say it's been a lifelong dream to be an officer. "I had no choice," I say. I don't want to be too open and have them judge me.

"Oh really? Why was that?" he asked.

"Well," I say after a long sigh, "I don't have family in the department, but things just didn't work out the way I thought, so it was this or nothing."

Instructor Gibbs doesn't acknowledge my answer before moving on.

"What you all do from now on is going to determine your maturity level, what kind of people you become, and what you value about life," he says.

One of the girls says something in Spanish to the girl next to her, and they both start laughing. Not only does our instructor answer her but he answers her in Spanish. We are all shocked.

"What? You all had no idea I spoke Spanish, huh?"

"Heck no," one of the guys says, and we all laugh.

"I thought you were Black," a bright blond guy says from the back of the room.

"We can all 'think' what we want, but when we treat people in ways that we think go with an appearance, we get what just happened, a shock, and usually a foot in your mouth."

Another girl raises her hand.

"Like when people say all cops are bad and they only had a bad experience with one officer," she says.

"Exactly. Black is not a character trait, neither is white, neither is sexual preference. So, let's just start by saying that most of the material you will learn is bullshit and only for test purposes. When you are out there in the real world, you'll learn really quick that stereotypes will hurt you. You are grown-ups, and most importantly, you are everyone and everyone is you. People commit crimes, people hurt other people, people do good things and can turn and do bad things. Knowing that behavior is not based on culture will be a good start."

Everyone looks like they are watching a puppet show, not knowing whether to laugh or acknowledge that puppets are not actually real. Why behavior is an area of scientific study for police officers is beyond me. Basically, we all have to learn how to act and treat people of different nationalities. Manners are a must, no matter what or who we encounter during our careers.

Why are these lessons? I wonder. Given my past, I might as well be part of the lesson of what happens when no one takes care of you and, by some miracle, you make it out of a jungle of sorts.

"Statistics show that what we see and hear from adults as children is the foundation of our early characteristics; we become what we dislike or like, even though we know some actions and views are wrong," our instructor says. "Remember, what you were taught and what you believe are two different things."

What is he talking about? I wonder. I was taught how to hustle and survive. I don't really have any other beliefs because the ones I had didn't help me at all. He obviously doesn't know me or where I come from. I am *exactly* who I was brought up to be.

I take everything day-to-day. Not only can I not imagine graduating but I also can't imagine making it through the next week. We work five day shifts one week and five night shifts the next. When people in the street recognize my uniform, which I sometimes hide by taking the jacket off and stuffing it into my bag, they say, "Good luck, pretty girl" or "Be safe."

One guy says, "Oh, you're going to be one of them, huh?"

"One of who?"

"A fucking pig."

I don't understand what that means. When I was younger, the street guys called cops DTs or the Po-po, but never pigs.

"There are worse, you know?" I reply, walking on as he drinks his beer and smokes his joint sitting in front of the funeral home on Saint Nicholas Avenue. I walk past Harlem School of the Arts, as I do every day, and wonder where my life would be if I'd kept dancing. I get lost in that thought and can't help but wonder if anything else will ever guide my life the way that dream once did. The streets are bare, and the light of the subway spills onto the pavement beside me.

As I start to descend the stairs into the station, I hear the *Woop woop* of a police car siren. I snap my head around and see two cops who have pulled up in their car. The passenger gives me the peace sign, and the driver motions two fingers from his eyes to me, reminding me that he's watching out for me. They both give me a thumbs up. I look down at my recruit jacket and feel good that at least there are some people who are happy about me being in the academy. I give them a wave before turning back and descending into the subway.

Maybe I've finally found my family after all.

The sun is boldly making its presence known, and sweat fills my eyes and fogs up my eye shields. My hearing protection earmuffs are slipping and soggy. A couple of the guys start swatting at bees, and one girl takes a few steps back and yells, "I hate bees!" So do I. It is a phobia I developed in North Carolina where beehives would pop up in the strangest places. I was once stung by a yellowjacket from a hive hidden under the porch swing and thought I'd be paralyzed. Now we have to deal with them at a firearm range in the Bronx.

The tower master starts screaming. "Knock it off, this is a disgrace! If I see one more person swat at a bee while holding a firearm, you will immediately fail!" Standing in a line, we all have our guns drawn. The target is a line drawing of a figure with no face. This is the practice round.

"On the tone, two rounds, on the tone." The robotic sound from the tower looms over us like a flock of crows. I close my eyes, my hand gripping the gun, and hope for the best. I hear a pop, and then, like fireworks, all the guns go off. With both eyes open, I look at my target. Nothing.

"Recruit, what are you doing? Fire two rounds! Two rounds! Why are you hesitating? Holster your weapon!"

I am holding my breath and panting at the same time. He pulls me off the firing line and leads me outside the range door.

"What is going on, recruit? Why didn't you shoot?"

"I—just got nervous, I guess this isn't something I'm used to," I say in a low voice with my head down.

"Pick up your head! It happens to many people; you remember what we said in class? Most people don't wake up in the morning wanting to harm or shoot people. This training is to get you to trust that, if you ever have to, saving your life and someone else's may depend on you taking action."

"Yes, sir."

"You came this far. Freezing now when we are in training isn't going to help you when you are in a serious situation. Relax, and remember: If you can't do anything, it's because you won't do anything. Do I make myself clear, recruit?"

"Yes, sir."

The next time I hear that beep, I close my non-shooting eye, hold the gun steady, block out all memories from growing up, and fire the gun. I actually hit the target within the lines. We progress to running obstacle courses in that dreadful heat—at times even in the rain—and we are tested on speed and accuracy. Something in me switches to autopilot during the training. I have no other choice. I can't afford to overthink things anymore. When I do, I get anxious, but when I am in "let it go" mode, I do well. When I notice what my mood does to my performance, I'm able to get it together. I truly hate feeling disappointed in myself, no matter how much I hate guns, so I don't allow myself to fail at this. I pass the course and let out a huge sigh of relief.

On the way back to the apartment, my classmate Sam asks, "How are you feeling, kiddo?"

"Like I finally did something I was scared of, and I didn't fall apart."

"You have been doing that every day you know?"

I had never really thought of things that way.

We spend a week at driver's training in Brooklyn, learning how to drive a police car the way movie stars do in action flicks. The thing is, it's fun for experienced drivers with the guts for speed and life-threatening situations, but I don't own a car, and the driving unit isn't nearby. Thank goodness Sam drives me to the field, otherwise I would have to rent a car. I'm extremely bad with directions, which would further complicate matters.

The real nightmare is now upon me. Four of us have to get into a police car with an instructor and take turns driving around the course. There are no words to explain how amazing it is to watch the instructor eat a sandwich while driving at an exceptional rate of speed, swooping in and out of cones set up so tightly it seems that nothing bigger than a two-wheel bike could fit through them. He talks to us the entire time, seemingly oblivious to the fact that the car feels like it is going to flip at any second.

By the end of the course, those of us in the car wear different facial expressions, varying from "This is great" to "I am so excited" to "I can't wait until it's my turn." Then there is my expression, which says, in no uncertain terms, "I am in a horror movie. I need to throw up, and I can't feel my head."

While the other classmates take their turns, the rest of us are lined up on the outer perimeter of the field, ready to retrieve and replace any run-over cones. We are told to stand back a bit because the orange cones indiscriminately take flight depending on the way the car hits them. We don't like it when someone hits a cone; it's a workout in itself just to make the trip to retrieve the cone and put another in its place. You can imagine the fury my classmates feel when it's my turn on the field, as I totally obliterate the course. It looks like a scene from *Police Academy*. Cones fly left and right, and those that aren't hit by the car are simply flattened. In the rear-view mirror I can barely make out the recruits rushing to grab them while trying not to get blown away by the storm.

Before long, the field looks more like an ocean. It feels like that rain comes from hell, shoots upward to the sky, then comes back down just to torture us. While some of the cones float away, I continue to blatantly run over most of them, making my fellow classmates struggle through inches and inches of water to fix a course I have utterly destroyed.

"Out of the car," the instructor says without even looking at me. The rain is screaming at me through the windshield, and the wind is whipping the car so hard it shivers. I look at him with tears in my eyes, partly because I can't imagine why someone would ever have to drive a car like it was a rollercoaster, and also because I am mortified to be the only person kicked out of the car.

"Sir, don't you think the rain was a bit much? I can barely see anything."

"Out. And by the way, you failed."

"Don't be so down on yourself," Sam says as I sit down in the classroom. "This is the only thing you can fail and still graduate. You just won't be able to look at a police car, let alone drive one, until you pass. They even have tutoring, and it's not so scary. That's what I heard anyway."

Another voice pipes up from behind me. "Don't worry, we aren't mad at you anymore for making us pick up almost every single cone you crushed out there. You are still family to us, and we know you will pass next time."

As a group of us laugh, I have to admit it was a scene that had gone bad fast. The cones flew up left and right, and those that didn't get hit by the car were simply flattened. In the rear-view mirror I could barely make out the recruits rushing out to grab them while trying not to get blown away by the storm.

Leaving that training on the last day is bittersweet. I know I'll have to return at some point, and I can only wish it will be on a sunny day.

Despite struggling through drivers training and firearm training, I manage to get my gun and shield. We still have a few months left in the academy, but it's a significant milestone. Sitting in the classroom waiting for our test results, I'm ruminating in my pit of sorrow. I still have nowhere to live, and at the same time, I have to work my butt off to graduate the academy. My classmates are laughing and confident, while I am wallowing in the homeless blues.

Instructor Gibbs hands me my test paper, and I see a big F on one portion of the test. He leaves the room, announcing that he'll return in a few minutes. Amidst my chattering classmates, I feel distant. Trying to fit in and believe that things will work out makes the room feel small, tight, and suffocating. I'm beginning to feel as though I don't belong here either, and that the other crushing shoe is going to drop at any moment. Will I ever have something in my life that lasts longer than my doubts?

In this moment, I make a decision. I am going to resign instead of waiting to get crushed by a "you failed" blow. I might as well get ahead of it and save myself the heartache. After all, it's better to give up now than keep trying for something that won't happen, isn't it?

I worked so hard at dance, yet my mother made it impossible

for me to succeed at it. And now that she got us evicted again—this time for good—I've been distracted from my studies. Beyond that, I need to find an apartment because even if I *do* graduate, the NYPD places you in a precinct based on where you live. They have no idea I am homeless.

As I push my chair out it squeaks across the floor, but nobody looks around, as they are too busy celebrating their test scores. I leave the classroom to go to the main office to quit. On the way up the steps, I see Instructor Gibbs.

"Where are you going, Allyn?"

My resolve crumbles and I dissolve into tears. I tell him everything I've been too embarrassed to tell anyone that I've been through. I've never told anyone except Emily, for fear people would turn me away. I really admire him and fear he may look down on me or be disappointed as well as I ramble through every disappointment and failure in my heart, mind, and soul.

My words tumble out… the constant threat of homelessness… the fear of failing at everything… losing dance to my mother… Lord knows where my father is… I am a reject half-orphan trapped in a city that beat the crap out of me. Why would God— or my deceased grandmother—ever really help me? I am always on my own, and everything in my life seems so much harder than it does in the lives of other people. The words and tears spill out, nonstop, and the resulting flood surrounds us in that staircase.

When I finish, my eyes are swollen and I am panting like a thirsty puppy. He folds his arms, nods his head, and turns up the corners of his mouth in a smirk. Then, he puts his finger on his chin, looks up, and says, "Well, you went through all this in your life. YOU made it to the Academy. YOU made it with no father. YOU made it this far."

He stops to let a few recruits pass us on the stairwell. They salute him and continue on their way. He turns to me and says, "Look at me, Allyn."

"Yes, you did not pass a portion of the test, but you know you can take it again. So, everything I heard you say was a bunch of sorry excuses. You're using excuses to give up. The life you had before is behind you. You've obviously started making choices that are working for you, so if you give up now, that is your fault and your fault only. Great job, rookie. Let us see what you do with this awful life you have."

With that, he turns and walks away, leaving me standing in what seems like wading waters. I feel like I've been given a swift kick to the gut. He didn't feel sorry for me, and that's what I really wanted—for someone to tell me that all of my complaints are legitimate, and I have the full right to give up. I'm a little annoyed. No, I'm a lot annoyed.

The reality of my situation hits me. *If I resign, you won't have any place to live or a paycheck.* There is no way I'm going to end up like my mother. Not knowing where she is keeps my stomach in knots. But if I do see her again, I'm not going to tell her that I quit. I head back down the stairs and follow Instructor Gibbs into the classroom.

Determined to pass my test the second time, it's time to buckle down and study. Living with Emily is beneficial because she helps me make studying fun. We make flash cards of the proper legal terms and crime classifications and use them while we drink and listen to music. Luckily, my life has been one big series of crimes, and we have plenty of material to draw upon in our study sessions.

Possession of a controlled substance? Misdemeanor
Rape 1? First degree felony
Assault 1? Felony
Burglary? Felony
Grand larceny? Felony
Possession of marijuana? Misdemeanor

It is like watching the parade of my life pass before my eyes.

"Okay," Emily says while putting her drink down and placing an index card face down on the bed. "When you were with Steve, hint," holding her finger up like Sherlock Holmes, "his stupid ass was much older than you."

I blow smoke out of my mouth while looking up as if listening to the Final Jeopardy theme music before belting out, "Rape!"

"Right," Emily says. We laugh and give each other a high five. I think about that answer as Emily is shuffling the index cards like a pro Blackjack dealer. *Why wouldn't he have known that? I guess since I was willing it never crossed my mind. But who would have been brilliant enough to tell me at the time?* I think, sipping my tequila. I am feeling elated about not having to say I am *currently* being raped, voluntarily or otherwise.

"Here is another good one," Emily says.

"Okay let's have it; we're on a roll."

"Ron punched you in the ribs and face," she says, looking up at me holding up her finger again, "and you punched him back many times, so you both actually did this." She stubs out her cigarette.

"Assault," I say, barely able to get it out I'm laughing so hard.

"You crawled down the fire escape and went into your old apartment through the window because the super didn't let you get your shit after they kicked you out."

The whole sentence stung me like a punch from Sugar Ray Leonard. I feel a bit ashamed and don't want to go on. Emily looks up at me. "Don't start feeling bad. Look where you are now. You're doing good for yourself. Stop with that and answer the question." I laugh because I knew she was going to say that.

"Burglary, and cheers to that," I sing along to the beat of Sade playing in the background, and we clink our glasses together.

"The money you took from church, even though those people were phony as heck, but you were still in a religious building."

I take a deep breath and glance out of the window. Jezebel is playing on the CD player.

"Grand larceny." And yes, they may have been phony, but I did like the building for a time.

"You held that crack for Ron, and in your house. It was less than ten bags."

I wince. One thing I despised was how I felt I was getting back at my mother by being with Ron. She knew him before I did, and I was so embarrassed when he told me she bought from him. When I held his drugs, I was supposed to sell them. I felt lower than low and wasn't going to let his drugs ruin my life. He already helped my mother do that. We had a fight when I gave them back to him. I held them over the sewer and said I'd drop them in if he didn't take them back and promise to never speak to my mother again. She was already getting her stash from other dealers, so it hadn't really made any sense to throw around such a pointless threat. I was trying to save her, but taking away one dealer would have no impact.

"Freaking jerk," I say, "and possession of controlled substance."

"Girl," Emily says while swaying her head back and forth to Bobby Brown's "My Prerogative", "You are going to slam that test this time." She continues, "What we smoked in the staircases when we were younger."

"Possession of marijuana." I am so happy that I only drink now, and I hope I'll pass this time.

CHAPTER 14

My patent leather shoes reflect the lights above me, not a scratch on them. I waited until the last minute to get a pair because I didn't want to jinx myself. I spent hours on 34th Street looking in different shoe stores to find them. On the train home, I peeked into the box they were stored in God knows how many times; my smile made my cheeks cramp. They remind me of my first pair of tap shoes, the ones that had a big black ribbon laced into them.

"Oh my dear, how amazing and sweet you look," Grandma had said when I first wore them. These shoes are not tap shoes, but for the first time in years, I feel as though she is looking down at me from somewhere in Heaven.

Maybe my sense of joy also comes from the fact that I found an apartment a month ago. Every time I wake up in my new apartment, the sun spilling into the living room, I am grateful. I have my own apartment, *and* I am graduating. I feel amazing.

Backstage at Madison Square Garden, we're all taking pictures with our now colleagues, who were once our instructors, and I see Instructor Gibbs standing with a few of my classmates. As I approach him, he has his usual smirk.

"See what happens when you don't feel sorry for yourself?"

"Yes, but see what happens when someone gives you a kick in the butt?"

134

We both laugh, and I lunge forward and hug him. "Congrats… officer," he says.

I look in a mirror set up backstage. My dress uniform is pristine, my shield and name tag placed perfectly on the left side of my jacket. We are all wearing blue. No more gray shirts. Holding my hat, I run my fingers over my cap device and trace the numbers of my shield.

We take pictures with each other, our instructors, and the NYPD bagpipe band, who are practicing in the corner, providing a joyous musical backdrop to our experience. The instructors are so happy for us. They are as giddy as we are. It is as though they are starting over again with us. My heart sinks when I look at the people, I have spent more than nine months with. Sam catches my eye and winks, a broad smile crossing his face. I run over and hug him; I would never be here without my friend and personal chauffeur.

Part of me doesn't want to move on, and I start to feel lonely, despite the throngs of people around me. I reach into my pocket and pull out the Nokia phone I bought last week. No missed calls. I told Emily to be here at ten, but I can't find anyone I know in the crowd now flooding the arena. I hope my aunt and cousins made it.

"Everyone get in line; the ceremony is about to start." The sergeant from the ceremonial unit is stiff as a board, his mouth moving more slowly than the flashing lights around him. We all take our places and wait. I can see the arena from backstage. The lights all go out. It is pitch black, and then monitors display the NPYD logo. The voice of James Earl Jones narrates as the audience watches video clips of NYPD rescues in helicopters, boats, foot pursuits, major drug, and gun arrests, helping the elderly across the street, finding a lost child, or starting or ending a riot.

What if I were in one of those situations? I wonder. I am smiling, taken by the thought. I picture myself in the less dangerous situations: saving a lost child, helping a woman have a baby, getting hugs from old people.

Then, the video changes to images of officers who were killed in the line of duty. I remember the stories we were told in the academy about how most of them died: assassinated while conducting an undercover operation, a sudden health issue, or a fatal accident. The coffin being carried by six fellow officers, the American Flag draped over the box, the perfectly ordered unity marching to the drums. The audience erupts in applause at every face that appears then fades away. I'm wiping tears from my eyes as James Earl Jones repeats, "Heroes, always heroes." All the lights snap back on, and I jerk at the sound.

"And now, introducing the NYPD graduate class of 2000!"

New York New York by Frank Sinatra starts blaring over every speaker in the arena. The first group of officers starts marching out, disappearing from behind the curtain and into the bright light spilling from the stage. The camera flashes and screaming make me feel like a celebrity. I am tapping my foot and rubbing my hands together while waiting for my class to walk into the light.

"I wanna wake up, in a city that doesn't sleep…" The past nine months seem like a blur as I sing along with ol' blue eyes because I finally made it somewhere.

"If I can make it there, I'll make it anywhere…" I cover my mouth and bounce on my tip toes. Then I start swaying back and forth and lock arms with the officer on either side of me.

"It's up to you, New York…New York."

We start walking out, and the cheering is so amplified that my ears are ringing. I am panting and can't hear the music anymore over the cheers. The audience looks like mountains of autumn trees. I see waving, clapping, and endless smiles, family members yelling the names of the officers as we all stare straight ahead at attention. When the applause finally settles down, the department chaplain approaches the podium to give a speech and offer a prayer.

"Parade rest!" the ceremonial sergeant commands, his words echoing to the roof of the arena. We all snap into rest position with our hands behind our backs and our heads lowered. I hang onto every word the chaplain says and want to put him in my breast pocket to protect me.

"Atten---tion!" I hear the sound of our shiny shoes clap together, and our heads pop up at the same time. A perfect dance.

I glance down and see my reflection in the tips of my shoes and feel I am on a performance stage again.

"May God be with you all," the chaplain says at the end of his prayer, as he makes the sign of the cross.

Mayor Giuliani takes his place on stage. "I, as the mayor of the best city in the world, am proud to see another graduating class from the New York City Police Department. As I walk around this city and watch how far it's come, I am so pleased with the hard work of the citizens of this beautiful city and the officers who risk their lives to protect and serve each and every day. Today, ladies and gentlemen, is the first day of life as official police officers, the first day of a new chapter in your life and the first day being part of an amazing law enforcement family. And now it is time to induct you all officially into the police department with the solemn oath."

The ceremonial sergeant commands through his microphone, "Present arms!"

Our right hands go up with such force it makes a vacuum-like sound, almost slowing down right before the end, when every white glove is facing the front of the stage, staving off bad energy.

The mayor starts the oath that we must repeat. "I solemnly swear..."

If Grandma could see me now. I repeat the prayer she said most nights when she was home: *The Lord is my Shepherd*. The God who may never forgive my past. I have been too ashamed of it to ever ask, but now I get to erase it, let go, and abandon everything I have hated about my life.

"I solemnly swear..."

Even though I feel so far away from the God, she taught me to trust.

"To uphold the constitution of the United States of America..."

I shall not want.

He restoreth my soul.

"To uphold the constitution of the United States of America..."

He led me through green pastures, my cup runneth over.

"To protect and serve... To uphold the law... With integrity and dignity to the best of my ability."

Everything and everyone disappear; I am standing in that arena alone. A blur in the world. Who is really paying attention to me in this sea of blue? Through the lights above, who can see me?

Goodness and mercy shall follow me, all the days of my life.

"With integrity and dignity to the best of my ability."

"So, Help You God."

Everyone reappears again, the lights flashing.

"So, help me...God."

The ceremonial sergeant barks, "Order arms!" and we drop our hands in unison.

Mayor Giuliani finishes with "Now we will give thanks to all the family members and friends who supported you all while you were training for the life you now have."

"Right and Left face!"

We turn to face the audience.

"Present Arms!"

When we turn and my heels click together, I give my salute. The first person I see is Emily. She is jumping, clapping, waving, and screaming. I'm so lucky to have her as a friend. Right next to her is my mother and Shelly. They are doing the exact same thing, surrounded by a few of my friends, cousins, and my aunt. I am not allowed to move out of formation, but I feel overwhelmed with emotion, realizing that I hadn't even allowed myself to expect my mom to come. Down by my side, where nobody can see, I ball my fist in a celebratory mini air-punch.

She's here. I cry like a baby and smile like a champ. *This* is the best day of my life.

CHAPTER 15

Roasted chicken, café con leché, and rice and beans scent the air as I walk along Broadway at 183rd Street. La Caridad restaurant is on the northwest corner, and the senoras are dancing while serving up the food I can smell. There are cars parked on both sides of Broadway. Traffic is moving slowly, and someone is blasting Spanish music from their obnoxious trunk speakers.

On the side of the red brick building with dusty windows that make it look like an abandoned school is a huge decal that says 34th Precinct, Police Department City of New York. I walk up the stairs and see a police car zipping out the side parking lot with sirens on, drowning out the Spanish music. The car moves into the wrong lane and drives north in the south-bound lane. The sirens fade as I turn to pull the door open. I hold the door halfway open for a moment. *I am in Washington Heights, as a cop. Wow.* I take a deep breath and walk in.

A female officer with a blonde ponytail is sitting at a small desk adjacent a metal barrier that holds a stop sign. Next to the small desk is a tall, larger desk on which a sergeant is resting his head. He looks like a mix between Ricky Schroeder and Richie Cunningham. They're both on the phone. The female looks up with her bright hazel eyes, smiles like the sun, and says, in an amplified voice, "Hi! My name is Doreen. We heard you were coming! What's your name?"

Before I can answer, she turns and pulls me through the gate and up to the big desk. "Sergeant Murphy, this is the new girl. Where do you want me to bring her?"

Sergeant Murphy waves his hand in the air as if he is swatting a fly. "Take her to Sergeant Walsh."

"Yay!" Doreen says, turning to look at me and squeezing my arm. "You are going to like him. He usually works midnights, but he is training the rookies because the hours work for the NYPD baseball season."

An officer walks out of the arrest processing room and stops in front of us. "Welcome to the rollercoaster, kid, and don't forget to bring your paperwork later today. Don't make me look for you."

I have no idea who he is, so I don't know how to respond. I raise my eyebrows and say, "Yes, sir?" and turn back toward Doreen.

"Jackson, shut your mouth and knock it off!" Doreen snaps. She turns to me and waves her hand in the same fly swatting move the sergeant made. "He is a moron! He always tries to make the rookies think he's important."

I like her, and I like how comfortable she seems to be. I was nervous as heck before I walked into the precinct, but because she is friendly, I feel as though I can get comfortable too. The bag I am carrying with my unform, gun belt, and bulletproof vest is causing my hand to chafe. "Hey, would I be able to put this bag down somewhere?" I ask Doreen as she leads me into the complaint room.

"Yup, put it in here; hang out while I see where Sergeant Walsh is. I think he has the rest of the group in the muster room..." Her voice trails off as she hops back in her chair. People who come into the precinct to report crimes sit in the complaint room. The large, glass-walled room is also where the administrative assistants type the handwritten reports that officers take in the field. There is therefore a typewriter on the desk in the middle and three other desks with computers and stacks of papers piled next to each one. I take the typewriter seat and glance around the room, aware that I can be seen from every direction through the glass partition.

A metal bookcase holds beaten-up books including the patrol guide, the law guide, and various manuals. Some of the covers are completely torn off. *At least the academy library looked better than this.* A few officers enter the precinct and walk up to the big desk. The sergeant's head is still down, and he's writing something. The officers wait.

I hope he doesn't ignore everyone like that, I think. I hear someone shuffling their feet and look up to see another sergeant appear—a can of Coke in his hand. His shoulders are slouched, his shirt barely tucked into his dull blue trousers, and his sleeves are rolled midway to his elbows.

He makes his way over to Doreen. He is holding a baton in the other hand. It is a straight stick, scuffed with chips all over it. *What the heck is he going to do with that? Who carries that thing around all the time? I hope he isn't the sergeant I am assigned to,* I think, cupping my head in my hand.

He spits into his can and puts it onto Doreen's desk. I gasp. He starts swinging the baton as if hitting a baseball. *Oh goodness,* I think. Doreen said something about Sergeant Walsh running the baseball team. *Jeez, that must be him. He looks a mess; he would have been in constant trouble in the academy looking like that. And what's with the spitting in the Coke can? How rude!* The judgement is coming full speed as panic rises in my stomach.

Doreen grabs his arm and heads toward the complaint room. "Hey, Sergeant Walsh, this is the new girl. She got here a little while ago."

I stand up, my eyes wide. Sergeant Walsh is within a few inches of me. His dark hair is cut in a low fade that accents his brown eyes that look at me, into me, and through me like a calm Neanderthal. Doreen is popping her gum and nodding as if this is a stranger I should trust. I wipe my clammy, slimy palms on my pants just in case he wants to shake my hand.

Out the side of my eye I see the sergeant and two officers staring at us. Sergeant Walsh gets my attention again when he says, in a low vibrating voice, "Well, I guess you're in my squad."

Sergeant Walsh is standing behind the podium in the muster room, where officers are given their assignments. It's like attendance for the platoon. The muster room is also a lounge, though there are no lounge chairs. Those would be found in the captain's office. A few vending machines are lined up against one wall along with an ink fingerprint station and a shoeshine machine on the other. Bathrooms and posters with crime stats sit behind the podium along with a huge sign that says "Report corruption to IAB" smack between the two.

I am quiet while one guy pushes buttons on the vending machine, another has on so much gear that he looks like the terminator, another keeps flexing his arms, another puts on lip gloss, and the last two stare up at the ceiling, daydreaming.

Sergeant Walsh takes rolled up papers out of his back pocket and a pen from his ear, looks at me, and asks, "What's your last name?"

"Allyn, sir."

He puts the pen down, takes a deep breath, and walks off the landing from behind the podium. We all take a step back. I want to run out the back door. *He looks like a dictator.* He stops and motions for us to come closer.

"Listen to me closely." I stick my nose out a little like a cat sniffing for food.

"Don't call me 'sir.' You are not in the academy anymore. It's just sarge, sergeant, or whatever." He hits one hand with the rolled-up papers in the other. "The most important thing you need to do is listen. Got it?"

"Yes, Si—sergeant," we all respond.

He swings the rolled-up paper again, as if on a pitcher's mound, and asks, "Who passed the driving course?"

Everyone else raises their hand, even the girl who focused on her lip gloss.

"You didn't, huh?" He is still swinging that paper, looking straight at me.

"No."

"No police car for you," he says. A couple of the others laugh, and I feel a burn of shame rising in my cheeks.

He stops swinging midair and points to each of the laughing

officers. "You, you, and you will be on a foot post for the first week. What's so funny about someone not being police car qualified? I bet I can have a dozen cops smoke you all with their eyes closed in a car battle." He points the paper at me last and says, "You will learn and pass when your ticket is up. And Allyn, just call me Sarge."

"Yes, Sarge." I am smiling like Celie in *The Color Purple*. Something in the way he says "You will learn and pass" sounds so confident that I can't allow myself to have any doubt. I start to trust this fake baseball-bat-swinging, dictator-looking sergeant.

My locker is in a row up against the right far wall of the room, so I'm afforded a bit of privacy if anyone walks in while I'm changing. We all have a break before heading out to the assignments Sergeant Walsh gave us. I am a little nervous about my assignment at a protest and need to pull myself together.

One of my favorite songs starts to play in my head as I pull on my uniform shirt over my bulletproof vest, "If you're blue and you don't know where to go to, why don't you go where fashion sits…"

Tapping my feet, I button my shirt and look in the mirror. *So long to the Margarette I once was*, I think, grinning at my reflection. A roach scrambles for its life under the bench; I smash it with my patrol boot.

I put one pant leg on, "Trying hard to look like Gary Cooper…" I slip on the other leg and tuck my shirt in. My nerves are giving way to excitement; I feel like I'm getting ready for a show.

This is how backstage feels when everyone is running around like crazy. It's a high like no other, I think as I pick up my gun belt and close the buckle, "…Super…"

I pick up the gun and look at it. I don't feel like it's a perfect fit, *but hey, we are in a show,* I say to myself as I shrug my shoulders and holster it in my belt.

Fixing my collar and giving myself a once over, I wipe my crisp new patrol boots, slick a strand of hair behind my ear, and look in the mirror again.

"Puttin' on the ritz… puttin' on the ritz…"

I wink at myself and shut the locker door.

"Puttin' on the ritz…"

Downtown is flooded with people leaving for home after work. We are in front of the North Tower of the World Trade Center for a protest by a group of people having a problem with May Day. We've been here for over four hours and there is no protest in sight.

It is one of our first assignments as a group outside the confines of the precinct. I am relieved we were not met with an angry May Day mob. After having lunch, we stand around cracking jokes with each other. Sarge leans up against a giant cement planter, looks around and says, "One sergeant and eight cops at the World Trade Center because of a protest that isn't going to happen."

"What should we do now, Sarge, can we just go back to the precinct?" Brown says. He is the tall cop who often farts in front of us and acts like Homer Simpson.

"No, Brown," Sarge says, "We just don't ditch an assignment because nothing's happening. We make the best of it and relax for a change."

Night has come upon the scene and people are scattered about. One or two people exit buildings now and then, and the streets are no longer packed with the earlier afternoon traffic. The main lobby lights of the north tower shut off and there is a soft layer of dim light that gives the front of the building a welcoming feel.

"Who wants to go up to the top of the building?" Sarge asks.

I raise my hand. "I'd love to, I've never been up there before."

"Why would you have been up there? I don't think any of us have," Dixon says.

"I've been up there plenty of times," says Weiss. He always must one-up someone.

"Ok, Allyn, Fuzz, and Dixon can come up with me," Sarge says. "The rest of you can man the lobby until we come down."

"You are not missing much," Weiss says as Sarge waves him away and we head into the lobby.

The elevator is like an inner tube shooting upward like we are in the Star Ship Enterprise. I am so elated—to be in this building and to get a chance to go all the way to the top is something I've never imagined having the opportunity to do.

I notice Sarge looking at us as we gaze around the elevator like we are in Disney World. The doors open and we are led through another door and walk up a few flights of stairs. The door opens to the roof top and my breath is knocked out of me.

If I didn't know any better, I'd swear I could reach up and touch a star. "We are way above the pollution. As high as a plane. The sky is clear as a bell, and look how many stars there are," I say.

"Isn't it priceless?" Fuzz says, looking up next to me.

"Look down," I say. "I can't see anything below the grey clouds. This is so cool; I don't know what do to with myself. I think it's romantic."

"It's something, that's for sure." Dixon says.

"You know what I think about?" Sarge says, standing a bit behind us. "Many people built this building. When we are absorbed in our lives, going here and there, we never think how these buildings came to be."

"Yeah, that's true," Fuzz says. He continues, "Back home in Puerto Rico, you have to hear it from every generational woman who built this house or that house. But no one says how the bridges got there, the dams, the roads…"

The hands that built this building and the others surrounding us. I feel humbled to think of this in a way that makes me appreciate being on the top of this particular building even more. *I hope they were under the same stars as we are now,* I think as I stare up, remembering the stars in North Carolina.

In the police van on the way back to the precinct after the non-existent protest, I am sitting in the last row by the window.

"Come on, Brown, you are so gross!" Rosie says as she taps Fuzz's shoulder, urging him to open his driver's side window.

"Brown, who would ever date you?" Fuzz asks as he opens all the van windows.

Sarge is leaning out the window, but the traffic is preventing much of an opportunity for breeze. "You ought to be ashamed of yourself!" Sarge says.

"I can't help it; how long should I hold it? It's natural, you know?" Brown pleads.

I'm truly happy I chose the back row.

"Speaking of dating, who lost their boyfriends or girlfriends since joining this job?" Dixon asks, his hand already in the air.

"My ex had the nerve to say he didn't feel like he could handle me being a cop, and it wasn't because he was worried about me," Rosie says.

"I don't know if I could have a cop girlfriend myself, but I guess it also depends on how she is as a person. I would worry, but if she really wanted to, I would support her," Fuzz says.

"Of course, you would, Grandpa," Weiss says, referring to the fact that at thirty-four, Fuzz is the oldest rookie. We all laugh.

"How about you, Allyn, any relationships?" Fuzz asks, looking at me in the rearview mirror. I thought I had slouched far enough behind the bench seat in front of me to avoid being involved in the conversation. I want to have rubber arms that stretch to the driver seat so I can smack Fuzz upside the head.

"I am as single as they come. The last guy I dated—no, had a fling with, wasn't as I thought. He never took me anywhere, even when I offered to pay. Turns out he was married. When I complained that he never bought me anything, he showed up at my apartment door with a truly sorry limp bouquet of flowers."

"That sucks big time!" Rosie says. She turns around and wags her finger in the air, "I hope you dropped him. What an insult."

"I felt so crappy; it was worse than him never doing anything. They looked like the flowers no one bought so the store put them on sale for ninety-nine cents just to get rid of them." We all laugh. We have grown comfortable with each other over the past few months.

Yet I feel ashamed for even telling the story. I don't know why; it seems the gate flew open, and I when it did, I lost control of it.

I stare out the window as we slowly make our way uptown. It's 1:30am and I feel sleepy. *What a funny bunch we are,* I think. I doze off while listening to them chatter away about horrible relationships.

"Allyn, wake up. We are at the precinct." Rosie is shaking my shoulder.

"I didn't even know I fell asleep. That went quick, huh?" I say, climbing out of the van behind Rosie. I'm the last one out, and when I step down, I look up to see my fellow rookies (and Sarge) standing in a half circle facing me. All of them with grins on their faces. Fuzz is holding a dozen roses and hands them to me.

My mouth drops open. "What—how, is this for me?"

"No one deserves dead flowers," Fuzz says, giving me a hug. He continues, "Sarge suggested we stop at a deli and get you the real thing."

I look at Sarge, then at each of my fellow cops, fighting back tears. "I don't know what to say," I wipe my eyes and give each of them the tightest hug I can manage. Rosie also gets a kiss on the cheek. I literally jump up on Sarge's imposing frame and hug him last.

I can't imagine having a different sergeant and group of cops to work with. May Day turned out to be Love Day for me.

CHAPTER 16

I take a deep breath and put my hand on the steering wheel. Sarge decided to help me practice driving late at night when there isn't much traffic. Plus, he's smart enough to know that driving in traffic at this point would be a horrific idea. I am nervous as heck, but I have developed respect for him. Like they taught us in the academy, I had judged him based on his role as a sergeant, and assumed he'd be nasty to us. I feel like he truly cares, and I haven't felt that way about a grown up in a very long time.

We are parked on the roundabout at Fort Tyron Park. A couple is holding hands, walking their dog. The street and roundabout sidewalks are lined with trees and flowers in full bloom. The black streetlamps remind me of a magical forest. It is a peaceful place to hang out in Washington Heights.

Before I ask what the plan is, Sarge asks, "Where are you, Allyn?" while looking at the couple walking down the street.

"Uh... in a police car, Sarge."

He rolls his eyes. "Again, where are you, Allyn?"

I quickly remember my public speaking professor in Borough of Manhattan Community College telling us to never say "um." I'm running through possible answers and can't come up with anything profound. "In front of a bush?"

"At the stadium, but way in the back of the parking lot," he says, opening a can of Coke. He takes a sip and raises the radio to his mouth. "Diaz, on the air."

"On the air," a voice says from the other end.

"You alright?"

"We got it under control."

He looks at me and says, "Diaz and his partner are at a domestic job."

"If he goes on the radio and requests help, I know where he is. I don't have to waste time asking the dispatcher for his location." He spits into his empty coffee cup. I have grown to love the smell of his chewing tobacco. "If someone shot me right now and you had to ask for help, where would you say you are?"

I feel like I have been kicked in the stomach. "Yes, you're right," I say.

"So where are you?"

"Forty Tyron Park, at the roundabout, in front of the museum, to the left of Castle Hill Avenue." I'm smiling like I won Final Jeopardy.

He starts laughing hard, a first for me to see.

"Okay, well done, but let's not make a paragraph out of it. Keep it as short and precise as possible."

"Yes, Sarge, and I hope that never happens."

"What?"

"That you get shot."

He grabs his .38 from his right thigh, and the Bible from his bag, and says, "I'll be alright and if not, just do the best you can. Let's get driving. Here is the plan; if something serious comes over the radio, I'll hop out of my seat and roll over the hood and you just climb into the passenger seat, got it?"

"Why can't I hop out and roll over the hood like the Dukes of Hazard?"

"Because, Allyn, my legs would probably get stuck trying to get over to the driver's seat. You would have no problem. I am too tall for that plan. Just trust me, okay?"

I trust him.

It's not just right now, in the car. Sarge is always so calm and handles everything with such confidence. No man has ever stepped in as a father figure for me, and in this moment, I officially give him that status.

"Don't brake until you are supposed to. Let's keep the speed smooth, okay?" says Davis, the instructor testing me.

"Those cones look like they are closer together than when I came for tutoring."

"They are," Davis says. "When you come for practice, we don't want the cones all over the place, so we use a different set up. Are you worried?" he asks, then takes a bite of his sandwich. A piece of lettuce falls out, which he doesn't bother to pick off his shirt.

He glances sideways, waiting for my answer, but I think my terror-stricken face was response enough.

I think back to when Sarge and I practiced at night when traffic was light. He had me drive down the narrowest streets in Washington Heights, even down blocks with double-parked cars. He spit his tobacco, drank his coffee, and occasionally said just the right thing when I was about hurl or lose my patience.

"Allyn, be scared but don't panic. Trust your decision, don't stiffen up, look ahead. There may be a kid running in the street for a ball. Where are you when you stop the car? Don't hug the inside. Good job, well done."

"Rosie has been taking me to tutoring. Why are you taking the time to help me practice?" I asked when we took a break one night.

He always played classical music or Shakespeare on tapes, and I was glad when he turned it down while we were practicing. Romeo and Juliet did nothing for my nerves at 2am.

"That's exactly why, Allyn; you're trying to help yourself. You are not as standoffish as you were when we met. You have come a long way, and you are doing a good job; it's a pleasure to help," he said.

Sitting in the car, ready for my test at the same training field where I wiped out last time, I don't want to let Sarge down—or

Rosie. Thinking of them calms me down and I loosen my grip on the wheel a little.

"Okay, are you ready?" instructor Davis asks. He claps and rubs his hands together in gleeful anticipation.

"I'm ready, instructor," I say, smirking.

He counts down while holding a stopwatch in his hand. "3,2,1, *go!*"

I take off and the wheels screech. I'm calm as I increase my speed.

"Okay," Davis says, "We are coming up on the first curve; remember what to do."

I accelerate a little more and gently press the brake to make the sharp curve. I hit only one cone. *YES!* I say in my head, not wanting to get ahead of myself.

"Good, good, now the next," Davis says, glancing at the stopwatch.

We use Crown Victoria clunkers with a gear shift so big I could pull it off and use it as a golf club. They're made to withstand the treatment they get on the streets. I slow down for the next curve, and as soon as the car makes a three-quarter clearance, I hit the gas again. No cones down! *Woohoo!*

I take the next curve at a steady speed. I am straight away now, and I keep my eyes ahead, just like Sarge taught me. I see Davis nod his head out the corner of my eye. My heart is racing. I am desperate to finish before I screw up the end.

"Here we are, almost at the end; don't forget what to do."

I nod my head and pick up speed, just a little. I cut the first curve, then slow down and make it around the second, then go full speed, slam on the brake, jerk the gear to reverse, push the gas pedal to the floor for a few yards, then hit the gear again to drive forward. I get the last curve and drive straight at full speed for another few yards before coming to a sudden stop.

"Woo!" Davis says and presses the button on his stopwatch. He slaps me on the shoulder and smiles. "You passed, kiddo. I am impressed! How do you feel?"

I take a deep breath, like I've been underwater for hours. I let the air out, wipe the sweat off my brow, and turn to Davis. I leap over, hug him, and scream so loudly that the other instructors can probably hear me from all the way across the field.

In the middle of Floyd Bennett Field, under the fall sun and surrounded by hundreds of standing cones, I feel like I am the Indie 500 champion.

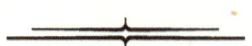

"Do you like to read?" Sarge asks one day when we are sitting at the George Washington Bridge. *Only Time* by Enya is playing on the radio. I love this song, though I don't really know why. The moon looms over the bridge, and the lights below seem to bow to its glory while taillights disappear into the darkness of I-95.

"I used to love reading, when I could live in someone else's world."

Anything was better than the world I really lived in. I slurp my coffee and gaze out onto the bridge. I would die for a cigarette right now, but he doesn't know I smoke.

"Why did you stop?"

"Hanging out, working, and feeling like I was getting too old for it." The truth was that I didn't want anything to do with little Margarette anymore. I don't say this because I don't want to hear myself admit it out loud.

He chuckles, "Too old, huh? You said your grandma and great grandma taught you a lot about church and God."

"Yup, that's why I hate God now. He took my grandma away, and my mom was a mess. You would think God would have let my father come around to help." This is the first time I've been this vulnerable with anybody at work, especially my boss, but he makes me feel supported and heard, and I know he won't judge me. So, I'm testing the waters.

Sarge has his Bible resting on his leg. That and his gun are always within reach. He seems to be comforted by them, but I am not sure about either. After all, they're both weapons.

The night air is warm, and he rolls up his sleeves a little, then looks at me and says, "Have you ever thought that instead of making it God's fault what happened to these people, maybe all those things were making you into the person you are meant to be?"

I don't want to agree with him. He's so comfortable with God and the Bible and believes in them so strongly. I'm not sure how that's even possible. He had a similar life to mine, but maybe he hasn't lost people so close to him. He hasn't had his heart ripped out because God took someone away. I'm ashamed to say that I don't trust God anymore because I'm scared it might be the only time Sarge will judge me. The mere mention of the word "God" makes my stomach hurt.

"Maybe you should get back into reading. It will also help you study for the sergeant's test," he says, bringing me back to the moment.

"You think I could be a sergeant?" If anyone could inspire me to become one, it would be him.

"Anyone can pass a test. Make sure you keep being you, with virtue. Not everyone can do *that*."

He tells me to carry two pages of the patrol guide with me to read when I have time. Becoming a sergeant will mean more study and more tests. I don't know if I can go through all that. As much as I see him as a faux-father, I'm reluctant to become *too* attached to him, because I fear that if I do, God will take him away too..

CHAPTER 17

I t's 8am and hundreds of officers are marching south from 57th Street and 5th Avenue to the entrance of St. Patrick's Cathedral. Hundreds of crisp uniforms and shiny shoes march to the sound of the bagpipers leading us, their sounds loud and clear over the early morning hum.

I feel a surge of energy from the buzz of the march as we laugh and hug former classmates and cops, we haven't seen in a while. Crowds of people stand on both sides of the avenue taking pictures of us going to get blessed by the Catholic Father.

When Sarge told us we were going to the annual Holy Name Society Mass and breakfast, I didn't get the feeling there was a choice in the matter. My stomach seized up, and I wanted to tell him that I'd rather sleep in. I haven't been to church in over ten years, and I'm not exactly excited to start now. Not to mention, I'm not used to getting up at the crack of dawn. I spend most of my time off alone or with Emily if she's around, but no matter what, I drink every night and hate getting up early.

Sarge had reminded us that we are technically working but assigned to attend, especially since he already bought the tickets for the breakfast at the Hilton. That was the only reason I didn't fully protest going. The Hilton and a fancy breakfast—that's the kind of scene I'd like to get used to.

I smell the frankincense and myrrh while walking up the stairs and toward the doors that look like they once belonged to the giant's house in *Jack and the Beanstalk*. As long as I've lived on the island of Manhattan, I've never been in a Catholic church, and my mouth drops open at the sight of the inside. Towering ivory-colored ceilings, titanic bronze doors, and stained-glass windows in every direction.

Thank goodness those bronze doors didn't slam shut when it was my turn to walk through them. I feel like a horrid imposter. Will the walls of St. Patrick's know what my past was like? Will the apostles' eyes send burning beams through me as I sit in the pew? Will the oversized crucifix holding Jesus looming over me know that not only have I not prayed in years, but I don't believe in anything when it comes to the people of the church or the church itself?

Yet the beauty of the church is breathtaking.

The choir is singing. *They don't sing this kind of music in the Baptist church*, I think, watching the young woman in front. It sounds like a lullaby sung in an operatic style — a potion within a song. Maybe something is trying to cast a spell over me. The bishop is standing at the wooden and brass podium to the side of the gorgeous high altar.

The reflections of light from the candles, stained glass, and organ pipes bounce from corner to corner. I am mesmerized as I try to fight how lovely the church is and forget about my hangover.

The balcony is full, and everyone is staring straight ahead. The service begins, and we kneel on benches that fold down in front of us. All I can do is listen; I am not as into this as everyone else seems to be. Sarge is in another world. I'm sure he isn't thinking about police work. Maybe his family. All I'm thinking about is how long we have to be on our knees.

Finally, we stand. The priest is talking, and Rosie is holding a string of beads. We get on our knees again. *Why do we have to keep doing this?* I think, creep back down and acting as if I know what I'm doing.

We stand again for another prayer. Officers in the front row, including the mayor and a few higher-ranking officers, walk toward the bishops standing in front. The bishops place something in each person's mouth and make the sign of the cross before they return to their seats.

"What are they doing?" I ask Rosie, who is already standing with her back to me, waiting for our row to enter the center aisle.

"It's communion, chica."

"What?" I say, in a slightly louder whisper.

"This is having communion with Jesus and God; you know, the body of Christ?"

I am shocked. In the Baptist church I grew up in, they passed a bowl or plate around with crushed Saltine crackers in it along with shot glasses of grape juice. I usually took more than one cracker because they tasted good, and I was usually hungry. The grape juice was a nice touch.

"Are we getting grape juice also?"

"Heck no," Rosie says as she turns her head back toward me. "We get real wine!"

"No!" I gasp. "That's amazing." My mouth waters at the idea of having even the smallest drink. A drink always relaxes me, and I want one so badly.

We make our way to the aisle and walk toward the bishop.

"Not today, though. That would be too much to give everyone here. But in smaller churches, they do it."

Just my luck, I think. I'm already in the aisle, so I can't turn around and squeeze past everyone to go back. Besides, I wouldn't want to insult Sarge.

I don't want to take the communion. I feel like it's admitting I have respect for the God who took Grandma and gave me a crappy childhood, like not speaking to a friend in a while, then hesitating to reunite without talking about what happened. I am holding my grudge.

Suddenly, I am next. I vow not to open my mouth, no matter how nice the priest is.

He holds the perfectly round disk in his hand and stares at me. I stare back with my hands folded.

"Hello," I say.

"Body of Christ," he says, holding the disc right under my bottom lip.

"Huh?" I respond, my mouth hanging open.

He pops the disk in my mouth, which I don't close because the disc is so round, and I'm not sure what I'm supposed to do or say.

"Eat it, child," he says and makes the sign of the cross twice. I close my mouth and bow my head. I feel defeated. "May God be with you, child."

I look into his eyes when I raise my head. I feel less apprehensive; he smiles. I half smile and turn to walk back to my seat. I look up at the apostles and Jesus. I take a deep breath. It is so beautiful, yet I never really feel like I deserve beauty. Back in my seat, Rosie squeezes my hand and motions for me to kneel next to her. She bows her head and looks so peaceful. I kneel next to her, as she continues to hold my hand. I don't want to pray, but I feel solace in her energy. It feels good to be in what feels like a safe space, if only for a short time.

I'm working with Velez tonight. He is a fellow midnight-shift officer with a few years on the job. I've worked with him a few times, and we've become good friends. At first, being the only female on this shift, I felt like I had something to prove, but overall, the midnight group of officers has seemed okay with having me. Plus, usually, when there isn't a partner to work with, I'm given a dead-on-arrival or a hospitalized prisoner assignment, as these are jobs you do alone.

It's a nice night; the weather is calm, and nothing much is happening.

Velez parks the car across the street from the restaurant on Vermilya Avenue. It is more of a nightclub after 9pm, and there have been a few big fights there which put it on the map as a public nuisance. Three women I recognize as dancers in the restaurant that secretly turns into a club are walking across the street toward our car.

"How's your girlfriend, Velez?" I ask, aware of his reputation as a flirt.

"Why ask now? Because they are walking toward the car?" he says as he laughs.

"I'm going to say something if you don't get rid of them quick. Last time, one of them stuck her barely covered boobs in the window. That may have been exciting for you, but I'm getting nothing here. Plus, they always think I'm dating the cop in the car. Like all girl cops must be dating their partner or something."

I light a cigarette. One thing I like about working with other cops is, they don't care if I smoke, even though I'm still way too shy to smoke in front of Sarge. I feel like I get a change to be a clean-slate daughter, and I don't want him to see me doing anything "bad."

One woman sits on the hood of the car, turns toward us, and waves. I wave back and blow my smoke out of the window.

"That's bad for you, *flacita*," the woman by my window says.

"How are you all doing tonight?" I ask.

"Good, what are you two doing?" she asks, using the window ledge to hold herself up.

"You been hittin' the José Quervo tonight, huh?" Velez says to the one on his side of the car. Now that he mentions it, I'd love a drink. *These girls are lucky they get to hang out,* I think as I gulp my coffee.

"Yup, you want some, papa?"

"You know I don't, but make sure you're careful going home. Get your friend off the car, please," he says, smiling at her.

"Okay, papi. Denise, get yo' ass off the car; come on, we have to go."

Denise slides off the car and stumbles toward her friends, who are waving at us as they saunter away like they are playing in fields of lavender.

"You are something else," I say, tossing my cigarette out the window.

"I can't help it if the ladies love the man."

"The ladies love the uniform—you said it yourself; you wouldn't get half the attention were it not for this!" I roll my eyes, shake my head and smile.

The dispatcher calls over the radio, "Sector David, the lieutenant wants you to go to the precinct."

I have a feeling about what's going on. The narcotics units do plain clothes assignments in drug-heavy neighborhoods for a few hours at a time. What that really means is, they arrest every drug addict from age eight to age eighty. Since I'm usually the only uniformed female working, I'm going to get stuck searching the women at the precinct before they're processed and sent to central booking.

"Sector David acknowledge," I say into my radio. I turn to Velez, "I wish they'd get a female to work with the narcotics unit. I hate searching all those women."

"Well, I get to take a nap while you search them," he laughs.

"I hope a roach crawls into your ear and the other cops sleeping in there are snoring so loud that you can't sleep," I say, lighting another cigarette.

I walk into the precinct to see women lined up against the wall opposite the desk. There is one arrest processing room, and the only cell is packed with men, so all the women I search have to be handcuffed to the bar bolted to the wall above a bench.

"Hey, Allyn," detective Cassio says. "Thanks for doing us a solid again. I know you seem to be the only female working when we do these stings. Here, we got you some coffee and cake from Malecon."

"Thanks, Cassio. This is a step up from the doughnut and coffee you bought me last week. I had to get a new pair of pants after some woman ripped them during the search. But this really makes my day." I roll my eyes.

I walk over to the line of women. "Stop flipping around on the floor like a fish out of water," I say to Sheila, the first of five women I must search. The second I walked up to her and touched her arm, she dropped to the floor and gave me an Oscar winning performance.

"I am sick! I have to go to the hospital!" she screams.

"Knock it off and get up; stop wasting time. You are getting searched before you leave here; just get up and get it over with."

She rolls over on her back and tries to get up. "Can you help me, please?"

"See? All that drama for nothing," I say, pulling her up.

"Keep it up, Sheila, and we'll hold you back for last!" Cassio says.

"I got it. She's alright. She does this all the time, right Sheila?"

"Yea, but I ain't got nothin'," she snaps, clenching her teeth and holding her legs closed.

"Sheila, I'm not in the mood. As a matter of fact, I'm never in the mood for this." I put my hand under the base of her head and use a pressure point technique to get her to pop her mouth open, at which point a small bag of crack falls out. I hand it over to Cassio who is holding a paper bag. "I knew it! You pull this shit every time, Sheila."

"Shut up, asshole," she says.

I grab her arm. "Come on, we are going into the bathroom. I know you have something in your crotch."

"I ain't… you don't have to do that, I just gave you everything," she pleads.

"You didn't *give* me anything, therefore I know you have something else."

We walk into the arrest processing room and toward the bathroom, which has stains on the walls that have surely been there since the building was erected a trillion years ago.

"Sheila, you got snagged, huh?" a male prisoner yells from the cell. He sticks his hand through the bars and tries to push her. I smack his hand down.

"Stop! If you know each other, take it up when you both get released."

"Officer, what the heck? Don't be such a hard ass." The other guys laugh.

"Thank goodness I don't know what a hard ass is," I say and close the door behind me.

"I told you I ain't got nothin' else. Let me pee, I gotta pee real bad," Sheila says, stepping from side to side, holding her knees together.

I swing her around and hold her up against the wall with one arm so I can wiggle the elastic of her pants with my other hand. She's trying to close her legs, but she can't because of the way I lock my foot against hers. I shake her shorts like they're a box of Cracker Jacks. A slightly bigger clear bag falls to the floor.

"She's hurting me!" Sheila yells.

"That didn't work before, Sheila, and it isn't going to work now."

Cassio is standing outside of the bathroom. "You alright in there?"

"Yup," I say, opening the door to hand him the bag.

I cuff Sheila to the bar, and she sucks in through her teeth. "You ain't shit, girl. You coulda let me keep that."

"You know, Sheila, I would love it if I never had to search you again, because maybe you stopped doing this, and maybe you can get help. The best way to get back at the detectives is to stop being the reason they get overtime." With this, I walk out to get the next one.

I move through them quickly and am finally at the last one. I look at the paperwork and see that her name is Elsie. I haven't seen her before, so I figure she must be new in the neighborhood. She was the one who was quiet as a mouse while waiting for me. She couldn't keep her eyes open and seemed to be dozing off while leaning against the wall the whole time I was searching the other women.

Cassio grabs Elsie by the arm and holds her up while I put on new gloves.

She is holding her head down, but I can see that she has short, curly hair. She is much smaller than the other women, no more than five feet tall. I walk toward her, and she slowly walks toward me. I take her into the bathroom and remove her handcuffs.

She lifts her head a bit and our eyes meet as I bend down. Her almond-shaped droopy eyes take my breath away. If I didn't know any better, I would have thought she was my mother. Same skin tone, eye color, and height. She turns to face the wall and puts her hands up.

My stomach feels as if it has collapsed. I open my mouth to ask her the usual questions, but I can't speak.

I don't want to search her; I feel like I am searching a replica of my mom and feel ashamed to do such a thing. I wonder if my mother was ever arrested, how many times she may have gone through being searched and had a Detective Cassio to deal with.

Elsie knows the routine and turns around to face me. I don't have to search much; her clothes are much larger than she is, and she has nothing on underneath. I rub my gloved hands around her bra line and up and down her legs.

"Can you open your mouth, Elsie?" She slowly lets her lower lip drop open. She had on red lipstick that is cracking and clumpy. My throat is tight. I think of the make up my mother used to wear before Grandma died, how she looked years *after* Grandma died.

I remove a few coins from her pocket as she leans against the wall with her eyes closed. I want to beg her to get off the drugs and the streets. I feel like a desperate, lost little girl in that dimly lit stinking bathroom.

"Hey Allyn, what's going on in there?" Cassio calls out.

A little started, I reply, "We're coming out now."

"Did she have anything?" Casio asks.

"No, she didn't have anything," I say, sitting her down next to Sheila. I place her coins on the table in front of the cell and cuff her to the bench. She rubs her stomach.

"Are you okay?" I ask.

"I can sure use something to eat," she says, her voice lyrical and soft.

"Do you have bills out on the desk that the detectives removed?" I ask, looking back at Cassio and his crew being loud.

"I only have what you took out of my pocket," she says, lowering her head.

I look at the change I took from her pocket and count thirty-eight cents.

"I'll be right back." I grab the coins and walk out of the room.

I get a ginger ale, potato chips, and a candy bar from the vending machine. I also grabbed the cake Cassio gave me when I came in.

"Here you are Elsie. Is this okay?"

"Oh, sure, this is good… I didn't have enough for all this," she says, trying to open the soda.

I open it for her. I also open the chips and cake and sit them beside her free hand. She picks up the cake and takes a small bite, then sips the soda.

"Why can't we get soda and cake? What the fuck?" one of the prisoners' whines from the cell.

"Well, next time eat a big dinner before getting arrested," another prisoner says, and they all laugh. The sounds seem to fade as I watch Elsie slowly eating the food.

If I am good to Elsie, maybe she will snap out of the life she's living.

Whenever I was sick, my mom managed to get ginger ale and Campbell's Chicken Noodle soup for me. And all of a sudden, I'm eight years old again and I can't contain my feelings. It was drilled into us at the academy that we are not civilians anymore, and our feelings don't matter. I've been fighting my feelings since my grandmother died, and I feel the dam about to break. Looking at Elsie, I can feel the tears threatening to bubble over and betray my tough cop act.

She lifts the bag to get the last of the crumbs out, and I can't hold it in any longer. I jerk my hand over my mouth and start crying, loudly. I turn on my heels and head out of the room, leaving the chatter and stifling air behind. I try to walk past the detectives before they notice, but Cassio steps in front of me. "What the hell is wrong with you?" Everyone stops talking and shuffling paperwork and looks at us.

"I just feel bad for her," I say, sucking air as I try to push past him.

"Why do you feel sorry for her? She is just a fucking skell!"

"She isn't a skell, you jerk! She is—she, oh God, you are such an asshole!"

I notice everyone staring at me.

"Can you jerks for once stop acting like you are better than the people sitting in that cell?" I say, covering my face and weeping.

"Allyn," Sergeant Grosen calls. He is usually the 3rd platoon sergeant, but he was working a midnight today and he's also Sergeant Walsh's best friend. "Head up to the locker room. Take a break for a while."

I nod and walk toward the door to the staircase. I want to look at back at Elsie, but I'm embarrassed for breaking down in front of everyone. I let the staircase door slowly close behind me.

I snatch the picture of my mother and me at my graduation from my locker door and stare at it, crying so hard I can barely see it clearly.

Someone knocks at the door. I open it and Sergeant Grosen is standing there.

"What's up, kiddo?" he asks, his cigarette hanging out of his mouth.

"She looks like my mother… I feel like they could be treated nicely, they don't have to be called 'skells'." Elsie's dark eyes in their sunken sockets look so much like my mother's, I have to look away. It is the look of a woman who has given up hope.

"Kiddo, you ain't wrong for feeling bad. Means you are right. Sorry about Cassio saying that to you. You always help them out, and sometimes they forget that we are all people."

"Thanks," I say. He hands me a tissue he had balled up in his shirt pocket.

Sergeant Grosen shows a little more emotion than Sarge, but he is also a bulldog. He's referred to as the Jewish Battle Axe. He's a bombshell when it is time to fight or give someone the smack down, but he's a pushover with me and anyone else he likes.

When I met him, he said, "Don't let my height fool you, kid, I ain't no joke. That's all around, remember that." I had smiled and he giggled. I feel like he's my lookout when Sarge is off. It feels good that he knew what I meant about my mom without me having to go into details.

The moment I finish my shift, I burst out the door and race home. I don't even stop at McDonalds for my usual breakfast. I need a drink, fast.

I look for Elsie every day for months, just to see how she's doing. On a night off, I am leaving Coogan's bar with some colleagues, and see her leaning against the wall outside. The sight of her, thin, disheveled, broken, I feel a tug in the pit of my stomach. I wonder if I can change her—if only she could love herself and see a better life for herself, her story could be so different. Her bad habits and poor choices are going to bury her eventually.

"Elsie, Elsie, it's me. Remember me?"

She looks at us, took a couple of steps toward us, then waves her hand for us to leave, walks away, and disappears into the alley.

CHAPTER 18

"You know, Mrs. Reynolds," I say as I swish the mop back and forth on the floor next to the bed, "as much as I enjoy spending time with you, I'd rather it not be spent cleaning up when you have knocked over an entire pitcher of water." I laugh.

Velez is across the room gathering a few papers that have fallen on the floor.

"I love to see you officers and the young ones. You are my favorite. Are they taking care of you over there, young lady?" Mrs. Reynolds asks, sitting on the side of the bed.

Mrs. Reynolds calls the precinct at least once a week when her home attendant is off duty, and she needs help with something. If there is an officer available and we're not very busy, the officer in charge of the telephone switch board will assign the visit to someone. We call it a wellness check, and it's a welcome reprieve to go to a job that doesn't involve violence and crime.

Velez and I have gotten to know her quickly. The first time we visited her she was stuck on the toilet but fortunately has a phone in her bathroom. The next time, she locked her cat in the bathroom, and tonight she knocked the water off of her side table and some of it spilled onto her sheets.

Velez walks over with a new set of sheets. "Okay, let's get you in the chair so we can change the sheets," I say as I hoist her up and we make it over to her Lazy Boy recliner.

"I truly appreciate this; you know my daughter will be visiting from Georgia next week. Velez are you dating anyone?" she asks while adjusting her nightgown.

"No ma'am, this job isn't the best for relationships." Velez had broken up with this girlfriend a few weeks before. "Besides, I am okay for now. I enjoy the single life." We put a dry blanket over the sheets and fluff her pillows.

"How about you, Allyn, are you seeing anyone? You are such a nice young lady."

"I don't want to date your daughter, Mrs. Reynolds." We all start laughing. I help her up and lead her back to her newly made bed.

"That's not what I meant, silly. I'm just wondering if you do, maybe you should consider that being on the street may be tough. You know young men may have a problem with that."

I think about the last time I had a so-called relationship and can't remember it. I don't even know how to have a good relationship. We work the most unpredictable hours ever, and I can barely keep up with the schedule changes. Between late jobs, lack of sleep, and my world outside NYPD getting smaller and smaller, I never give much thought to anything lately.

"Well," Mrs. Reynolds says, pulling the blanket over her waist, "I know God will give you what you need when you are ready."

"Yes, Mrs. Reynolds," Velez and I say at the same time. She and I see God differently and I don't want her to see me practically flinch at the suggestion He will ever be there for me.

"You both take care, you hear? Say hello to everyone down at the station for me."

I give her a hug, and we walk out of the apartment.

"You know, as much as I complain about these kinds of jobs, it's actually something I enjoy, as long as it isn't a naked or nasty situation," Velez says, holding the passenger door open for me.

"Yeah, you're right. Have you ever imagined being her age and having to call the precinct to help with little things like this?" I ask as I light a cigarette.

"One thing I notice about her is she never complains. She always seems to be in a good mood and encouraging. I am surprised I made it past the age of twenty. If I have half her attitude at her age, that will be nice for sure," I say, taking another puff.

"You won't be her age if you keep smoking those things," Velez says, wagging his finger at me.

"There are worse things I could be doing," I say with a wink.

"Sector Boy on the air?" the radio dispatcher says through the patrol radio.

"We are on the air," I respond.

"You have a job of a lost child; the call came from someone who said they saw a little girl walking on Saint Nicholas Avenue alone. She is described as three to four feet tall, dark skin, a pink and purple book bag. That is all we have; do you acknowledge?"

"Acknowledge, we are responding."

"It's after midnight," Velez says. He drives more slowly for fear of missing the child.

"She could be anywhere; how in the world will we find a child who could have walked in any direction by now?" I say, directing my flashlight toward the sidewalk.

"It only took us two minutes to get into the area, she couldn't have gone much further than where the caller saw her. Oh, look, I see a head over there." He drives the car into the opposite lane of Wadsworth Avenue and 186th Street.

She is walking in front of the buildings, holding the straps of her school backpack. Her head is down.

"Let me out; tell the dispatcher that we have her," I say.

"Hey, sweetie, where are you going?" I say, kneeling in front of her. She looks up at me and shrugs her shoulders. *She can't be more than six years old,* I think. "What's your name?" I ask. She shrugs her shoulders again.

I look over at Velez, who is now standing next to us. "I don't know anything so far," I say. "We have to take her back to the precinct, but let's take a few minutes to see if she can point out where she lives."

As we drive around, I'm not surprised by how she made it along the streets without being noticed; there are not many people out and about other than the late nighters, who tend to keep to themselves. I am sitting in the back of the car, looking through her bag. There is a composition notebook, an empty Twinkie wrapper, a half-chewed pencil, and a pink stuffed owl toy. She won't say anything or point out where she lives.

"Forget this, Velez, let's take her back to the precinct. Maybe the squad or Mrs. Matthews can find something in the computer if we get her name from this notebook."

"You got it," Velez says, handing me a lollipop from his stash. She takes the lollipop without hesitation. I smile and sit closer to her.

"Hey, Mrs. Matthews," I say as I lead the little girl into the complaint room. Mrs. Matthews is my midnight grandma. If someone goes into the complaint room uninvited, she'll certainly give them walking papers. She's very selective about who she tolerates, and I am amongst the very few, I think because I make her laugh.

"What do you have here? She looks just like you, Allyn," Mrs Matthews says as she wipes her mouth with an embroidered napkin.

"I thought that myself. Isn't she cute? But she won't say anything or point out where she lives."

The little girl finally looks up at Mrs. Matthews and walks over to her desk, then settles down in the chair next to her.

"I was wondering if you can look up any hospital records for her. I think I found a name in the back of her book. It's not the best handwriting; she is still young to write well," I say.

"We can give it a try; I'll just try the letters I can make out."

Lieutenant Brown walks into the office and stares at the girl. "Allyn, how long do you think this is going to take? We have a seatbelt initiative going on, and you can certainly get your summons numbers up." He might as well be talking to a wall. I ignore him.

"Lieutenant," Mrs. Matthews says, "do you mind letting us do our jobs? I think finding where this young lady belongs is way more important right now."

Most of us don't care for him. He is what we call a company man. He couldn't care less about anything other than the amount of arrest and summonses the cops have every month. He studders when the commanding officer talks to him and watches the clock like a bandit when we're in the precinct for lunch breaks. We barely speak to him unless we have to.

I smile and grab the little girl's hand, telling my colleagues, "I'm going to take her to the bathroom and get her something from the machine."

The little girl still hasn't said anything. She is probably scared and missing her mother or maybe even her grandmother. It makes me that much more determined to find her home and get her there as soon as possible.

Before long, we are back in the car with the little girl we now know to be named Kitri. She is eating the chips and drinking her juice, still looking out the window. Mrs. Matthews found her name in the computer. She had a physical at Columbia Presbyterian Hospital before she started school, and her home address was on the records.

"Isn't this exciting, Kitri? I am sure your mom is worried about you. We're going to take you home!" She doesn't respond. I wonder why we haven't gotten a call of a lost child the whole time we've had her. It's been almost two hours. It's almost 2am, so maybe her mom is sleeping and has no idea Kitri even left the apartment.

I bang on the door and look down at Kitri, who is blank faced at my side. *Maybe she'll be happy when her mother opens the door.*

A few moments pass and... nothing. Music wafts out the window of an apartment above, and over to my right I see a homeless guy sleeping under the stairwell. I go to knock again when the door swings open. A woman stands there, out of breath, her obviously pregnant stomach protruding out the door. She looks me in the eye, and I hold my breath, surprised at the avalanche of negative energy she brings with her. She looks down at Kitri and starts screaming at her in a language I don't understand.

Velez asks, "Is she saying thank you?", looking at me with a thin smile.

The woman reaches out to grab Kitri by the arm. I look behind her to see a mattress on the floor and a lamp next to the mattress.

"Why are you yelling at her?" I ask. "Maybe that's why she ran away."

Without saying anything, she doubles over in apparent pain and drops to her knees. Velez looks at me in panic. "What the fuck is wrong with her?"

A gush of water spills across the floor in front of us; it doesn't smell like urine and the sudden volume of it is disconcerting. Her water must have broken. She reaches up to grab my hand and screams at us at the same time. I look at Kitri, who has pushed herself up against the wall, just staring, wide eyed, at the scene in front of her.

Velez is quick to call an ambulance, and we watch as the drivers usher Kitri's mother inside. She is still yelling at Kitri, gesturing wildly, and occasionally cradling her stomach in pain.

I go with Kitri and her mother in the ambulance while Velez follows behind in the police car. Once at the emergency room, the woman is wheeled away by hospital staff, and Velez turns to me and says, "We're going to have to take her to Children's Services."

As much as I know this is true, my stomach drops in anticipation of leaving this poor girl alone with another stranger while her angry mother is off having another child to yell at.

At the Children's Services office, Kitri is eating crackers and sipping on a juice box while the case worker finishes up some paperwork. She looks over at me occasionally between sips, though I cannot read her expression.

When the time comes for us to leave her there, I walk down the hall and try not to look back. The temptation is too great, and I finally give in, looking behind me at her tired, worn face. Her chin starts to quiver and a silent tear escapes from the inside of her eye and rolls down over her chubby cheek.

I race back and scoop her up in my arms. "Hang in there, kid. It's going to be alright," I say.

I feel like I am leaving myself behind in that office. Another lost and broken soul, at only six years old.

It is the first week of September 2001, and the beginning of the school year... I remember my own dread at starting school every year after my grandma died; and now another school year has started in heartbreak. I hope that next few months are not so eventful in terms of jobs like Elsie and Kitri, which take me back to my childhood, which I'm trying so hard to move on from. I need a break from the constant onslaught of heartache.

The minute I walk in the door of my apartment, I crack open a fresh bottle of vodka.

CHAPTER 19

After finishing my midnight shift, I head the liquor store, where the television is blaring behind the counter.

"I think something is happening in Manhattan, and the radio said the bridges to all boroughs will be closed soon. Something about a plane crash," a guy next to me says, putting down the bottle of Jack he's been holding.

I approach the counter and stare at the TV, where a news anchor is reading from a paper someone's shove in front of him. "It seems that a plane has crashed into one of the World Trade Center buildings," the newsreader says in confused panic. "Our news crew is not able to get anywhere near the location, as traffic is jammed, and panic is growing."

I feel like I'm in a mental purgatory of sorts, staring directly at the TV and yet looking right through it.

Another customer walks in and calls out, panicked, "What happened? Why are the bridges closed?"

"There was an attack on the World Trade Center. They think it's a terrorist act."

I am in such a daze I don't know what to think. I head home on autopilot. My bedroom window faces the narrow courtyard in the center of the building, a gray, cylinder-shaped, upright tunnel. The apartment across from mine has a kitchen window that faces the same courtyard. The only way I'm able to sleep is from a combination of exhaustion and liquor.

I turn on the TV in the bedroom, wanting to see what all the chaos is about. The 12-inch screen blares black-and-white images no less graphic than a full-color version would be.

"Here is the playback from our reporters of the second World Trade Center building being hit as they are frantically running away. This is a dreadful day in America."

The first building starts to collapse, and the screen goes black. It then appears again with the news anchor speaking.

"This is considered to be a terrorist attack on America. All law enforcement and United States military personnel are being ordered and activated to assist."

What the heck is this? I wonder, drinking liquor straight from the bottle.

"Only Time" by Enya is playing over footage of people running for dear life as the second building slowly swallows itself, gray-like tube forming around the clouds of dust that surround it. A woman and man hold hands and jump from God knows how high. Tears drip on the bottle and my leg. The words sound like I am in an echo chamber underwater.

"Only time..."

"Oh my God, it's absolutely tragic!" the news anchor says, sitting grounded in his studio seat. My eyes, drowning in tears, start stinging from the tequila and cigarette smoke filling my room. Where my heart is, I have no idea; it seems to have dissipated.

I reflect to the time my sergeant and I were sitting in the police car at the George Washington Bridge, the moon illuminating the night sky above the bridge lights, letting us know there is life looking at us from beyond the calming, soft light that made the city under it special. That seems like an evil joke now; peace is fleeting, and life's harshness and human errors are as potent as a hungry child's cry for food.

When I sat in that car with Sarge, looking at the moon and listening to that same song, he had said, "We are but a tiny fragment in a vast space. We can make the most out of the moments here and now, not tomorrow or yesterday."

"We are now getting word that hundreds, maybe thousands, of

people are buried under two of the most historical building in this country, including police officers, firemen, and medical service personnel; God help us all."

"Only time..."

The song fades as the images flash frantically across the screen. I squeeze my eyes tight, maybe I am imagining the visual onslaught. But the scene not only changes, it gets worse. My head is spinning, and the room is caving in on me to the point that I can't move, my bottle almost empty.

"The National Guard is being deployed to the Pentagon as we air this broadcast. All passengers perished in the crash."

"Only time..."

I swallow the rest of the stinging liquid in horrid gulps, the pain in my head magnifying the beat of my heart, and I pass out.

It's 10pm when I come to. Was it all a dream? I have to stop drinking tequila. *What a nightmare,* I think. The shower provides both relief from and a reminder of the pounding headache and nightmare I just had about planes, towers, and people jumping to their inevitable death. I feel like I collapsed right along with the Twin Towers in my dream, and I'm not sure if I even care.

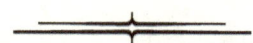

The cheering of the crowds of people along the West Side Highway is fleeting and confusing. We watch, blank-faced, at the slow-motion hand clapping, thank yous, and posters deeming us heroes as the motorcade of blue and white vans drives past the crowds and enters the frozen zone of Ground Zero. Standing at the site to which I have been assigned, the reality sets in. The eerie quality of the scene makes it feel like I'm on the moon. The ground is covered in ash, and there are crater-like holes sunk into the ground in every direction. Every building looks down upon us through the fury of blown-out windows, the life recently inside vacuumed into another universe.

When Neil Armstrong set foot on the moon, I wonder if he ever imagined his beloved home looking like it had morphed into the moon's surface. It is harshly surreal, and as I look up and search for the real moon, the dim light of it struggles to penetrate the blanket of smoke, smog, and sparse streetlights throughout lower Manhattan.

It does not feel like Heaven or hell but a new world where we are the only inhabitants, dropped there from the darkness above and expected to erect a homestead. I don't know what to walk on and what to avoid.

There is a bucket line of construction workers, their shadows larger than they are, moving back and forth, passing debris to one another. Everything is covered in layers of gray and black dust, and I imagine workers don't know whether they are passing a charred arm or a chair leg. When someone happens to notice a body, distinguishable by clothing and not crushed or burned to a crisp, he yells, "We found someone!"

Then, everyone stops what they are doing, and a bugle sounds with the song of death while we all watch the body pass from man to man until it reaches the waiting ambulance. Other than the lights from emergency vehicles, we make our way by the amber glow coming from what seems to be the center of the earth, telling us that the planet still lives, and we shouldn't forget about it.

I want to forget the last twenty-four hours, wish it never happened. We are given paper-thin hospital masks to wear. Who would imagine having to wear them outside of a medical setting? Not to mention the fact that they don't help. After ten minutes we must change them because the air turns on us, smacks us in the face, and punches us in the gut. We are followed, haunted, and infested with relentless remnants of evil I couldn't have conjured up, even in my worst nightmares.

We are posted on inner and outer perimeters of the building locations, mostly to make sure people don't wander into Ground Zero but also to look like we know what we're doing. An officer in a white shirt appears out of the cloud with a bull horn, demanding, "Get the cones straightened out; move the barriers over there; why are those officers standing there?"

"Why is he yelling?" I ask Sarge.

"They all need to be seen and heard, even in a tragedy," he says.

The chiefs and captains, recognizable by their white shirts, all come out from behind the death curtain, barking orders, sending the sergeants scurrying; changing our posts, mixing up stations, not knowing who volunteered and who was there because we had no choice.

"We found an officer!" someone yells from the wreckage.

Bugle sounds, hand over hearts, some salute, as he or she is passed on to God, Heaven, or wherever. I can't help the envy I feel for those receiving such honor and attention, even though the way it came was brutal and nonsensical.

After a few hours, which feel like an eternity, we walk to the only place open for emergency workers to eat: Nino's Pizza. With street signs missing, ash still covering landmarks, and the whole area in confusion, we barely know which way is which.

"I only have two years on this job, and most of it has been sickening. What is He doing up there?" I ask Sarge as we walk through the apocalyptic scene. "If there was a God, would He really let this happen?"

Sarge nods slowly, looking at the ground while formulating an answer. "God doesn't let this stuff happen, Allyn, it's humans who do that."

I don't answer him out loud. *Goodness and mercy, my butt. You're still a jerk,* I say silently to God, as I trip over another crater.

We finally get to Nino's, I see some of my friends, and we get food from the buffet. When we walked in, the small bistro-style room walls were lined with the tired, hungry faces of officers. Some were talking while others sat alone, gobbling food like they'd never see it again. The only place for us to eat is outside, waving dust away from our meals. Most of the executive officers are sitting inside on chairs at tables. They're dining on pizza, meatballs, baked bread, and coffee. We smelled it from a few blocks away. It carried my thoughts from dread to the hope of people gathering in cheer over food.

"Fucking figures; never fails, they're so embarrassing," Velez says, looking in the window and shoving a forkful of spaghetti in his mouth. "Here we are, standing out there for hours with no food, water, or even a place to take a break or a piss, and these assholes are hanging out like it's a party."

"They have to refuel and relax before they go back out there and start yelling at everyone," I say as I stare inside the restaurant, watching the comradery that's in strange contrast to the tragedy outside.

Sarge takes the last bite of his sandwich and says, "It's hard not to think they're all shoe flies when they're sitting there like they're having Sunday brunch at their mother's house."

"I can't help but feel annoyed. The only time we see them outside is when they are either looking lost or acting like pompous idiots. And yes, the females too," I say, gulping my water.

"Remember what we always say, Allyn," Sarge says. "If it bothers you, you're not wrong. And as far as your question about God letting this happen, the villains are not the problem. The cowards are. And they come in all shapes, sizes, and surely, different color shirts."

He was right about one thing: I have a habit of questioning what I truly feel about a person if it is not favorable. Always wanting to be the perfect daughter, dancer, or whatever else, I tend to go along with what I think someone wants me to say or do for fear I won't be accepted.

As Sarge gives me the green light to have my thoughts and feelings, I feel my confidence begin to grow.

We spend the next few weeks alternating between working at the precinct and Ground Zero for sixteen-plus-hour shifts. Officers who live far away sleep in their cars or pile up in the lounge and empty offices.

Because I live close by, I let some of my coworkers, including Fuzz, Velez, and Rosie camp out at my place. Our days off are canceled, and we have, at most, five hours between shifts. The few hours I do have off I spend drinking, even if only for an hour before dozing off. I stop by the liquor store near my apartment once or twice a week and start buying larger bottles. My usual routine is to watch "Little House on the Prairie." I love the reminder of North Carolina and close-knit-family love. But during this time, I can't even watch TV; every channel is taken over by the news, which seems to be force-hypnotizing me into permanent misery.

Every day when I leave the precinct, I want to mentally wipe out that night's shift. Alcohol seems to be the comfort I go to most often. During the days when I work at Ground Zero, drinking after my shift is a must. I can't get the images out of my head on my own, and my emotions are a constant mix of anger, sadness, and confusion. I decide to keep the television off and listen to music while I drink myself to sleep.

I become so absorbed in this harsh new world, that I don't answer the phone or stay in touch with friends. Shelly and my mom even show up at the precinct one day, looking for me.

"I was worried about you," Mom says, reaching out her arms to pull me in closer. Her movement almost startles me; apart from graduation, I can't remember the last time we hugged.

"I wasn't worried," Shelly chimes in over her shoulder. "I'm only here because Mom dragged me over."

Ignoring her comment, I release Mom and assure her that I'm okay, even though I don't believe my own words.

And I'm not the only one. I notice that there are no more bushy-tailed, wide-eye attitudes, even from the officers I graduated with. We are all tired, traumatized, and jaded. They didn't have lessons at the Academy about how to deal with something like this, at least not emotionally. Logistics, they just barely covered, but the impact on our souls did not even come close to being addressed.

This was not what I could have imagined doing. Before 9/11, I was already struggling to find some kind of joy on the job—the TV version of it, that is. But the reality is sinking in that it must be way better playing a cop on TV than in real life. Here, there's no director to yell "cut" right before someone gets shot or a child dies at the hand of a caretaker. There are no makeup artists, scripts to change, or obnoxious paychecks. I feel deflated, cheated, and useless.

My whole life feels like that flaming heap of ashes across from Battery Park City, and I struggle to imagine what it could look like if it were rebuilt—if that were even possible.

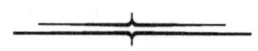

We're all sitting in the hood of a van on Chambers Street and Broadway, finally taking a break. My feet are sore, and my mouth is dry. Dixon pulls out a Tupperware bowl from his backpack, opens it, and starts eating.

"What's that?" Rosie asks.

"Ramen noodles with black eyed peas," Dixon says.

"Yo! I know you didn't bring Ramen noodles to work in your bag. Dude, that is so wack—and delicious! Gimme me some, you selfish prick!" Weiss says. We all break out into an amplified laugh.

"Don't even act like we all don't eat Ramen noodles like it's a gourmet meal," Fuzz says.

"I know I wouldn't mind some, instead of waiting on the Nino's line for the stuffed shirts to get food first," Weiss says.

Sarge chimes in; "You all don't know Ramen noodles until you put Spam in it."

"OHHHHHH," Rosie, Dixon, Weiss, and Fuzz blurt out at once, surprised Sarge knows about this secret.

"Sarge, you know you were eating cabbage corn beef and potatoes! You ain't never had no Ramen noodles—and especially Spam," Dixon says, trying to eat and laughing at the same time. Weiss takes his bowl and starts eating it.

"Not only do I know about Ramen noodles, but I also know about a lot of other things; you may be surprised," Sarge says.

"How about cold showers because the building has no hot water; I hate living in apartments to this day because of that," Fuzz says. We all agree, nodding our heads.

"Cold showers with the smallest piece of soap ever!" Sarge yells over his shoulder.

Weiss spits out his soup onto Dixon. We are laughing so hard the windows are shaking.

"Weiss! Control yourself; you're wasting my food!"

"Too bad they don't have a church with a cheese line going on. I'd be the first up front," Rosie says, then continues, "Pan con queso is da bomb."

"Yup, that's right for sure," Fuzz says.

I sit and listen. I've never told anyone other than Sarge much about my past, but listening to everyone, I'm starting to feel like I am not the only one who had hard times.

"Allyn, what about you? Any Spam or Tic-Tac-size soap in your past?"

"No Spam. That would have been an upgrade," I say. Rosie is laughing. I continue, "but I think one of my worst Christmases was when I got a pair of oversized boy sneakers wrapped in blue hospital bed paper for my gift. I would rather have had the cheese."

"If that ain't some shit. Meanwhile, I wish I knew you then. I would have asked you for those sneakers!" Dixon says. I can't contain myself as I slap him on the shoulder, laughing.

"I have you two beat," Sarge says, "I had to wait for my sister to get home to wear her sneakers to go outside, and on top of that, they had holes in them."

"Oh my God, Sarge," Weiss says.

Fuzz is choking and trying to speak, "Sarge I have an entirely new level of respect for you; I am imagining you in girls' sneakers with your bulldog look."

"I looked like a poodle with those sneakers on," Sarge says, his own laughter causing him to spit into his coffee cup.

Then, he stops laughing for a moment and turns around, "You all see what we are doing? We are not paying attention to what we don't like or ignoring the tragedy of what happened. We are still living and choosing to be of service to ourselves. Fix ourselves little by little, and we become more valuable to others when they need it. Got it?"

"What I got is a Ramen noodle covered uniform!" Dixon says.

I look around while we sit in the middle of a shit show, and I realize I'm proud to be with a bunch of cops who are somewhat misfits but also amazing. I let a little bit of my past through my shield, and for the first time since 9/11, we fill the space we're in with love and laughter.

CHAPTER 20

I started working the 4pm to 12am shift a few months after the 9/11 chaos eased up. The midnight schedule had worn on me, but the 4pm shift is much busier, and I rarely have a partner. I take advantage of the solo assignments by studying for the sergeant's test while watching prisoners or being stationed at Yeshiva University. It isn't the best set up; street cops have it harder when it comes to studying or having any life outside of the job. It's not like we can spend our time at work sitting in an office reading job material with nothing to worry about.

We all quickly fell back into the grind in Washington Heights. Sarge has always been a midnight shift person, so I don't see him as much these days, but when we're changing shifts, we catch a quick chat. He keeps reminding me to read the books he gave me, keep studying, not be so hard on myself.

"Can you believe it's been over a year since 9/11?" Rosie says as we change our clothes.

"I know. It's commonly said that time flies when you stop paying attention to it. The world really didn't skip a beat. Well, Washington Heights didn't as far as we know." I nudge her shoulder and laugh.

"You got that right, chica. How do you think you're going to do on the sergeant's test? I can't look at that crap anymore, I can't wait until it's over," she says, flipping through the pages of her study manual.

"Even though I spent a year studying for this test, it seems I've been doing worse on the practice tests."

"You'll do great, flacita!" Rosie snaps while nudging me back. "They make those practice tests hard on purpose."

"Yea, I'm not a fan of tests. I told you before how I struggled in the academy," I say, slipping my sneakers on, my feet finding welcome relief.

"Well, you're sitting here, just like I am. We've been on the job for almost three years. You know what they say about the first and the last person on the list after the test, right? They both get promoted to sergeant."

"I am so happy I know you. I hope we both pass. Wouldn't it be amazing for us to get promoted?" I say as we hug each other.

"No hoping. We are going to do it no matter what, the first time, because I will die if I have to take that test again." We laugh as we walk out of the locker room.

I see Sarge as I walk out of the precinct. "Hey, Sarge," I say, pulling on my coat. "The sergeant's test is tomorrow. Good thing I'm off for the next two days. How are things with you?"

"I heard. You can pace yourself." He picks up his bag, reaches in, and pulls out a book. "This is to cheer you up after you take the test. Don't force it; if you honestly did your best, then leave the rest up to fate. Be proud of yourself. Remember, Allyn, you were in a completely different place a few years ago." He hands Velez a radio, and the keys to the police car.

"Hey, Velez, what's up?" I say as we hug.

"Nothin'. You ready for the test?" he asks, throwing the keys up in the air and catching them.

"Do I have a choice? It's tomorrow whether I'm ready or not."

"Allyn, you got this, just trust it will work out," he says. "I can't be bothered with those tests. I have no patience to study. If I don't make the squad, I'll think about it…"

"Well, be careful tonight and don't bore Sarge to death," I say.

"Alright, Allyn, good luck—you don't need it, but I'm saying it anyway," Sarge says.

I smile at them over my shoulder and walk out of the precinct.

Sarge has been my main motivation for pushing through the utter punishment of studying. I want to be the kind of person Sarge is. He says he admires me exactly as I am, which surprises me. I admire how he is not a bells-and-whistles kind of guy, but a guy who has unyielding faith, courage, and true compassion for others.

If I get through this test, I will be the boss I want to see more of. If I have any influence on anyone, I want to have the same effect on someone else that Sarge has had on me.

It feels good that the others have so much confidence in me, but I don't feel as confident—not in my test preparation, and certainly not in myself. I've only gotten out of the studying as much as the alcohol allowed. Outside of studying, my days are lonely. I take random dance and workout classes when I can, but there aren't many dancing cops willing to jump on the bandwagon of studio life, and the people I meet usually have completely different personalities or schedules.

But not alcohol. That's there whenever I want it to be.

"Oh Jesus, we have a new captain. I hear he was a mess in IAB and a big boozer," Rosie says, brushing her hair as we dress for our shift.

It's been months since we took the test, and we've not heard anything. I'm tired of everyone talking about what questions they got right or wrong, and just thinking about it makes me sick to the stomach because I'm starting to think I got more wrong than right. I need this—it's going to be my make-or-break moment. Passing that test would mean becoming a boss, an example to other cops. Most of all, I'd make Sergeant Walsh proud, and it would be a great feeling for somebody to be proud of me for once.

"So. We always get new people here. He may be nice," I say, hoping I'm right about Captain Richards. I didn't realize he had come from the Internal Affairs Bureau; cops are never comfortable with people from that unit.

"Nope, I heard he botched an IAB investigation by having an affair with one of the target officers. What a dumb thing to do. And what does the job do? He gets promoted to captain and assigned to one of the better precincts. The good ol' boy crap on this job is so ridiculous."

"Well, when we pass the sergeant's test, we'll be part of the boss club too," I say, hoping it's true.

"We're still women, so we'll always get the double-edged sword—right in our backs."

When she leaves, I sit on the bench, slouched over, worn, defeated. Will I pass? I absentmindedly fiddle with the rosary beads Rosie gave me for my birthday and wonder if I will ever feel happy, alive, full of faith.

I've never imagined being a superior officer of any kind, let alone a boss. Sergeant Walsh is a kind of shield for me. I barely talk to other bosses, let alone captains, unless I'm directly addressed by them. I only know who the commanding officer is because his picture hangs behind his desk. He has his sidekick lieutenant and sergeant who run around bullying everyone and making decisions for the precinct operations, but actually finding him is like looking for the Wizard of Oz. If I become a sergeant, I'll be the friendliest boss around.

Over the next couple of weeks, I see the new captain in passing. Tall, dark, and chummy with the guys.

"He is attractive. I hear he is married and has a bunch of daughters," Mrs. Jenkins says. She pushes her glasses back and looks up from her admin desk in the complaint room. Middle-aged, warm, and sincere, she seems to know everything about everyone and refers to me as her "little buddy." We met when I was working evening shifts. She is the only civilian who handles our paperwork, and she taught me a lot about accurate writing and the computer system. She also brings me dinner most nights; it's the only time I enjoy hot, homecooked meals.

"Wow," I say, biting into a piece of steaming hot chicken. "I can't imagine having one kid, let alone a bunch."

"He needs to stop trying to be a college frat boy, lay off the drinking, and be with his family more," she says, indicating her own status as a happily married wife and mom.

"You should give him a good talking to," I say. Just then, Captain Richards walks into the office, and I freeze, my chicken caught at the back of my throat. I am supposed to salute him, but I remain frozen in place.

"Hello, Mrs. Jenkins," he says, leaning up against the wall and staring at me without waiting for her reply.

She looks over her glasses and says, flatly, "Hello, captain. How are you?"

"I'm doing just fine, just fine, thank you. Margarette, can you gas up my car and wait for me out back? I have to make a few runs."

Holding my fork midway between my plate and my mouth, which is wide open, I stutter, "Y-y-yes, sir."

He walks away and out of sight.

"What the heck?" Mrs. Jenkins says, staring at me over her spectacles and shaking her head back and forth. "Those arrogant ones just never get it. He knows he can do what he wants. When you get to where it is he wants to go, make sure you get out of the car and wait inside the building."

"Who's going to work in here with you? He didn't say anyone was replacing me," I ask, not wanting to leave her alone in the complaint room.

"Child, you know me, and God can handle this whole precinct just fine. Don't forget what I said. Don't be so bubbly either, just speak as little as possible."

I give her a hug and walked over to Sergeant Grosen, who's on the desk, to let him know I'm leaving to assist the captain.

With a cigarette hanging from the corner of his turned-down mouth, he looks up and says, "You can put gas in the car, but you ain't drivin' that asshole. Go upstairs after you gas the car. I'll tell him you have too many reports to do before the midnight shifts comes in. I'll call you when he's gone. Stay away from that snake." I want to jump over that desk and hug him. The time he supported me when I was so affected by Elsie was but one of many times he's had my back.

Straight after putting gas in the car, I head back up to finish my dinner. "I'm not gonna drive that captain anywhere," I say. "Sergeant Grosen told me to go upstairs until he calls me back down."

"I love Sergeant Grosen," Mrs. Jenkins says. "Enjoy your dinner, sweetie."

I manage to get out of driving him, even though he tries again a few weeks later. Given my position, there is no reason for him to speak to me, but he seeks me out occasionally and it makes no sense why.

We're all at the precinct club party that cops, detectives, and sergeants usually attend. This time, we're at an Irish pub on Broadway on the Bronx side. Some people play pool, and Rosie and I split up when she disappears to talk to friends, and I see a few girls I know.

"Hey, we are selling raffles; you wanna help?" one of the sergeants asks me.

I stream a few of the raffle ticket strips around my waist like a hula skirt and dance with a couple of my friends.

"Can you believe he's here?" one of my friends says though heavily liquored breath.

"Who?"

"Captain Richards, silly. They usually never come to club parties," she says over her shoulder, spinning on the dance floor.

"Well since he is new, maybe he wanted to get to know people," I say, giving him the benefit of the doubt.

He is sitting at the bar, another man standing close to him.

"That's his brown-nosing friend. He's a sergeant; they used to work together."

She saunters off to get another drink. Captain Richards signals and waves at me to go over to him.

"Hey, Captain, you want raffles?"

He and his friend start laughing.

"For starters. How much?" he asks, putting down his drink and turning his body to face me.

"Well, I think, wait, let me ask…"

His hand grabs the front of my pants. He pulls me in too quickly, and I have no time to move. His friend blocks him from view of everyone, and his hand takes a plunge into my underwear. The more I try to back away, the tighter he holds onto my waist with one hand and the more he digs into my crotch with the other. My waistband is cutting into my skin, and I wince with the pain of that plus the urgent stabbing of his fingers. They are both giggling like shy schoolgirls, and I am mortified, petrified, and desperate for a way out. I look around for my friends, and Rosie walks up. He withdraws his hands quickly.

"Hey guys! How do you like the party? Did you get any tickets?" She is completely oblivious to what is happening, despite me staring at her intently.

He nudges me away and his friend distracts Rosie by putting his arm around her neck and leading her away. The captain then turns back to the bar, picks up his drink, and lights a cigarette. Everyone and everything freezes. I snatch the raffles off my waist and throw them onto the bar. I run into the bathroom, go into the stall, and sit, still throbbing from his grip.

What do I do now?

"I'm a little tired. I'll take a cab home," I say to Rosie as she is laughing and dancing the night away with her friends.

"Are you sure? You haven't even had a drink yet."

She's right. Probably for the first time in years, I am stark sober in a bar.

"No, it's okay. I'm just a little tired. I'll see you tomorrow." I can't think straight and need time to process what just happened.

"Okay baby doll, are you okay? You seem off."

I wave away her concern, not ready to say anything yet.

The captain never moves from that stool, never looks up. My insides feel as empty as the glasses in front of him. All I hear in my head is what other people had said about him: "A sneaky asshole," "An entitled brat," "The good ol' boys club criminals," "He knows he can get away with anything." Yet it still feels like my fault. I usually don't talk to Captains and was probably being too friendly.

I spend almost a week at home drinking and calling out sick. It feels easier to drown in my sorrows than face up to them. Maybe I give off some kind of scent. Maybe he knows I am a rat trap girl and have dark behaviors in my past. Maybe it is just something I will never get rid of. Maybe this is who I am, and he knows it. Maybe that is why he did it.

Deep down, I know he was wrong, but he was so pompous and arrogant, like he had the right to my body. He is just like that drug dealer, Ron, only with a white shirt and a badge.

Sergeant Walsh calls and asks if I am alright.

"Something happened at the party, and I've been feeling too embarrassed to go back to work," I say, taking a deep breath.

The story spills out, and I can feel Sarge holding his breath on the other end of the phone.

"One of two things is gonna happen. I get the guys together and we beat the holy shit out of him, or you're gonna say something," he says.

"They're not gonna believe me; he's a captain," I say, knowing its truth as I say it out loud.

"This happened to you because somebody else didn't do anything. The job just rewarded him by letting him be a captain. And you're gonna be the person who stops him from doing this to anybody else on the job."

I respect Sarge so much, and his pep talk convinces me that I need to speak up. *You're no coward.* I hear his voice in my head. *You can be scared, but don't panic.*

I go into work and straight into Sergeant McKillop's office. She's sitting behind her desk, typing intently on her computer. I close the door behind me and sit down to tell her everything.

She writes a letter to IAB, which clearly makes its mark, because twenty-four hours later, everybody in the precinct knows.

When I walk into work the next day, all eyes divert. Rosie ushers me into a corner. "Why didn't you tell me what happened? Some of the cops in IAB told some guys here that you filed a complaint against the captain," she says in a hushed voice. "They said you ought to be ashamed of yourself for screwing up the captain's pension."

Before I can open my mouth, she says, "You know what? Fuck 'em, chica! You don't have no nasty track record. If you never spoke up, he would do that shit to somebody else, like he did before you. You are no victim, flacita. God didn't make victims; he made warriors to survive and angels to help other people."

Rosie feels like one of my angels. I stare over her shoulder and see the captain laughing and walking down the hallway with some of the guys who ignored me moments ago.

"I have to go to the DA's office tomorrow. They said he may get criminal charges," I say.

"He should've gotten charges a long time ago. This is what happens when self-centered morons get away with small things; they get bigger and bigger. You can do this. You have the right people in your corner. Don't turn your back on God and faith for the sake of those jerks. I'll be a call away if you need anything. We all will."

The problem is, I have not felt anything for God in so long, I don't even know if he would recognize me.

Over the coming weeks, I don't feel supported. I feel like the town slut being burned at the stake in front of everyone. People who were once partners, people I worked with side by side, people I ate dinner with and met their families were suddenly strangers to me. The only support I had was from my core group of friends, who were scattered throughout the precinct, so couldn't hide behind them.

The Bronx district attorney and the PBA union representative are out in the hall talking. One is louder than the other, then they both whisper. They both again raise their voices, then abruptly stop. I am staring out the window at the cars passing and people scurrying by on 161st Street. The criminal court building across the road is dingy, its tinted windows thick with filth. I sigh, my head throbbing from the night before. I have been to the DA's office for so many arrest cases, but never myself as the complainant.

The district attorney, a balding man with thin spectacles hanging from his neck and his sleeves rolled up, opens the door, comes up to the front of his desk, and leans against it. He looks down at me, sitting upright and ready in the worn chair, sighs, and says, "I'm sorry you went through this ordeal. I don't wish it on anyone. But, at the least, we have a misdemeanor charge of sexual abuse and official misconduct because he—" He then takes a deep breath, rubs his head, and says, "… well, he is an executive officer. It will be all over the papers and an embarrassment to the department."

He reaches out and touches my shoulder. "None of this embarrassment is on you, of course. He had a rocky past and screwed up before, and the job let him slide. All this comes out if we go to trial, and even if we don't, the process before that will be more than you deserve. Do you understand what I am saying?"

My eyes glaze over his moving mouth as I absorb bits and pieces of what he's saying. "Executive and embarrassment and what I deserve" sound like a muffled echo.

"As always, the spoiled jerks get a pass at her expense. The job should have booted him a long time ago!" the PBA rep says.

"We have to decide what we're going to do, not go on and on about what the job should have done before," the DA snaps. "I know it sounds crazy, but if we keep it within the job, they'll deal with him without this all getting out."

As I sit there listening to the rep grunt and curse the job, and the DA mumble legal jargon, I mentally slip into what feels like total surrender.

Back at the precinct, what I thought was bad becomes worse. Even though I agreed to let those in charge take care of things, people still see me as the enemy, mostly bitter men, some of whom outright call me a liar.

I walk in for roll call and overhear a group of cops speaking go quiet when they see me. "She only said that cuz she wanted to get a special assignment," one of them sneers as I walk towards the front of the room.

"She probably wanted him, and he rejected her," another one says, nudging the guy next to him. They all snicker and my face burns with anger.

"The way he rejected you two scrubs?" I say.

"Haha, burn!" one of the others says, and they all point and laugh, cooing and jostling each other.

Before the first guys could retort, Sergeant Grosen walks in and calls for everybody's attention. I roll my eyes at them and turn to the front.

I realize that my circle has gone from what I thought was a large family to a few true friends. The people who were never loud or popular, the people who never sought attention, and most of all Sergeant Walsh. "Always keep your trust off people and on God," he said the last time we spoke.

I don't know how to trust anybody anymore. I especially don't want to be told to trust God. I feel lonely and ashamed—keeping it within the job is like keeping it within a newsroom. Details of the incident run through the precinct like a fungus with no boundaries. I start getting phone calls from people asking me to pull back the complaint because they believe he's a good guy who's made a small mistake.

In the end, I don't pursue criminal charges. The feeling of being gutted by the job I'm so proud of is too much for me to bear.

When I tell Sarge and what's left of my friends what happened, they react the way we did when someone was killed in my old neighborhood. "I understand why you didn't pursue it criminally, because this job is not out to help you at all. They just want to avoid admitting that he's like that because they kept excusing his past actions," Sarge says. "But I tell you what, we can have our own trial and jury. I will get the guys together tonight and beat him within an inch of his life."

I know he is serious. This man would literally take a bullet for me and others he respects. Other people he would throw in *front* of a bullet, Captain Richards being one of them. Even though I'd love them to get revenge that way, I know it's not going to solve the problem.

"Just like you said, they're going to turn that around on us if anyone finds out," I say. "He'll get his punishment; you know he will. He has to live in his own misery."

"You really do listen to me, huh? Now you're giving me my own advice." Then he looks me in the eye and says, "You're right, Allyn, we have our dignity; he doesn't. If you change your mind, let me know."

Right now, I know I'm giving up, but it's normal for the victim to take the bullet. It happens all the time.

CHAPTER 21

"I'm leaving the precinct," Sarge says. "My friend is the commanding officer of the 33rd precinct, and I think I've been here long enough."

We're in the muster room on a break. He's holding his Bible and closes it to tell me this. I want to snatch that Bible right out of his hands and then choke him.

"Why leave because of that?"

"Why not? That's what you always ask yourself before doubting a decision. People can tell you many reasons why you should do something, like stay in one place forever, but you have to always think, 'Why not try something else?'"

Anger fills me like a dam that never stood a chance against the force of rage. What the heck is God for? What the hell is life for? Why would the nice one leave us here?

I finally feel like I have gained a father, and now he is leaving me too.

I want to tell him that, but I am too choked up.

Maybe I should take his advice and try something else myself. Things have not improved at the precinct, and I need a new scene. I pass the sergeant's test but find out that my score was low, so I am way down the list of promotion order. I don't want to wait around at this precinct, especially with Sarge leaving, so I apply to be an instructor at the Police Academy and am accepted.

It's scary to imagine being an instructor, as I looked up to so many of them during my time, but it's also way less intimidating than staying at a precinct where I have become the town leper. It's difficult to say goodbye to friends like Rosie, Fuzz, Dixon, and Weiss, but we don't get to spend too much time together anyway these days.

My phone rings and it's Velez. "Hey girl, as much as I hate to see you go, I know it's something you have to do," he says. "But you know we love you and we always have your back."

It is good to think about somebody having my back, rather than stabbing me in it. I grab my bags and walk out of the 34th Precinct for the last time.

After a month of instructor training, I am thrown straight into the action. The gym has not changed, the grimy walls outdone only by the murky light and slimy floor. I walk in on my first day shift, and a shiver runs down my spine at the memory of D-Day week when they tortured us to weed out the weaklings.

Am I going to be the one doing the torturing now?

There are two other physical and tactics unit female instructors on the day shift. Pam was an instructor when I was a recruit, and Sandra was in the same academy class as I was.

"Wow, long time no see! When did you become an instructor?" I ask Sandra while we're changing in the instructor's locker room. I never thought in a million years I would see the other side of the curtain.

"I've been here about a year. Before this I was in Queens at the 109th Precinct. We know where you came from already. People around here talk, so be careful to keep your business to yourself," she says, giving me a gentle warning.

I thought it would be a fresh start, but my reputation has preceded me. They know where I came from— a whirlwind of disappointment, left behind some of the most courageous people I've ever met. I'm running from chaos and hoping for some kind of new start. I recognize a few of the other instructors from when

I was a recruit. I'm surprised that they never left. Maybe I should have stayed here and saved myself five years of misery.

I have to learn the curriculum and class schedule. After reading a few pages, I slam the book shut. Handcuffing techniques, take down tactics, baton lessons, the use of mace, and on and on. None of them make much of a difference if we can't use the best assets we have: the ability to feel confident and the skill of communication.

I wish I could expand on all my lessons in that realm. Confidence, communication, and trust will save you in so many situations on the street, although I learned the hard way that they might not help you in the precinct.

All the recruits are lined up in formation outside the gym, staring at the head in front of them. As the instructors pass them, there are sound offs of "Atten—tion!" and the snapping of feet coming together in the proper position.

Sandra walks right past the recruits, not looking up, down, or sideways. Her golden bob hairdo bounces in the hot, thick air of the cinderblock-lined hallway. The corridor is tight and hazy, and the screaming of commands echoes in my brain like shotguns in a cave. I have a headache, again, and the yelling does not help.

A few of the male instructors nod their heads and return the recruits' salutes. I look at each company class, salute, and slowly wave. A few eyes meet mine and quickly dart away. I remember the way my eyes frantically searched for light in those hallways a few years ago, searched for personality in the instructors, searched for someone to tell me that I'd made the right decision.

The instructors stand around the gym with rosters, waiting for the command for the recruits to enter the gym. The lieutenant, four sergeants, and six of us police officers.

"Fall in!" Sergeant Woodward yells.

The new recruits come spilling in through the double doors like a waterfall, wearing gray shirts and blue shorts. They spread out over the gym floor, and I can smell their fear as they rush, scramble, and sway, like trees in a strong wind. They all take their places and stand still facing the front stage. The lieutenant steps up to the podium.

"Welcome to the police academy. I am the commanding officer of the physical training unit. For the next two weeks, we are going to make sure you have what it takes for the long haul. If you can't hack it in here, you will get crushed out there."

No Sinatra quote this time? I think, standing behind my assigned class.

"You are not babies; your parents can't hold your hands, and this is no place for whining and laziness. Everyone around you is now your family."

Looking at the group, I wonder how many of them come from families where parents hold their hands. I walk around looking at them, wondering if they are as scared as I was when I was in their shoes. Are they taking care of children? Following in their parents' footsteps? Looking for stability? Or outright homeless like I was, with nowhere else to go?

Sergeant Olsen takes the stage and gives a series of commands to get the recruits in another formation. Then, the hell begins. It starts with simple jumping jacks that quickly trigger my memory. The other instructors start yelling at the recruits who can't hold a push up, others are sliding their feet on the puddles of sweat on the floor, which is still as disgusting as it was when I was a recruit. Still others are huffing as if they just ran two miles. They are put in the push-up position and have to stay there for eternity.

There is a female looking to the side at one of the instructors while picking up her jumping jacks pace. She gasps when I step in front of her.

"Don't worry about where they are. Pay attention to where you are. Try as hard as you can, because you choose to be here, and you will be just fine," I say.

She cracks a small smile and says, "Yes, ma'am! Thank you, ma'am!" I smile back and remember the first time an instructor encouraged me. I also had an instructor who was soft-spoken, and when he addressed us, he was encouraging. I respected him, and that made me want to try harder. I want to help them feel the same way. It felt nice to get a break from the constant verbal whippings we delivered by most of the other instructors. For the first time today, I forget I have a headache.

Then there are push-ups, bear crawls, and sit ups—a lot of them. That's just the warmup. They are all in line to start the run. I can't bring myself to yell, even though the other instructors are right on board with it. There must be a philosophy that scaring the recruits is a positive, and I know it scared me when I was a recruit, but I don't want to be that kind of instructor.

The run starts off okay. The sergeant is at the head of the gray wave, and the rest are in the middle.

"Left right left. Left. Left. Left right left."

It seems like only a minute ago that I was in that group. Running, moving, never stopping. The constant movement in the gym is a metaphor for my life. I am now afraid to stop anywhere, make connections, put down roots, trust people. Things seemed to crumble any time I stop moving.

A few of the recruits fall out of formation and are immediately swarmed by a few instructors. "Get back in line! Assume the position! Can't you keep up? We haven't even started yet!" Oddly, this is gentler than when I was a recruit. The poor souls are practically crawling to the middle of the floor, a spectacle for the others.

The huffing and puffing take over the sound of their steps. Some start coughing, and the pace picks up to a slow run. More and more fall out of formation, and soon there is an island of recruits in the middle of the floor, getting tortured by the instructors. Some of them are screaming at others to keep up, help each other, and not give up.

I imagine myself in the pack, out of breath, legs cramped, running for my life. I am tired just watching them. It doesn't help that I did not sleep much last night. By the time I finished my bottles of wine and half quart of vodka in front of a movie, it was 2am, and we had to be at the academy by 7am. I don't remember getting so little sleep when I was a recruit.

I decide to jog next to my group. "You won't die; it's nothing you can't handle. Don't focus on the run, focus on making it out of here," I say as they look straight ahead in terror, searching for a life ring to save them.

"Thank you, ma'am," a few manage to say, sucking in air.

Each day I am there, I grow more and more miserable. I

normally feel at home in a precinct, and the academy is not where I feel I belong, although I am starting to feel attached to the recruits.

At night, I drink and watch movies until the early hours. In the morning, I catch the train because I usually don't feel alert enough to drive, and I can sleep on the train. The only thing that gives me joy is spending time with the recruits. They are what I wish I was: young again, starting over again, not knowing what was going to happen to me. I don't envy the fear I used to have when I was in their shoes, but I do long for the naiveté.

Six months later, I am on my lunchbreak and desperate for some fresh air. I walk past a church on Park Avenue that has been renovated into a club called Club Limelight. How I wish churches were truly a place to be saved; how easily they've become a place to drink.

Seeing the recruits going through the process I went through five years ago has sucked me into a funk. Where am I going? What will I become? If I were a sergeant, maybe my life would be brighter. If I hadn't lost dance, maybe I would be happier. If I still played the piano, maybe I would bring joy to others.

Looking at the church again, I wondered if maybe being Catholic would save me. I absolutely hated the thought of acknowledging any concept of God for fear of being punished for hating Him so much. Panic is in me all the time, and I am still not quite sure where it is coming from or how to quiet it.

It's no secret that my time in the physical training unit is a disaster. I don't fit in, and it feels like I am constantly fighting something or someone. The commanding officer suggested I leave the academy, and the other instructors feel that I'm not a team player and that I treated the recruits too nicely. "Instructor Allyn has to work on being more assertive with the recruits," they said during my evaluation.

Never mind that the recruits respected me and worked hard for me. All my fellow instructors and bosses could see was that I didn't yell at them enough. Laying heavy hands on them does nothing for their faith or confidence, plus I believe that a mix of approaches is important. I also don't hang out with the other gym instructors during our downtime, and it clearly makes them uneasy.

The gossip runs through the building. It seems I've become the rebel instructor, the misfit who causes trouble in the dungeon of the place that was my home when I was a new officer.

It becomes clear they need to move me, so we decide I should try teaching in the classroom instead. I have just told my small group of recruits that I am being reassigned.

"Why have they taken you out of the gym? You are the nicest one here."

"Are you going back to the street?"

"Will you be punished?"

The questions fly at me like wild, beautiful birds as I stand in front of the group with a smile and a sigh of relief.

"Well, no doubt I'll go back to the street when I get promoted to sergeant. I have no idea when that is. And I won't be punished. I will say this: Never try to be what you are not. You will see the results of your decisions, good or bad. I can't feel better by making other people feel worse. And I can't find happiness living out someone else's demands."

The moment I say this, I feel like I'm connected to something. There is something light and lovely in saying it. I mean it, and I am embracing myself.

But I can't hold on to it, and the feeling slips away at three o'clock when it is time to go home, alone and lost.

Every half hour I have to give the recruits a break so I can get to the bathroom to hurl up the contents of my shredded stomach. During morning inspection, my breath lingers in the air like an annoying fly.

Maybe my years of hard living have caught up with me. *Why am I so damn sick all the time? Do I have some sort of blood disease? Or is it something worse?*

"Jeez, instructor, hanging out last night, huh?" one of the recruits says while we are damn near touching noses. I am mortified.

"Yup, and remember, I don't have any studying to do young man, so when you graduate, you can hang out too. Don't get caught out of focus. They are watching us from the tower."

I smile and move on to the next recruit. Covering up my shame by being funny is my way of trying to appear that I am really enjoying a social life rather than showcase the reality that I'm completely isolated and spend all my free time alone. Weekends are a dread. I can't even fight against drinking so much, but I know that the people around me drink less and also seem to be less miserable. I hate being alone all the time but that's what I am. I don't relate much to anybody and I can't take anymore disappointments.

I decide right there on that muster deck, the deck on which I have spent plenty of minutes in the push-up position praying to God to help me and not let my hands burn on that asphalt, that I need a change. Maybe if I move to the classroom, things will be easier and I'll feel better. At least I won't have to do push-ups while I feel as rotten as I do.

Despite my marginal optimism, the move from gym instructor to classroom instructor launches me into Groundhog Day, and I feel trapped in the merry-go-round because I haven't heard anything about my sergeant's test results yet. I wake up, make my way to the academy, nurse my headache, greet my group of recruits. I'm about to start teaching my fourth group once my current group graduates. But every session is the same. I get to know them, recognize their enthusiastic faces, and support them on the days they feel they can no longer go on with the virtual torture of the academy. They have no idea that my own life feels like one long, drawn out torture, too.

I like having a group to nurture, to inspire, to encourage, or at least that is what I hope I am doing. It's hard to be light and inspirational when I feel so low. As instructors, we are never allowed to get close to the recruits, so I try to maintain my distance, but much of the time I feel more connection with them than I do with my fellow officers.

I have a fondness for each group. They are always professional and always maintain a slight distance, but they are there. It feels nice to be admired and looked up to, and I wonder if this is what respect feels like.

I long for the days when I was younger and slightly more optimistic about my future with the force. I've made so many mistakes and I can never get that time back. I want to be the Margarette who makes good choices, has good friends, and has a lifetime of good days to look forward to. Not the Margarette who has left a trail of destruction behind her. I envy the recruits' opportunity to have a fresh start.

When each group graduates, it feels like an arrow through my heart. I love to see them graduate and move on to the next chapter in their career, but at the same time, every time they leave me, I fall deeper and deeper into my lonely hole of solitude and regret.

Today, my third group is celebrating their graduation at Madison Square Garden.

They are hugging each-other, cracking jokes, fixing a collar here and a tie there, and twirling hats in the air. The chatter in the audience is at a low rumble, the bagpipers overtaking the space with their musical enchantment. The police commissioner and executives arrive just before the ceremony starts. It is an automated visit, another stop on the campaign trail.

I sit in the audience, looking at the more than 1,000 seats, one for each officer graduating from the academy. Nearly six years earlier, I sat in one of those seats, moving from one world to another. Another number in the ranks of an ever-changing family, the families in the audience and my new brothers and sisters standing right next to me, behind me, and in front of me. The stage family, the actors who forget their roles and script lines over time, who are ultimately replaced by the next attractive prospect.

BOOM, BOOM, BOOM! Is followed by six more fast booms from the bagpipe drummer. It doesn't matter if one is on a float in a parade or a casket in a procession; all are led by that man with the staff. Marching to the *boom boom boom*, swaying one arm back and forth while steadily holding his golden rod with the other.

I've realized that I love teaching, but I dread this day—the day that the recruits graduate and go their separate ways. The recruits who started off as scared as I was when I wore that gray shirt but now look up to me and stand at attention when I enter the room. Who respect me. And who are now leaving me.

I get up from my seat and look at the stage, the place where I danced when I was with National Dance Institute. There we were, joining together in artistic unison, people from all over the world moving like an ocean that brought New York a show it would never forget. In the sea of colors and movement, I see my little self, her smile as bright as the lights, her arms and legs swinging, twisting, and jumping around my dance friends and family. She spots me in the audience, and I wave, jump, and clap to let her know that I've been here the whole time. Maybe she didn't notice that I abandoned her when Grandma died.

I feel for the first time an unbearable sense of guilt and shame. That girl dancing is not the hungover, rotten, used-up specimen in uniform, the person who wants to erase the past by running as far away from it as humanly possible.

I thought that wearing this uniform was like wearing a costume in my make believe show, but instead, I keep getting punched in the face by judgement and disappointment. People and things have always left me feeling a sense of despair worse than before.

Maybe the little me is in Heaven and I am left in hell. How will I ever know? And how will I ever know if she could ever forgive me?

Now, she is all grown up and in uniform, graduating from the police academy. She is looking off to the side, searching the audience. I glance over to what she is looking at, and there is her mother and family, giving her a standing ovation, just like she got when she was dancing, tears running down her face accompanied by the same smile.

Everything is in slow motion, and I wonder why I am so miserable. I am tearing up and cannot understand why I am so utterly sad. I could not save her, and I have no idea how to save myself.

One of my literary summer schoolteachers reviewed Shakespeare, and I've never forgotten the quote from one of the greatest writers in history: "All the world's a stage, and all the men and women merely players." Where do I fit in on the stage and why do I keep ending up feeling alone? Where do all the men and women go? I wish the theater of my life would never be empty.

As I walk down the steps toward the opening backstage, I watch the recruits through my hazy eyes. They looked so damn happy, innocent, and free. What will happen to them? To Officer Kinsey, who struggles with words but has a heart of valor? Who will be the first to receive the fighter jet sendoff? Who will be a chief?

The time until they leave me is ticking away, and it is unbearable.

My little group spots me in the wings. "Hey! Our dear instructor! Instructor Love Bug!" they cheer.

Then, Officer Kinsey picks me up and puts me on his shoulders as they all clap, and I pump my fists in the air while waving my hat. Everyone is looking on, clapping, cheering, and hugging. I stand in the middle of my class, surrounded by people who have given me a glimpse of purity, hope, and love. My arms reach around them in an embrace, a desperate desire to be where they are.

"You all take good care, be good first, and if you ever forget where your feet are, just look up. That light always shines on you," I say.

"And now, introducing the graduates of the New York City Police Department!"

Start spreadin' the news...

I'm leavin' today...

I want to be a part of it...

The roaring applause once again takes my breath away.

I close my eyes and imagine walking out into the light with them. But it is not my moment in the spotlight—it's theirs. My time has passed, and I messed it all up.

And this is when I decide to go home and shoot myself in the head.

CHAPTER 22

I barely remember making it back to my apartment. I'm sitting on the edge of the sofa, dangerously close to tumbling off, but my knees are up against the table and stop me from falling. The room (or my head) is stuffed and feels heavy. My eyes want to close; I want to finish what my thoughts started earlier.

The ashes from the cigarette hang on for dear life; I see myself through the smoke. Or rather, I see what seems like a rolling film of my life, images in my head that flash by like a movie reel.

It is enchanting and frightening at the same time. Where did Ralph go? What was Alice saying? I push myself up a little. I must sit up straight. *When I get to that last DVD, it's over*, I remind myself.

All my thoughts are slow as molasses and yet darting in and out like a kid playing peek-a-boo. As I gaze out the window at the hideous sun, the short circuit memories of my life fade in and out like actors on a stage, looking for their marks in the dark. Each event surfaces like a flickering candle that's quickly extinguished by a swift, teasing wind, a breeze that doesn't last long in scorching heat.

I hear the music of my piano teacher, *A, B, C, D, E, F*. Then the *tap, tap, tap* of my dance lessons. The drumming in Harlem School of the Arts. LaGuardia and "Fame". The screams and boom of the World Trade Center collapsing. I thought I had what it took, but I have no idea what it takes or who I am anymore.

My mother appears in my thought or on the sofa. She's rocking back and forth watching the Giants. The scent of new ballet slippers that look like satin candy, sweet as a sugar plum. The sting of the blows from Ron, and my insides rotting from all the pain I both gave and took.

What ever happened to little Kitri and Elsie? Are they living the same pathetic life I seem to have?

I feel like I'm trying to hold onto a past I had no control over. It seems everything that went wrong was my fault. It feels hurtful to let myself off the hook and trust something, anything. I imagine the little me reaching out, but she's unrecognizable when I gaze at her sitting next to me on the sofa.

The cigarette burns my index finger, and I jam it into the ashtray. I shift sideways, lean over, and fall to my knee. I stay there with the glass in one hand and my gun in my other.

The faint sound of a voice is pushing its way from deep down in my mind, from my gut. I see my grandma's face. I look at the gun.

She seems to be sitting on the sofa behind me, next to little me, and they are watching me struggle. If she watched me all these years, then she knows I don't believe anything she said about God. Knowing her, she took his place to watch over me all this time.

Could she have been the closest thing to believing in something I loved that I once saw and touched? What will she think of me if I kill myself? What if I meet her in Heaven? What if I don't go to Heaven at all? It's a stabbing thought to ponder.

I hear little me's voice saying, *Mommy does not deserve to be told you shot yourself in the head... remember, remember...* the Fame music and the little voice meld together. *She'll never learn how to fly... it's too high.* The gun is getting heavier, and I hold it tighter. I want to point it at little me. Shooting her would stop this unbearable chatter. I don't know if she is haunting me or trying to save me.

I see Mom's face again; I turn the gun around so the barrel is facing me, tears in my eyes. *Why am I doing this?* I wonder. The thought is sucked out by the barrel of the gun like a vacuum. The alcohol seems to have taken on a life of its own, as if it's controlling me. Any nice thought or memory is immediately crushed by a stabbing pain in my gut. I take another sloppy gulp of vodka, put the barrel in my mouth, and bite down.

The father of the female detective we found dead from suicide on the bench is in my head. I remember his blue eyes, as blue as God's sky. *Did that detective think of her dad before she did it? My father would hear of this; it would suit him right for ditching me!* I put my thumb on the trigger.

She doesn't deserve to be told... The voice is louder. It sounds like my grandma's voice.

"You beautiful child," Grandma would say.

I don't want to be mad at anyone anymore for the life I've had. There is no physical fight left in me. I want to be out of pain. I try to think of a solid reason to put the proverbial nail in the coffin and justify what I'm about to do.

"I'll see you when it's your time child," the voice says again. Maybe that was Gram. If I stand in front of them when this is over, will I be able to look them in their eyes and tell them what I did? I don't think I'll be able to, but I also can't imagine living with this pain anymore. My brain is hot; my scalp feels like it is melting. My stomach is cramping violently, and my vision is thick and blurred.

Will my mother be rocking back and forth, staring at that damn TV, watching the news or the Giants when she gets news of what I've done? Will I be a six-second slot on the news? Will the Giants make a touchdown? I bite down on the metal barrel again to hold it in place, making a screeching sound when my teeth slip a bit.

"Your mother doesn't deserve this!" I hear louder.

My mother will surely pay for this and get what she deserves: a lifetime of sorrow for being a horrible mother. God and Jesus can both burn in hell for being liars. The shepherd and the staff that comfort me—ha! What comfort?

"You remind me of your grandma all the time," my mother says. She is sitting on the sofa next to grandma. Little me is fading away; I feel my heart beating hard enough to crack my ribs.

I again bite down on the barrel with my teeth to distract myself from my nerves. I start crying so hard that I don't notice the falling night. The sun has left me, but the light from the TV remains.

The barrel is cold, like the clearest water from a barrel in North

Carolina. The city is closing in on me, and the dirty, headstoned buildings have no room for my name. My name. Remember, remember, remember the music the lyrics of the songs I love, the inexplicable way I feel when I'm around people I love, people who love me.

My grandmother and little me may be holding my hand. I want to reach for them, I want mercy and forgiveness. I take a breath so deep and fast it burns my chest, and I try and stand up while holding the gun. I fall onto the table. The gun hits the table first and jams the inside of my cheek. My head hits the side of the table, hard, and I hear a loud crack.

It's the last sound I hear.

When I open my eyes, my vision is blocked by a massive headache. I squint to keep the light out. Lying on my back on my living floor, I look toward the TV, which is streaming steady white noise.

I lift my hand to my forehead, where I feel a lump and a wet gash. My phone is ringing, but I can't lift my head, let alone roll over to get up.

What happened? I reach down to push myself up and see my gun next to me.

I start to remember what I'd planned.

Am I dead?

I can't be—unless I'm in a bad version of purgatory. Whose head would hurt like this if they were dead? Did I miss and I have a huge hole in my forehead? My stomach is doing somersaults. I roll over and start to crawl toward the bathroom.

My vomit smells like a brewery on steroids. I have been vomiting almost every night and at times during the day while at work. There is blood in the vomit again. I lean against the tub and lift the back of my shirt to feel the coolness of the porcelain.

The sink feels like a cool pillow against my head. I tilt my head up toward the ceiling. *You jerk.* I think. *Why can't I just die?* I can't remember how many times I've asked so-called God to not let me wake up. I tried to help it along last night and woke up in more physical pain than I can bear. The events of the night are not clear and dealing with the day in this condition is overwhelming to think about.

I feel at a loss for any kind of emotion. In a brutal effort to shower, I push myself up using the sink and get a glimpse of myself in the mirror. The lump on my head reminds me of when Ron slammed my head into the glass door the night we had the big fight. There is a gash across the lump and the blood is clumpy and dried around the edges. My cheeks are sunken in. It's not the image of a person with defined jaw line. I'm damn near skin and bone, my yellowing eyeballs protruding, my teeth grey.

The water runs over my head as I sit in the tub and hug my frail knees. I'm too weak to stand and wash, and the crying isn't helping my strength. My stomach is clenched so tight I feel it may rip as I cry.

"Oh, Grandma, if you are really watching over me, please help me; please," I say through my sobs. The hardness I once felt seems to be melting away and flowing down the drain.

"Hello," I say, barely able to open my mouth.

"Hey Margarette, it's Rip. What the heck happened to you?" he says.

Rip is short for Ripple. He is the union representative for cops at the academy. He was also one of my instructors when I was a recruit. It had been a pleasure to become close friends with him.

One of the things I like most about him is his passion for the people he works with and for his recruits. He is usually the person speaking up for the underdog, the so-called misfits. He also runs the tutoring sessions for the recruits having a hard time with the study materials. He's like one of the academy big brothers.

I frantically try to remember what he's talking about. The room spins faster the harder I try.

"What are you talking about? Did I say something inappropriate?" I ask, rolling to the other side of the bed and throwing a blanket over my head as if the conversation were a secret. I haven't been able to remember anything past a certain time after drinking. No matter how much I've tried to slow the drinking down, I've always thought I was fully aware of what I said or did.

"No, you didn't say anything rude, but I can't imagine what would have you so miserable. You said you were tired of your life. That you couldn't fix the past."

I have tears in my eyes. My stomach is cramping again. He continues, "Margarette, I'm worried about you. You certainly had me fooled at work. You're one of the happiest people I work with. It was heart breaking to hear you on the phone last night."

If the bed would swallow me up, I would be utterly grateful. Trying to come up with something to say that would make me sound good is giving me stabbing chest pains. I can't come up with anything other than the truth.

I need a break. I'm so tired. I'll never show that at work. It's my job to make everyone else happy, but while trying to find my way, I seem to have lost all sense of direction. I light a cigarette, and take a puff, the nausea too much to handle. I drag myself to the bathroom while holding my hand over the receiver.

The phone is under the bathmat as I begin hurling again. *How can I vomit air?* As I reach for the phone, I glance at my stomach. It's so sunken in I can clearly see every rib.

"Margarette, are you there?" Rip is asking.

"Yes, I'm here. Sorry, I had to get a drink of water," I say, wiping my mouth with my shirt.

"I've given your number to a friend of mine. He's going to call you later today. I suggest you listen to him. He's from a program I highly respect."

"What program? I don't need a program, Rip," I say as I rub my head. My speech sounds amplified, like I'm screaming.

"You need more than a program, Margarette; you need to trust me. You need to trust anything other than yourself right now."

I try to take a deep breath, but the sharp pain in my chest halts it. I touch the lump on my head. *What do I have to lose?* I tremble a bit from the cold and rising fear.

"What is he going to say? I am not sure what kind of program you are talking about."

"I know one thing: if I see you at work on Monday, I'm going to tell our boss, and he will force you to get help. You know what that means, right?"

"No, I don't! And what do you care anyway? Why bother if I go to work or not?" I'm lying on the bathroom floor, cold and unforgiving beneath my protruding bones. Nobody really cares; I'm just one more thing for them to gossip about.

"Have you ever stopped to realize that people truly care about you? If I say nothing, or do nothing, I am not only an asshole, but I am helping you destroy yourself. For the sake of our friendship, give this a chance and trust me. Please?" He is pleading with such kindness I feel I owe him just that much.

"Okay, I will listen to him, but that's it. When did you say he was calling?"

"Later today, its already after 1pm. Maybe around four or five; if he does, let me know, okay?"

"I'll let you know," I say, holding back tears.

"Margarette? You deserve better. You are a wonderful young lady. I swear you won't regret talking to my friend."

I put my hand over my heart and feel it beating fast. I let the tears stream down my face. "I am grateful for you, Rip. I'm sorry for snaping at you. Thank you for being a hard ball prick. I guess that's what I love about you." I giggle, surprised my stomach doesn't implode.

"You got it, kid. Remember, I'm here for you, let me know what happens."

I manage to make toast and coffee, then sit on my bed with the pillows supporting me as I eat in silence. My life starts flashing in front of my eyes, like I am Dorothy from the *Wizard of Oz*. I see the house in North Carolina, Christmas balls, Gram in the garden. I don't want to remember anything anymore, but the images keep coming. The dance studio, music notes and a piano, Grandma's headstone, my mother, the two of us standing outside our apartment.

The images keep coming, even as I go back under my covers. I doze off, hoping answers will come to me once I feel better.

The phone rings jolting me out of a half sleep.

"Hello," I say in a haze.

"Hi, this is Tom. Rip gave me your number. He said you are someone who could use some help."

"Hi. I don't really know what I need, but I think I am doing well," I say as if I'm late for my flight to the Oscars.

"Well, I think you may be doing better—right this minute. But would it hurt for us to meet for lunch just to have a chat?" Tom asks.

I don't want to see anyone, especially today. If I can push it, I can convince him that I just had a bad night, and he and Rip don't have to worry about me at all.

"Sure. But I am busy tonight, how's next week sound?" I say, holding my breath.

"Sure," Tom says. I let my breath out, feeling victorious. He continues, "How about Tuesday?"

"I can meet you after work. Is there a place you prefer?" I ask, like I'm setting up a drug sting.

"We can meet somewhere in midtown on the west side."

I think about the Gin Mill on Columbus Avenue near the 24th precinct. I love that place. When I open my mouth to suggest it, I figure I better pick something else.

"We can meet at the diner on 110th and Broadway; is that out of your way?" *I'm feeling much better about getting out of this.*

"Yup, that works for me. Enjoy the weekend and see you on Tuesday." Tom says, chipper as a Smurf.

I roll my eyes as I say, "Same to you, looking forward to it." As I end the call, I spy the gun still sitting on the floor and kick it under the couch. *I'll deal with that later.*

Thank goodness I can relax for a few days and think up an excuse for the behavior that's caused Rip to think I need help. For now, I'll enjoy the weekend and go to work Monday refreshed.

"Chica, you ready for me to pick you up?" Rosie asks.

"Oh crap. I forgot I said I would go with you to the Yankees game. Yea, I'm ready. Where are you?" I ask, smashing my cigarette into the ashtray and downing the last half of my glass of tequila.

After getting off the phone with Tom, I'd gone to the liquor store and the Jamaican restaurant. Nothing like island food to help a hangover. What I didn't realize was that I'd gone to the liquor store on autopilot. I thought I wouldn't drink after my stomach almost caved in earlier, but once outside, I couldn't resist it. I'm relieved to be reminded about the Yankees game. Hanging out with Rosie and our friends will give me a break from sitting in the house alone.

"Falcita, get yo ass downstairs. I'm already here!"

The Yankees are playing against Oakland. It's the third inning, and I'm on my fourth beer. I see the liquor stand and decide to get something stronger. Plus, the beer is making me feel bloated.

"Chica, what's with the drinking?" Rosie asks, popping her gum.

I light a cigarette. The stadium seats are worn, chipped, and dirty, but I love it. It gives me a feeling of warmth, the idea that people who love something deep down have sat in these seats for decades. The field is green as a country lawn, the players gleaming specs under the stadium lights.

"What do you mean, 'What's with the drinking?' You know I like to drink liquor, not beer," I say.

"I'm saying that I don't know what the heck is going on with you, ever since that shit happened with the captain and you went to the academy, you changed. You are flaca as hell and your eyes are mad dry, mama. You don't seem like the girl we all fell in love with years ago in that van."

"I guess I'm just run down, looking for my place, finding my way," I say as I stare at Alex Rodriguez swinging his bat. I think of Sarge, always practicing with anything he can use as a baseball or bat. I feel like my batting score card is screaming zero zero zero!

Back at the apartment, Emily is waiting for me with a bottle of tequila.

"Girl, I think I might need to chill out with the drinking," I say. I sound foreign unto myself. I don't feel like I can concentrate on things lately.

"Since when do you have a drinking problem?" Emily says. "You work too much to have a drinking problem."

I'm too ashamed to tell her how much I have been drinking when I'm alone.

"Yeah, maybe you're right," I say as we crack open the bottle.

The night, like all the nights before it, passes in a blur.

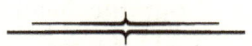

I am woken by the shrill ring of my phone.

"Hi, Margarette?"

"Uhhhh, yeah…?" I reply, no idea who it is.

"This is Bella; I'm working with Tom. He mentioned that he was a little concerned and thought that we shouldn't wait until Tuesday to meet."

I mumble in agreement with the plans she suggests, still drunk from my night with Emily. When they arrive, Tom takes one look at me and says, "You look tired."

The tears flow before my words. "I am tired," I say, sinking into my chair. "I never thought I'd be so damn tired at thirty-one."

"I need your gun and shield, kid."

The ark completely sinks. The reality, like a bat, cracking my head and heart wide open. That gun and shield is all I have to remind me of how hard I worked to get them.

The day I was handed those two things in the academy didn't just mean I was going to graduate. They meant I made it despite not having a home when I started. They meant I wasn't going to end up in the street, dead, or in jail. And they meant that no one handed anything to me that I hadn't earned. I worked my butt off for those two items that represented way more than something to show on my hip and chest.

I was so proud of that gun and the shine on that that shield.

The glint on that gun is now a stunning reminder that only two days ago I turned that very same gun to my head… the words of sarge echo in my head in the same memory, "You can't shine shit." And now *I'm* the shit in this situation.

What choice do I have but to hand them over? I am scared as heck, and I feel like I am handing over my ability to breathe.

Just when I start to panic, Tom reaches over, grabs my hand and says, "You need to take a break, kid. And listen, if it doesn't work for you, you can always go back to what you're doin'."

Oh, seems I do have a choice. Great.

My hand moves in slow motion and makes short circuit jerks as I hand him the gun. The shield is tucked underneath the barrel. *I truly hope I haven't made the biggest mistake of my life,* I think as I watch him slip them into his bag.

I start mentally preparing myself to take a few days off and then resume my normal activities with a fresh head.

"In order for you to take the break at rehab, you need to go to detox first."

"Rehab?!! Detox?!!" What on earth is this guy talking about? I thought I was just taking a few days off work. "Detox for what?!" *Oh my God I should have made a different decision before turning over my gun.*

They both look at me with sad eyes.

"Hey, kid, I know you've been drinking. But who knows? That might not be your problem... Let's just get you there to see how you do."

Is it that obvious? I surreptitiously take a whiff of myself. I smell like I have showered in rum and dried off with tequila. The perfume I hastily sprayed on before they arrived has done nothing to quell the stench of my long night drinking.

"What place are you talking about that I have to go to first?" I ask, not convinced at all. I don't even know this guy and he's talking about detox and rehab like I'm some junkie. "Why are you helping me? You here on overtime?"

Bella laughs.

"No, I retired three months ago," he says. "Kid, I know you don't trust me, but I haven't had a drink in thirteen years, and I bet I felt the same way then that you feel now. It started with taking a break."

He's retired and here on his own time. Maybe I can listen to him, for a bit. What else have I got to do? I'm still unsure and nervous, but something tells me he won't leave me hanging. I agree to spend a few days in detox and decide what more to do after that.

Tom says he'll come back for me after I've spent three days in detox, and I have to admit I feel slightly better. But on the drive to the detox center, the fear rises again, and I begin to panic.

"What will they do to me there?"

Tom patiently talks me through the process. He assures me that they just want to get the alcohol out of my system and make sure I'm physically well enough to go to rehab afterwards.

I still don't understand what alcohol has to do with anything. Everybody drinks. Maybe not quite as much as I do, but is it really something I need to go to rehab for? During check in, I hang on to Tom's leg, slumped on the floor, crying like an abandoned three-year-old, begging him not to leave me there.

"I promise I'll come back on the fourth day; I promise," he whispers, holding back tears himself.

"We won't hurt you darlin, you will be okay," the nurse says, on her knees trying to comfort me. Bella turns away, wiping tears from her face. I'm still scared to death.

I watch them walk away, leaving me alone in this place. *What have I gotten myself into?*

CHAPTER 23

Tom and I have been driving for almost three hours, though it doesn't seem that long. The gray overcast has been sucked up, the buildings are few and far between, and homes seem miles apart. The world is much bigger and brighter here.

We make small talk here and there while listening to jazz music, guessing who composed the piece. On either side of the car are farms, fields, oak trees, and ponds. The air is crisp, the sun spotlighting everything in nature I've long forgotten. Horses and cows graze peacefully. An occasional tractor puffs smoke into the air. The clouds seem to be resting, little pillows that welcome a nap.

The morning's events flash through my mind.

"Told you I'd pick you up, kid," Tom said without turning toward me.

As I had watched the detox center disappear in the rear-view mirror, I had tears in my eyes. I felt safe there. Taken care of. Nobody knew me, and I didn't have to live up to any expectations. I was given copious amounts of Librium to prevent alcohol-withdrawal seizures and had therefore been pleasantly spaced out the whole time, fairly clueless about the surrounding events but feeling good, nonetheless.

"Nice music, nice scenery. My senses are enjoying the colorful space in the world," I say, feeling like I should interrupt the silence.

"Well, believe me, if you like the scenery now, you will love the place we are going. I told you not to judge anything from the three days you had to spend at detox. You needed that before going here."

"I barely remember what happened there," I say, feeling a bit embarrassed at not having the slightest clue about what happened over the previous seventy-two hours.

"It's the medication. Keeps you sleepy and unable to get nervous or scared. I know you were very put off, but it wasn't horrible, right?"

"From what I remember, no. I had two nice roommates. One woman was seventy-five years old and started drinking after her husband died; another was a young nurse hooked on pills." That much I remembered.

"It's not all that surprising how many people are alike and how many people suffer from the same things—things we think we can't see," he says, swaying his head to the music.

"I remember the nurse asking about the bandage on my head. Said she could look at the bruise for me." A small scar and bump remained from the massive lump I got when I hit my head on the coffee table. "That fall sent me to the moon for sure."

We laugh, I more nervously than he. "I actually thought I was gone," I say.

Linus and Lucy by Winston Marsalis starts playing. I tap my foot to the melody.

"Charlieeee Brown, here we go, buddy!" he says, tapping the steering wheel.

I wonder if I really wanted to be gone. The memories of my childhood creep in, the times I spent watching "Charlie Brown" and "The Muppets". The times I was oblivious to things that didn't go well. The times I believed in magic and fairytales. Will I be able to live in this world as it is? Will I be able to keep what works and chuck the rest? Do I want to see what tomorrow holds? Can I even get through today?

I notice I'm not feeling miserable but I'm not feeling good, either. I feel sedated; at least the chaos has stopped. What were those drugs they gave me in detox? Maybe I need more of that.

The fields glide by like a spinning top slowing down, a tree peeking in the window, a bird saying hello, a cow moving past as if on roller skates.

"We're almost there. Do you want to stop off at the local shop to grab a few things? You are going to be here for a month—well, that's if you like it, which I think you will, but if you…"

"Okay, I got the point." We both start laughing. "Yes, let's stop off for a few minutes."

My hands are sweaty, and my heart starts pounding. I am not in Kansas anymore (or at least not the safety of a small detox center, with people drugged up and not able to really feel or realize what we did to ourselves).

The mountain air smells like fresh water. The little town of Walton sat nestled in a nook, its small homes and neat roads stark against the dark rock walls decorated with sprinkles of trees and reflections of the sun.

The town reminds me of a western cowboy town. Train or trolley tracks run right through the middle of the road, store fronts on both sides, a mountain with farms, fields, and beautiful air. As I pick things up that I need in the town store, I remember the shop down the road from the big house in North Carolina.

Soda pop, Vicks, cigarettes, beer, toiletries, hairbrushes, and snacks are all the same here. The store seems stuck in the past, everything neatly lined up and in order. I'd stood in that little store in North Carolina with jelly shoes on and a bottle of Mellow Yellow, happy as a ladybug on a lily pad.

This is not a gas rest stop; it's a Dollar General. I've never seen one of these stores before. There are toys and jackets for sale alongside garden tools and cigarettes. There is a Goodwill next door, as well as a lumber house, a post office (or post closet—it looks so small), and a few other places. It all feels simple, safe, and free of drama.

At the counter, I look through the window and notice Tom fiddling with his phone in the car.

"That'll be $23.75, please."

Her country accent surprises me.

"I didn't expect you to have an accent," I admit.

"Well, that's how we speak up in these parts. I notice your accent is different."

"Yes, but we are from the same state," I say, giggling.

"Yes, I reckon you are right indeed. Well, are you visiting a relative or somethin'?"

"Yes, I am. Just for a few days." I'm glad I was quick with that response.

"Who is it? We all know each other round these parts."

"Mr. and Mrs. Batson." *Please don't ask me any more questions.*

"Oh, my Lord, we all love them. You make sure you tell them Sadie from the General said hello, you hear? And they'll take care of you. Don't you go bein' a stranger now."

Back in the car, I ask Tom, "Did you have to make a call?"

"I tried but reception is horrible here."

"I had no idea people spoke with a country accent," I continue.

"Yea, this is considered the country. Everything was open fields and country landscapes until cities were built and took over."

"It's beautiful. She said she knows Mr. and Mrs. Batson."

"Everyone does. They are the best, you'll see. Remember, if you hate it in a week, I'll come get you. I promise."

"You got a deal."

There's a big red barn up the road to the right, and a pond and maple tree to the left with a few ducks waddling by the edge. The house is three stories tall, Victorian, with a porch that stretches across the whole front. There's a free-standing garage between the house and barn, a dirt and gravel driveway, and birds singing to each other like they are announcing that someone has arrived.

The oil painting, I love from my grandma's apartment where I grew up looks strikingly like this place. The music stops and I take a quick breath.

This is New Direction, my new home for the next thirty days.

"Here we are. I'm going to go in and say hello before I leave. You know our deal, but you are in good hands. I was here myself. Here, I'll take your bags," Tom says. He walks ahead of me towards the house, carrying my suitcase. He shakes hands with the man playing the guitar before walking past the porch swing and through the front door.

The man is playing an Irish tune and sings as beautifully as the birds accompanying him. The chickens peck and graze around the coop, their little ones trailing behind. The ducks relax in the pond, and there are a few koi splashing around.

I notice a path that leads up to a high hill and smell the grass that looks like a green waterfall. At the very top, barely peeking up and reaching for the sky, is a cross.

I don't know where I'm going, I don't even know where I am, but as far as I can tell, I'm not where I used to be, and maybe there is nowhere else to go but up.

I feel a release of tension in my body and heart. Being angry at God and rejecting a spiritual higher power is not what I want anymore. I think I'm ready to let myself want peace.

I want to listen to the rivers singing, the oceans yawning, and the animals breathing. I want to watch the wind ruffle the leaves and flowers while geese fly south for winter. I want to watch birds chirp and listen to woodpeckers, truck horns, and church bells. The crying of a baby and the wail of a man.

I take a deep breath to steel myself and walk towards the house, pulling my jacket tighter around me, desperate for some semblance of a hug to take away my nerves.

The door opens and a woman comes out. She is short and cuddly, and her green eyes peer at me over half-moon glasses, which she takes off to hang on a string around her neck. Her smile is warm and immediately disarming.

"Welcome, Margarette," she says, opening her arms for a hug. "Come on in."

CHAPTER 24

I stare at the wallpaper in my bedroom. The snack that Ching, the house cook, made me is a meal that descended as a treasure from the sky. I never enjoyed a turkey sandwich with macaroni salad so much.

The food back at the detox facility was half decent. The nurse weighed me on my last morning, and I had gained five pounds. She gave me a high five, which I gladly accepted. It was huge progress from my ninety-six-pound frame when I first arrived, and it looks like I may add to that in my time here.

Margaret Batson sits from across me on a twin bed while I look around the room. She is going through my bags to make sure I don't have any loose pills or alcohol.

"I don't know why I bother to check your bags, my dear," she says in her British accent. I absolutely love listening to her speak. I'm reminded of the Australian dancers I met while performing at Madison Square Garden. It's fascinating how people from so far away can come together and be kind to one another. I never forgot those dancers, and I get to hear Margaret every day, even though she's from a different country.

Her husband, Matt, is a former alcoholic. Margaret met him before he went into recovery, and they opened their home and named it New Direction to help people like me rebuild themselves.

"Yes," I say and laugh. "I did drive up here with Tom. I doubt he would have let me stop and get anything I shouldn't have."

"You know when Tom was here, what was it, thirteen years ago now? Well, he was a dogged mess." She's folding my clothes and putting them in the drawers.

I'm the only one in this room. It's the kind of room I wish I had when I was little. There is a closet and a nightstand in-between the beds. The flower wallpaper reminds me of North Carolina, along with the lace curtains that lightly shield the pitch-dark night on the other side of the window.

I couldn't leave here if I tried, I think. There is no way I could see two feet in front of me. There are no streetlights, and only an occasional car passes here and there. If I left, I'd surely get eaten by a bear or some other kind of mountain creature. For some reason I don't want to leave anyway.

"I do this automatically," Margaret says. "Occasionally, someone tries to bring something in. This isn't a hospital, so we can't have anyone taking anything illegal. It's automatic safety I guess," she says as she closes the last drawer and sits in front of me.

"How do you feel, my dear?" she asks. Her green eyes are soft, and her hand on my shoulder is comforting.

"I'm tired," I sigh, squeezing her hand. "I'm confused and a little nervous."

"Why, my dear? You will be just fine here," Margaret touches my face and hands me a tissue.

"I may be fine here, but what about when I have to leave?" I start crying softly. I am nervous the people in the bedroom next door may hear me.

Margaret gets up and closes the door, then sits right next to me.

"Let me explain one simple truth to you. It isn't easy at first, but you will learn to leave tomorrow to the universe. You are here today, now, not where you were yesterday. I ask you to keep your thoughts in the day and notice how much less you think."

I nod my head, and she hands me a composition notebook that reminds me of when I was in kindergarten and looked forward to showing Grandma my alphabet and handwriting. "I want you to write in this book. Write about your feelings and ask for the patience to give something new a chance."

"Ask who?" I ask, almost snatching my hand away.

"Ask God, or the sky, or someone you know in your mind, but just honestly ask for patience to give this a chance. Don't worry about what's going to happen. Look at what's not happening and be grateful for that."

"Thank you, Mrs. Margaret, and thank you for putting my clothes away," I giggle. "You didn't have to do that."

She touches my face again. "There is something about you, my dear; my heart hurts for you. I pray you give yourself a chance. I truly believe you will live a life beyond your imagination. Many people have come here in tremendous pain and left as miracles. You are a miracle, too."

I'm a miracle. No one has said that to me since Grandma. She has a point; I've spent a lot of energy worrying about what would happen before anything happened. The last three days have felt more relaxing than any other time I can remember.

"I have another book for you to read," Margaret says as she reaches over to the other bed, grabs a book, and hands it to me.

It's a book about alcohol. I squint my eyes and wonder why she would pick this kind of book.

"You have tons of book lining the shelves. Why give me this one?" I ask. Margaret lets out a royal British laugh, which is at once coddling and slightly devious.

"My dear, this is all I can give you now. You can pick something else tomorrow. This was the closest book to me when I grabbed everything to come up here," she slyly says while I smirk at her. She knows what she's doing; choosing that book was no accident.

"Okay, but I'm going to pick something from your library tomorrow."

"Of course, and dinner is at eight sharp, so see you then. You can meet everyone."

Margaret closes the door behind her, and I stare at the book. I start to think about what will happen when I go home, or when I go back to work, and I feel as if I've been smacked against my head. *Ask for patience*, I hear. *You are not in tomorrow; be grateful for what's not happening right now.*

As I think about Margaret's words, I notice I haven't vomited in almost four days, I haven't had a splitting headache that made my brain feel like it was being torched, and I haven't thought about suicide. I look up and whisper, "Thank you." For once, I really am thankful.

The table is set, and there is a salad bowl at each plate. In the middle of the table is a dish of pork chops, and others of apple sauce, baked potatoes, and broccoli. *Oh, my goodness, I am in food Heaven.* It is a replica of Gram's house or my childhood apartment at Thanksgiving. My nose is treated to the sweet scent of the apple sauce, spices in the pork chops, and fresh baked bread. I have an appetite for the first time in years. I want to go under the table and dump the whole plate in my mouth like a cartoon character, but I remember the lady of the house is a royal Brit and contain myself.

"I'm Susan. Welcome, Margarette. Let me introduce you to everyone else," Susan says as she passes me the breadbasket. Susan is one of the clients staying in the house with me.

"Grace first," Matt says.

Everyone stops chatting and holds hands. Matt is on my right, and Brenden is on my left. Brenden grabs my hand and gestures for me to bow my head. Matt takes my other hand. Margaret is standing to Matt's right with her hand on his shoulder and her head down. She motions for us to follow along.

I haven't said or remembered grace at dinner since Gram's house, who said it before every meal. It was automatic to me. I have no clue when I stopped giving grace or when grace deserted me.

"There are people out there suffering, for many reasons, may we all be grateful that, right now, right this second, we are fortunate to have a meal prepared for us by these lovely people who help Margaret and I run this house, and may we be grateful we are not hurting ourselves or others. Give us patience to be kind, understanding, and supportive. Amen."

I feel a bit apprehensive. I feel fake bowing my head like I've been praying all these years. But Matt and Margaret seem heartfelt about what they are saying and passionate about providing their home to help people. That is something I can believe, just for now.

"I already met the model from the magazines," Brenden says. He is the guitar player with the Irish accent and the only person I already met earlier today. Now he's gushing about me looking like a model. *But I don't know any model that looks like me.* Sitting next to me, he takes a bun from the basket and puts it on my plate.

"Yes, we all know you are the house greeter," Susan says. She points toward the woman next to her and says, "This is Tessa, Rusty, Sharon, Mike, and Maggie; Maggie's real name is Marguerite! Isn't that so cute? You both have the same name!" They all wave, and I smile at them.

Matt takes a bite of his pork chop. "Young lady, how are you coming along so far?"

"Not bad, thank you. Everyone's been so nice. You have a beautiful home; it reminds me of my great grandmother's house in North Carolina," I say as I shove a forkful of potatoes in my mouth.

Margaret walks over to me, touches my wrist and kisses my head. "Eat child, you will be just fine."

Matt nods his head, "You are going to eat right here, young lady."

Everyone nods in agreement. As everyone is talking and eating, I think about how delicious the food is, and how long it's been since I cooked myself a meal or went to a dinner with family or friends. Dinner conversation flows, and throughout the evening I find out why everybody else is here.

"What's your drug of choice?" Susan asks.

Is she talking to me?

"I don't do drugs," I say, and a few of them giggle.

"Why are you here then?" Maggie asks.

"I don't know," I say, the tears springing forth before I can stop them. I compose myself after a few moments and dab my eyes with the corner of my shirt.

"For me, it's coke and alcohol," Tessa says. *Ahhh, coke.*

"Dope and alcohol," says Rusty. *Ahhh, heroin.*

"Alcohol and weed," says Mike from the end of the table. *Weed...*

These guys all do drugs, and I got that under control years ago. "But I don't do any of those things," I say.

"Alcohol is the bridge to everything else," Matt says. "If you didn't have alcohol, you would still be doing those other things."

Silence.

The air is heavy with the weight of that statement, and they all know it.

Alcohol is the problem?

But... I can control my drinking. Drugs made me feel horrendous, but alcohol is my friend. How else can I relax after work with the job I have? It shuts down my insecurities. It helps me come out of my shell. It allows me to live a fearless life. When I don't drink, all my fears rise to the surface, and I don't want that in my life. These people don't even know me.

As they share their stories with me, it clicks. Most of them have been here two or three times. It's basically their version of a vacation, a break from lives riddled with the effects of drugs—drugs I broke free from years ago.

I don't belong here. I'm a cop. I don't need to be taken care of. I know how to fight and deal with pain, and maybe I don't feel good sometimes... well, most of the time... but I'm still here, aren't I?

I'm a success story compared to my mother. She has a good job and some friends, but I know she's still doing drugs. I called her on my way up here, and she was incredulous at me going to rehab.

"Why didn't you tell me something was wrong?" she said. "I could have helped you."

It's because of you that I'm going there.

We wrap up dinner, and I head up to my room.

I can't understand what Matt said about alcohol being a bridge to everything. Do I really have an alcohol problem? I grew up around drugs, even people with food issues at LaGuardia. I remember a girl vomiting after binging on food in the locker room. I was pissed. "I can barely get food and you are throwing yours up in the toilet?" I said with seething anger.

I decide to take Sarge's advice and escape into a book, the only one I have is the one Margaret gave me. The topic of alcohol is clearly a theme, so it looks like I can't escape that being drummed into me over the next month.

I may as well just read it, since it's the only book I have right now.

I look at the table of contents and see stories written by actual people. I pick a random story and start to read. The story is about a woman who started out in life as a happy kid. She lived with both parents and had a couple of siblings. Her mom drank all the time, and her father used drugs and gambled. She grew old enough to notice. She watched her home tumble into ruins and her parents' constant fighting. She became disconnected at school and heartbroken for her mom and dad.

One day, she came home and her mom was gone. Her dad had kicked her out. She didn't know what was better, being left with her dad or wanting her mom. She drowned her fear in alcohol throughout her late teens and drank for years. She ended up in the debt of alcohol. Her words sink in. She comes out of the book and sits right across from me on the other bed. I can almost hear her voice in my head.

"The alcohol is something we have in common, sweetie, but you know what else?"

I already know. It's the feelings she had in relation to her life.

I am so at one with her in that moment, and I can hear her so clearly that I can't even tell if it's her voice or mine. *"When something happened at home that scared me as a child, and no one helped me through it, I never learned how to articulate my feelings. My insecurity grew, and that was paralyzing. Alcohol shut that down for me."*

That's me.

It was supposed to be a savior, but alcohol brought nothing but pain and chaos.

That's me, too.

Her story talks about recovery and how the pain has completely left her. Trusting in something she couldn't see, like faith. Knowing she deserves a better life, and that she can make choices that move her further from pain and closer to peace.

I am mesmerized by how identical she is to me. I would never have been able to explain my feelings the way she did in her story, nor would I admit them. I'm not weak, and I never ask for help.

Although the woman in this story doesn't feel weak. Maybe there's something to this. I haven't felt any mental, physical, or emotional torture in a few days. I don't know if I'm moving closer to peace, but I do know I could be moving further away from the misery I have lived with. I close the book and lay my head back. I look over to the bed and smile. *Maybe,* I think. *Just maybe I have a chance to live in peace.*

If things don't get worse today, maybe I'll ask for the patience to stick around another day.

Our twice-daily meetings are mandatory. "Two of you are going to make it out of the ten of you," our counselor, Bobby Jordan, says to the group sitting on the plush leather couches below the high ceilings of the converted barn where we hold meetings. "That's just the way it is."

"What do you mean two of us are going to make it?" I ask, sitting forward. Make it? Are the rest of us going to die or something?

"Stay sober without relapsing," he says. "Everyone is here because of choices. Which life do you choose to live? It's as simple as that."

Bobby Jordan sits back and looks around the room at each of us. No judgement in his eyes, just wisdom from a place of personal knowing. He said they'd had to literally drag him into rehab twenty-eight years ago, close to twenty years into his NYPD career. Several years into retirement, he is here with us, supporting our choices.

"What about the choices other people make? Like, the ones that affect us?" I ask.

Everyone looks from me to Bobby Jordan and nods their heads.

"Your reaction is your responsibility," he says, without missing a beat. "Those people aren't sitting here. You are."

He goes on to talk about our childhoods and how blaming our parents or circumstances has to stop somewhere.

"Yeah, but–" Tessa says.

"Everything after 'but' is bullshit. Stop making excuses. Every one of you are here because of your choices. What you chose before, what you're gonna choose now, and what you're gonna choose after that."

We absorb his words. Maggie squeezes my hand reassuringly. It's okay for her; she's leaving next week. Maybe she can be my inspiration for what lies on the other side because I don't want to be Brooks from Shawshank. When I leave here, I'm never coming back, no matter what happens.

I look around the room and it hits me. They are all full of excuses, living their crappy lives, miserable in their relationships and neglecting their children. They remind me of my mother, and it pisses me off.

I don't want to be a repeat client, that's for sure.

Maggie's final day arrives, and the air is charged with positive energy. She isn't the first to leave since my arrival, but we have grown close, and I see her as a big sister and mentor.

We all gather out the front to farewell her. She hugs each of us, saving me for last. She gathers me into an enormous embrace and whispers in my ear, "I love you; I love your young, happy spirit," before taking the amethyst from around her neck and pressing it into my hand.

"I'll see you when I get out," I manage to say between gulps of tears.

As Maggie gets into the car, Matt rings the beautiful, large brass bell that's saved for special days like today. It's ring peals across the open field and fills us all with hope and optimism. He continues ringing it until Maggie's car disappears over the hill and we can no longer see even the dust marking her departure.

I know she's left me for now, but it's only temporary. I'll see her when I get home. I have a point person in the outside world now. *If she makes it, I can hang out with her when I'm sober, and I'll be fine too,* I think.

The weeks fly by, a collage of long walks, impactful conversations, group meetings, and a lot of time spent in nature. Matt sits with us outside sometimes, smoking his cigar and speaking about his own sober journey.

"You know you don't have to do it," he says, leaning back in his rocking chair and chomping on the back of his cigar.

"Do what?" I ask, smiling. I love our talks.

"Drink."

We've watched movies and read books to the point that I've finally come to accept that alcohol is a problem in my life, but his words still land heavily. We can't control the negativity that comes into our heads, but what we choose to do with it is our choice, and I've come to accept that I don't have to let the default negativity lead my choices and feelings.

Still, I'm not naive enough to think it will be a simple process. "It's easy while we're sitting here on this porch," I say. "Going home is another story."

"You're gonna look back and have a story to tell," he says. "How do you want that to sound?" he asks, easing out of his chair and patting my shoulder on his way back inside.

Simply put, I don't want it to sound like I was a victim who made excuses. I don't want to continue to hurt myself over people who aren't in my life anymore or things that happened years ago. I don't know what will happen when I go home, but I don't want to come back here and tell the story of my relapse.

The day before my own departure date, we're picking leeks in the garden for dinner. I've chosen beef stew, biscuits, and sweet potato pie for my final dinner here.

I hear tires on the gravel driveway and turn to see a car stopping outside the house. It is a silver Mercedes, and I know immediately that I've seen it before.

I walk over to the car and see a woman in the driver's seat, her head in her hands. The big blonde curls look familiar, and my stomach drops.

"Maggie?"

She lifts her head and looks at me through the open window. Her eyes are swollen and bloodshot from crying, and she says, "I'm so sorry, baby." I'm reeling from the shock of seeing her. She is my sobriety touchstone.

Standing in shock, her amethyst around my neck, I have no

words. Neither does she. She simply hugs me and walks past me into the house.

A few hours later, the farewell dinner I have been looking forward to feels more like a wake. I try to smile and respond to the encouragement I'm being given from the others, but inside I'm in turmoil. *Will* I *be back in a week, too?*

"My husband gave me a list of what he wanted me to agree to in our divorce, what money I'll get, what days I'll have the children…" Maggie interjects across the table. She had reacted to the paperwork, called him to argue, and invited a friend over to drown her sorrows in marijuana and liquor. "I hate him. I want to get revenge. He's an asshole, and I never feel like I'll have the upper hand," she says.

I finally look up. I can see it so clearly now. "Don't you think the best revenge would be to be the best mother and woman possible?" I ask.

She touches my hand and nods her head in silent agreement. Maybe I'm telling her something she already knows but isn't strong enough to do. I wish someone had told my mother that when I was a kid. Perhaps it would have saved us years of anger and pain.

Matt gets up and puts his hand on my shoulder as he walks into the kitchen. "You don't have to, young lady…" he says, as though he's reading my mind.

CHAPTER 25

"I am Margarette, and I am an alcoholic."
Relief washes over me like a thousand waterfalls during my final meeting on the morning I'm going home. I feel like a thick chain has broken, releasing all the chaos and the misery of the past. I'm ready to give myself permission to not let my past define me anymore, which feels like a high all on its own.

I have been holding on desperately to what I've been trying to fix and admitting that I don't need to live in my past anymore is the reprieve I have been waiting for, for what seems like a thousand years.

I no longer feel ashamed of my past; I don't want to try to fix it. I also don't want to be Maggie. Her return rocked me at a deep, primal level. She has relapsed multiple times, but seeing her get out of that car, so deeply ashamed, has really sunk in how important it is for me to own my past, my present, and my future.

I have to stop doing what I've been doing if I'm to have any chance of surviving. Stop the denial; stop the excuses; stop the anger. Just stop.

I left the gates of New Direction and walked into my new life.

That new life took me to my first meeting back home in Harlem. At the start, the chairperson asks, "Is anyone at this meeting for the first time who would like to introduce themselves?"

I remember what Bobby Jordan said to us at New Direction. "You are going to get out of it what you put in; do these three things and the pieces will fall into place: raise your hand and say something, anything; fold your chair and put it away; and most importantly, shake the hand of the speaker."

So I say, "I am Margarette, and I am an alcoholic. This is my first time at this meeting, and I have forty days."

The room erupts into applause and people shout 'Welcome!' from all sides. If I'd been looking for a supportive audience all my life, I finally found one, although I don't think about it that way. I meet people who are kind, friendly, supportive, genuine, and determined. I'm surprised at the breadth of backgrounds: people with money, people without, people with two parents, one parent, no parents. Every kind of situation and story you can imagine, and we all have *one* thing in common.

New friends suggest other meetings they love, and I attend meetings every day, at least once. I also explore new ones all over the city.

I make friends with a younger woman named Tina at a meeting uptown, and she suggests a meeting on the ground level of a church on 88th and Lex. She lives on Staten Island and drives there to meet me.

There are at least fifty people in attendance; it's the biggest meeting I've attended since New Direction. Everyone talks, laughs, and snacks on the huge buffet that lines the counter by the kitchen. I feel like I'm at an early evening party on the Upper East Side, and I didn't even have to wear a tight peacock dress to fit in.

I meet a woman named Christine. "This is a good meeting," she says. "We can have coffee after." Tina is not planning to stay afterwards because she has to drive home, so it's good to know I'll be able to debrief with somebody. When the meeting starts, Christine she gestures for me to sit next to her.

The chairperson announces that the sponsor liaison will be available to help anyone who needs to find a sponsor. I haven't been willing to ask anyone to be my sponsor; I know that it's a big decision, and I've been weighing up my options. What kind of person do I want? What if I ask the wrong person and end up with somebody strict or demanding or unforgiving?

I know that it's my responsibility to solidify a true sponsor and work closely with her to move forward with my sobriety.

Christine leans over and quietly says, "I would offer to be your sponsor, but I travel a lot for work, and it wouldn't be fair."

I bite my thumbnail and look around, wondering who the sponsor liaison is, when a woman across the room stands up and says, "Hi everyone, I'm Nona, and I am an alcoholic."

"Hi, Nona," the room says in unison.

"I am the sponsor liaison, and if anyone is new, or not new, and needs a sponsor, I have a list of people willing to sponsor you. Don't be shy, and make sure you see me after the meeting." She looks just like Annie Wilkes from "Misery", and all I can imagine in this moment is her breaking my ankles if I don't do exactly what she says. *Thank goodness she's the liaison,* I think, imagining I'll get a pixie-dust-frolicking-in-a-lavender-field woman to coddle me through this process.

"Okay, let's all stand for the serenity prayer," the chairperson says. We all form a circle and hold hands.

"God, grant me the serenity—"

I look around the room and wonder, *How am I going to feel comfortable? When will this be normal to me?* I don't want to ask Nona for a sponsor, and I want to leave right after the serenity prayer. The room is so crowded, no one will notice me leaving anyway.

"To accept the things I cannot change, the courage to change the things I can—"

That voice telling me to leave sounds sweet and reasonable. I wonder, once I'm standing on the other side of that door, facing Lexington Avenue, will I be proud that I didn't ask? Or pissed?

"And the wisdom to know the difference."

Everyone starts clapping, snapping me back to the room. I don't want to be pissed; I want to just go for it. I spot Nona and make my way over to her.

"Hi," I say, as Nona sticks her hand out to shake mine.

"I'm Nona, what a pleasure meeting you." Her demeanor is very chipper.

"My name is Margarette, and I'm looking for a sponsor." I bite my lower lip.

"Well, you are in luck, deary." Jeez, she even *sounds* like Annie.

"Oh, that's good news," I say, ready for her to point me in the right direction. I look back at Christine, who is walking up to us.

"How long have you been in recovery?" Nona asks.

"Forty-seven days," I say, exhaling.

Nona claps her hands together and rubs them like she's concocting a plan. "I'll be your sponsor; I absolutely love newbies!" she says, laughing to herself. My eyes pop open at Christine, who is smiling as wide as a Cheshire cat.

"Hello, my Christine, how are you my dear?" Nona says as she reaches out to hug her. They hug while I stand there, mouth wide open, imagining how I'm going to escape Annie. *Who wrote* this *part of my life?* I ask myself while I watch Nona and Christine talking. I can't imagine how I will ever like this woman or get anything out of the program with her as my sponsor.

"Christine and I have been friends for... how long now? At least five years, right?"

Christine takes my hand and says, "Margarette, Nona is great with newcomers. She helped me a lot when I first came in. You won't be sorry and I'm so glad you asked for support."

I turn to Tina, who has walked up beside me, and hug her. "Thank you for coming all the way out here to meet me. I'm so happy to see you doing well," I say.

"When you left New Direction, I was so sad," Tina says as we loosen our hug. "I was worried if you would make it or not... if *I* would make it or not... but like they say, be with the people who seek a solution that doesn't include destruction, and we will be okay."

"Yes indeed," I say. Tina walks out of the room, and as I watch her, I whisper *thank you* under my breath. Nona and Christine have moved on to chat to other people, and I take my opportunity to slip out the side door.

On the way home, I think about the people I've met, and the idea of Nona as my sponsor. It's a whole lot to adjust to, and even though I feel good, I am waiting for something to go wrong, like it always does.

Back in the apartment, I look out of my twelfth-floor kitchen window. The view is of Fifth Avenue South. The sun's rays are playing peek-a-boo from behind the clouds, and there are a few people milling about. I look at the Goodwill store where I bought the armoire that sits in my living room.

I never thought I could be in this space again after what happened here before I left for the detox center. When I came home from New Direction, the apartment was exactly as I had left it. Tom, Bella, and I lugged two large garbage bags full of empty bottles down to the dumpster, but there sat the pile of clothes I'd folded that night, my uniform shirt on top. The ashtray was overspilling with cigarette butts, and the stain of blood on the coffee table remained.

The apartment was a reminder of the feeling of trying to walk on water, unable to get to solid ground.

"It's not the outside space or the people around you that make you comfortable, it's the trust you have in your ability to get better, the love you can have in yourself," I remember Matt saying when I hugged him before getting in the car to come home.

Yesterday, I had spoken at a meeting on West 46th Street. The room was small but held over fifty people. The walls were covered in a rainbow collage of sayings like *One day at a time, Live in the solution, Live and let live.* Everyone sat around, sharing chairs, or sitting on laps of friends while drinking coffee, soda, or water. A small spread of food sat nearby.

It was the first time I was the speaker at a meeting since New Direction. Christine was the chairperson of that meeting, and when she asked me to speak, my instinct was to say, "Hell no!" But then I remembered what Bobby Jordan said: "Many people came before me, and without their courage to tell their stories and diligently reach out to help another person, I wouldn't have had this chance."

The least I could do was speak at the meeting. Even if I sounded like a mess, at least it kept me and the people there sober for an hour. To my surprise, not only does the meeting go well, but I meet a new group of friends and feel like I'm in a real-life scene from "Rent". The meeting is held in the theatre district, and the creative, colorful, cool people in the room are reminiscent of my fellow dancers from the old days, although much more supportive, kind, and encouraging. They yell out in agreement with things I say and give me hugs and back slaps after I finish. I never imagined hanging out late at night with a bunch of people who are extremely pleasant to be with. And I'll remember the whole night when wake up tomorrow morning, sober.

My kitchen smells like sweet potatoes and baked chicken. I cook again, real food, and replace the liquor in my fridge with my favorite drinks: Coca Cola and Hawaiian Punch.

Talk about Heaven.

Working with Nona has been surprisingly pleasurable. I follow her suggestions and call her every day, even if she doesn't answer. The last few days, she's answered every time.

She gets a kick out of me being a cop. I tell her I don't know if I will get my job back, so I'm more like a cop in limbo.

"You are the true Margarette in the making; the label is irrelevant," she reminds me.

"I couldn't agree more," I say as I watch a woman cross the street with a little girl. "There's something about ridding myself of these labels and definitions. I thought I had to be one thing or another. I was always trying to *act as if*, and I felt awful every time I went against my true feelings."

"What do you think loving yourself means?" Nona asks.

"I can come up with all sorts of things that really don't mean self-love, like shopping, keeping phony friends, popularity, but all that wouldn't make me respect myself. I can only imagine it's not doing anything that harms me," I say, letting out a breath of air that relaxes my whole body.

"That's a nice way of looking at that. Remember when you had a hard time with the word surrender?" she asks.

"Oh yes; I also felt that cops don't need help. When I stopped thinking about myself as some kind of emotionless machine and looked at surrender the right way, it made so much more sense." I light a cigarette and pour milk into my coffee.

Nona listens and then says, "Isn't it nice to look at surrender like you are turning over all the thoughts, things, places, and people that just don't work for you to another universe? Where it all goes is not your concern. They are replaced with people places and things that bring you peace and joy, even in the hard times."

Since being home, I've been able to show up for my friends instead of sitting in my apartment for hours, drinking my life away, alone and in misery. I do the exact opposite of what I did before I put the drink down. The days are passing by and the nights are pleasant; one day at a time I'm moving away from what I knew and closer to embracing myself. I'm showing up with grace, dignity, and comedy. *I am funny,* I remind myself, and it starts to feel good.

The other line beeps on my phone. "I'll call you back, I'm getting another call," I say to Nona.

I click the button on my phone. "Hello?" I say, glancing at the Manhattan number I don't recognize.

"Hello," a woman says on the other end, "this is Sergeant Willcal from One Police Plaza. How are you, Officer Allyn?"

I gasp. *What the heck?* Tom and Gene said I wouldn't hear from NYPD before they made sure I was clear to go back to work. *Am I getting fired? Why is a sergeant calling me from One Police Plaza?* My stomach drops at the sheer mention of the place.

"Uh—" I gulp my coffee, "I'm doing okay, is everything okay? I'm a bit surprised to be getting a call from a sergeant at One Police Plaza." I hold my breath.

"Well," sergeant says, letting out a chuckle, "I notice you haven't been to work in a while. That kind of gets in the way of you becoming a sergeant."

I slap my hand over my mouth to keep from screaming. "What? Are you kidding me?" I say, tears suddenly appearing and dropping into my coffee.

"Congratulations, Officer Allyn. You're getting promoted, but you have to come back to work by this coming Monday. That's when your training starts."

"Oh my goodness, thank you, sergeant. Thank you so much! I'll be there with bells on, don't you worry about that!"

"Sure thing," she says, "and take care of yourself. Congrats again."

I start running around the apartment and jump on my bed like I'm five years old. Little me is jumping along with me as Grandma sits on the edge of the bed, watching us and laughing. I feel my shine breaking through even stronger.

"Hello?" I say, closing my book and lighting a cigarette. I glance at the clock; it's almost midnight. Nona and I spoke for two hours, and I'm surprised to get another call so late.

"Hello baby..."

As soon as I hear the voice, I know who it is. "I was worried I wasn't going to hear from you. Last we talked, you said you were coming to my promotion ceremony. You are still coming, right?" I ask, holding my cigarette midair.

Maggie went home from New Direction a couple of weeks ago, and I've been to her house in Roslyn to visit. We had such a nice time, and when I found out I was getting promoted, I was excited to invite her to the ceremony.

"Sweetie, I can't make it I—I..." She sounds like she's underwater.

"You drank again?" I snap.

"I'm so sorry. I tried, but Victor—he's such a jerk and I miss my boys. I can't—"

I cut her off. "You know, Maggie, what about your boys? I can imagine how they feel. I feel like them more than I understand you! You remind me of my mother. Every time I foolishly asked her to show up for me or do anything for me, her empty promises and lies were beyond hurtful."

I hear her whimpering on the other end.

"Are you still there?" I ask.

"I'm here, and I know I disappointed you. I feel... awful."

Cigarette ashes fall on my leg, and I jam the butt into the ashtray.

"Disappointed me? You disappointed yourself and your boys, yet you keep talking about your ex-husband like he's making you do this to yourself. I truly pray for your boys, but I have no judgement toward you at all. Take care of yourself, Maggie. I wish you well." I go to hang up the phone.

"Sweetie—wait," Maggie says.

"What?" I snap.

"I'll get better; I promise I will," she says, still sounding like she is drowning.

"For your boys' sake, I hope you do. I have to go, it's late.

Goodnight," I say, looking for the end call button for a second. Then I press it.

I lie in bed exhausted—not because I'm angry with Maggie but because I understand that I was attaching my success to hers. When she relapsed while I was in New Direction, I was scared to death, but I thought if I stayed sober, she would, too.

I finally get it—not just Maggie, but everything.

People can't and shouldn't change because of what I choose to do with my life. My mother continues her life the best she knows how, showing up as best she can. When I was younger, she fell short in many ways. But wanting people, places, and things to change to accommodate my fears or self-doubts has caused so much wasted energy and piles of anguish.

I extended my expectations to others as I got older. When I wasn't accepted or acknowledged the way I wanted to be, I believed it was my fault, that everyone else's pain or failures were my fault in some way. I'm sick of it, and I won't take responsibility for anyone else anymore.

I sit up in bed and look out my window toward the sky. I can't see the stars, but I know they are there. I say, "Grandma, I'll see you at my promotion tomorrow." And with that, I smile and lie down.

Before I walk into the muster room, I check myself in the mirror. I straighten my Midtown North collar brass and tap the gun in my holster. Getting my gun back was a significant moment, as it meant they trusted me to use it in the intended way, not the way I attempted in the messed-up scene only two months ago.

I have to wait until I get to One Police Plaza to get my shield. I think about where I was just a couple months ago. How I felt like I had given up the last bit of my soul and slither of respect when Tom took my gun and shield.

I am not getting my cop shield back. I am getting something better. My dignity, the self-love I always had inside of me. I don't know how to live sober yet, but I know I couldn't live if I had to give up my gun and shield again. Not if I can help it.

If I am the reason my life ever gets destroyed it would be too painful to deal with.

If I am going to trust anything at all, it has to be the people who have faith in me. It's not so much about the gun and shield; I feel like I am touched by a true miracle. A miracle I will cherish as best I can.

I stand in the middle of my classmates and slowly wipe my shield, number 3735, and I tear up. It was Sergeant Walsh's shield. He retired with twenty years of service while I was in sergeants training.

The day he told me he turned in his shield at one Police Plaza, I called the shield office and asked if I would be able to have it when I graduated. Sergeant Edleman who worked there, said, "Well, you are in luck, we haven't sent it out for re-glazing yet. Yes, you can have it, but it won't be gold. It will be silver, like a cop's shield." *The irony*, I thought as I laughed and held my heart.

When Sergeant Edleman hands me the shield, I hug her so hard. "Wow! Thank you, Sergeant Allyn," she says while laughing. As much as the phrase 'Sergeant Allyn' is music to my ears, she has no idea how happy I am to be able to wear sarge's shield. The shine is not shit by any means!

"Newly promoted Sergeant Margarette Allyn!" the ceremonial Lieutenant announces as we salute each other on stage. and flashes from cameras light us up like fireworks.

Sarge, along with mom, Emily, Rosie, Fuzz, Weiss, and the rest of my friends and former students cheer so loud I could swear Brooklyn hears it. I stand on that stage wearing his shield as I assume the rank of sergeant and raise my hands in a fist pump like I am dancing on the moon.

I look around the audience, at the people who took the time on so many levels to show up for me and think, if my life was a mirror, I can't imagine a better reflection of who I am, in the faces and love of these people I love.

A week later, I'm standing next to the patrol sergeant, Sweeny. We are behind the podium in the muster room at Midtown North Precinct. It's the 18th precinct, but I couldn't care less. Out of the seventy-three precincts in the city, I was blessed to be assigned to this one. It's nestled on 54th Street between 8th and 9th Avenue. Smack in the middle of Hell's Kitchen. Sweeny's going to give roll call, but I want to talk to the officers beforehand.

The precinct covers 59th Street from the Henry Hudson River

to Lexington Avenue and south to 44th Street. I'm in the middle of it all. Rockefeller Center, The Time Warner Building, some of the best restaurants and clubs in town, and most of all, the theaters. *The theaters.* My heart beats faster every time I think of it.

I spent a month in sergeant training at the academy. I'm able to see all my old friends and coworkers, including Rip, who I couldn't stop hugging the first time I saw him again. They're so proud of me and welcomed me to chat with their recruit classes. I'm honored that he, along with some of my former co-instructors, felt I was worthy of speaking to their classes about my experience in the precinct.

Being back in the academy with a clear mind feels surreal. I have a nervous excitement that reminds me of happier times when I was about to perform on stage or do something even simpler like show my grandma an art project I worked on at school. This time, I'm sharing my excitement with myself.

There are twenty-five officers standing in front of Sergeant Sweeny and me. They're lined up in formation. "Relax everyone," I say before they all take off their hats and soften their bodies a bit.

"I wanted to come in and introduce myself. My name is Margarette. I'm sure you heard you were getting a newly assigned sergeant here. I can safely say that I am new to the rank of sergeant, but not to life or this job. I love this neighborhood and feel honored to be working here."

I wipe the sweat from my head and stick my hand in my pocket.

"Welcome," a few officers say.

"I would also like to add that this is your world. You have worked in this area longer than me. I look forward to learning from you all and working together. I'm sure we'll all get along just fine."

One of the officers raises his hand. "Excuse me, Sarge, I'm Officer McDaniel. I wanted to say, that was really down to earth introducing yourself like that. We thought you looked like a bitch behind the desk, but so far you seem nice," he says, looking around and slowly lowering his hand.

"What the heck is wrong with you, you dope?" the officer

behind him says. Another officer belts out, "Why would you tell her that to her face, you idiot?" while pushing him to the back of the group.

The entire group is belly ache laughing, including me. Sergeant Sweeny turns to me and says, "Welcome to the theatre district; meet the actors."

I look at them joking around with each other, laughing, and horsing around, and feel right at home.

"Listen, you wet back piece of crap, don't screw up my order again! All you have to do is ask for black coffee. How freaking hard is that? Damn rookies!" Denis snaps as he slams the desk phone back onto the receiver. He reaches his arm back toward me and says, "Sarge, sign these." I chuckle as I grab the papers and start signing.

Officer Denis is my desk assistant. I never call him by his last name, and I refer to him as my desk *angel* because he is a nineteen-year job veteran and knows everything about the precinct. His job is mostly to work on the desk and help the sergeant during the day. He basically runs the whole circus and took care of me in my first few months as a sergeant.

Sergeants usually don't like being assigned to the desk because precinct operations can get hectic. Sarge always told me to learn how to do something in and out the right way, and not assume anyone is going to hold my hand.

Denis is in his daily position, feet crossed on top of the desk while reading the paper. He throws the papers I signed into a basket. He has nails holding the soles of his shoes together, so they don't fall off, and his pants are six inches too short.

"Denis, when the heck are you going to get new shoes?" I ask.

"Boss, I have nineteen years on the job. Why bother now?" He chuckles and hands me something else to do. I have grown fond of him.

I watch Denis run that desk every day. He manages two phones, adjusts the roll call after we are finished with it, and takes care of computer reports. Chiefs call and ask for him, and he knows everyone's schedule like the back of his hand. Today I've been assigned to the desk because Sergeant Sweeny *never* wants the desk—unless he is off work the next day.

Gulinello and Howard walk over to the desk after roll call. They are two officers in my squad, and I think Gulinello, with his blue-grey eyes and little crinkly crow's feet when he smiles, is cute. I have been trying to spring up small talk when they come in for their lunch break, but his replies are always two- or three-word sentences.

"Hey, boss," Howard says, reaching over the desk and handing me a set of keys, "our car is on the fritz. Sergeant Sweeny wanted us to ask you for another one."

I take the keys and turn to Denis, who knows what cars we're able to give out.

"They can use the extra sergeant's car, but don't fucking crash it," Denis snaps, tossing the keys over the desk.

Gulinello catches the keys. "Thanks, Sarge," he says, giving Howard a high five.

"It's not every day we get to ride the boss's car, huh?" Howard says before they wave at us and walk out.

"Remember what Denis said. Be careful!" I yell after them.

"Okay, Sarge, you got it," I hear from the vestibule.

I turn to Denis and let out a sigh. "Denis, I keep trying to strike up small talk with Gulinello, but he barely talks to me. How can I get to know him without being obvious?"

He looks up from the book he's writing in, turns to me, stares me straight in the eye, and says, "You're a *fuckin' sergeant*—take him to drive you."

My eyes pop open and my mouth drops. I lean in to speak when Officer Long walks up to us from the telephone switchboard station, "Boss, Denis, the guys want to know if you want your regular for breakfast."

Denis and I both wave him away, muttering, "Yeah yeah" at the same time.

I lean in a little closer. "Oh my goodness, Denis—that is a genius idea! Would've never thought of that."

Denis pats my shoulder and chuckles. "That's why we like you, boss— because you wouldn't have thought of that."

"Huh?" I ask, confused.

"You didn't come here the first day barking orders at anyone. You stood behind me and watched me do my thing. The guys say you ask their opinion on the street when you see them at jobs. They feel like you include them, and they like that about you. It's nice you don't think or act like a lot of the cocky jerks we get around here—and that's the last nice thing I'll say about you; I'm not the mushy type."

I giggle and give him a quick hug. "Well, I do have my reasons for being the way I am. Cockiness without humility doesn't get anyone very far, no matter how differently they think. Anyway, how are we going to get Gulinello to drive me? He and Howard are partners."

"I know," he says, picking up his papers as he stands up. "Since you can't just break up partners for no good reason, your timing is perfect. Gulinello has traffic court tomorrow. I'll take care of everything. We'll go over the plan tomorrow morning."

"Denis, why are you going to help me with this?" I ask while walking with him to the desk door.

"I have one good deed left in me before I retire. I like Gulinello; that's saying a lot. Besides, if it goes to shit, I'll be long gone before you can catch up with me." We both laugh.

I sit back down at the desk and look around at the outdated arrest processing room, the old monitors and torn posters on the dingy walls and feel like I've landed in Disney World.

CHAPTER 26

D r. Buzel hands me a mug of coffee and sits across from me. I settle into her oversized lounge chair and take a sip. She was assigned to me when I left New Direction, and I was required to see her in order to get my job back. At first I hated it, but then I really started to like her, and now my therapy sessions are a welcome respite from my week.

"I find it hard to believe that you don't drink coffee, yet you make it so well," I say, and we both laugh.

Her office is on West 73rd Street on the ground floor of a townhouse. She has a Persian rug, mahogany bookcases, and plants on the windowsills. It feels like I'm in her home, hanging out in the living room.

I've gotten way more comfortable with her. A long way from the first time I sat in this very same chair and cried for most of our session.

"Well, bub," she says as she picks up her cup of tea. "I want to hear about this officer you are going to work with tomorrow. You do remember one of the most important rules of relationships within the first year of sobriety, right?" She looks at me over her glasses.

"I'm only taking him to drive me, nothing more. Plus, if he's a clutz or clueless, then I'll find out sooner than later," I say, shrugging my shoulders.

"Well, I trust you are not going to move too fast since you are doing so well. Relationships are one of the big things you and I are working on. How do you feel about what we've talked about?"

She's referring to my relationship with myself. Over the last couple of months, I realized that I saw little me as a burden, a fungus, a disease that had to be eliminated. Dr. Buzel gave me homework, which was to imagine me letting little me hang out with present-day me, letting her feel like she could depend on me.

"Ever since Maggie relapsed before my promotion, I've been thinking about how long I've wanted to feel good through other people." I put my mug on the table and stare out the window at passersby. "My motivation to do anything depended on what other people did."

Dr. Buzel sits forward in her chair. "And you suffered, bub, that little girl could have had a better life, but she's sitting right in front of me, creating a better life right now," she says, smiling adoringly at both current me and little me.

"A woman at a meeting talked about how she's been sober for a number of years now, and two of her adult children absolutely refuse to speak to her." I blink my eyes. "She didn't say it like she felt sorry for herself. She said she understood. They were traumatized by her behavior when she was active. I kept trying to love my mother when I was little, but I'm a grownup now, and I've found it hard to admit that I didn't like her and at times, outright hated her as a person."

"Sweetie," Dr. Buzel says, taking off her glasses, "you don't have to like your mom; who said you must like *anyone*? Your only job is to like yourself. How you treat others is a direct reflection of what you feel inside. Speak up for little you, and give yourself permission to know your life sucked—because of other people at first, but then you made mistakes that you are not making today. Let yourself be kind to yourself. You're not doing the same things anymore." She hands me a tissue.

"It's hard to fully let go of things. I did do some crappy stuff way after I didn't need my mother anymore." I wipe my eyes and continue, my voice breaking, "mostly from being scared. Once I knew she was not telling the truth most of the time, and why she wasn't truthful, I hated her, and it hurt to hate her. The fact that she did what she did seemed to make it tolerable to hate at all."

"As long as you do this work with me, you will know how to handle those triggers that take you to the negative places in your mind. You never deny what you feel, but you don't have to panic anymore. You landed on your feet, right?"

That saying reminds me of Sarge: *Be scared, but don't panic.* In meetings, they say that if we get a bit overwhelmed, we should just look down and come back to the moment. I'm feeling more and more grounded each time I say out loud something I was previously too afraid to say.

Just as he said he would, Denis concocted an Einstein-level plan to get Gulinello to drive me. I was a nervous wreck, but I followed his instructions to the letter. Shortly after we started our shift, we were called to a hotel stabbing. I was hoping he'd be on point. I'd be crushed if he were just an empty suit. But he stepped up as soon as we got out of the car, and just like the other bosses mentioned to me, he was intelligent and confident in the way he worked. Not to mention, he paid for my breakfast that morning, so he'd already passed some tests.

Over the next few months, I took him to drive me once more. Today is our third day together. I'm getting more comfortable with him, and I keep a conversation I had with Sarge in mind. When I told Sarge that I liked Gulinello, the first thing he said was, "Don't kiss him... Do you want to be a forgotten fling or a respected mentor?" I couldn't face Sarge, Dr. Buzel, my sponsor, or my friends from meetings if I made a silly mistake over a crush on a guy.

It's been over two years since I've had any kind of fling. And I've never had a long-term healthy relationship. Dr. Buzel and I are working on how I view relationships, and I don't want to start off with old habits, especially since I don't have alcohol to run to if things go wrong.

We're sitting in front of Tiffany's while I eat my breakfast, and I peer into the window.

"You know, Gulinello, have you ever wondered what people's lives are like as you watch them?"

"Sometimes. I actually like knowing that people are not any better off or worse off than we think they are."

"Yea, that's true," I say, and take a bite of my bagel.

"Sarge," he said, "this is the third time I'm asking you to come out with the group of us after work today. The guys and gals said you keep putting it off. Why won't you go?"

I have been putting it off. The first two times I said I had a doctor's appointment. but I don't want them to start thinking I have an ongoing medical issue. The thing is, I'm just learning how to get out of social invitations without having to lie but without outright announcing that I'm not comfortable hanging out in a bar.

When he asked me the first time, I thought I could just go and have ginger ale, stay for an hour, and leave. I called Nona on my break to run it by her, and she said, "There is a common saying that goes, If you sit in a barber's chair long enough, eventually you are going to get a haircut,' missy."

The same goes for the fact that people who rob banks don't hang out with priests.

I have over two years of sexual energy stored away. Coupling that with the smell of alcohol, a guy I like, and a bunch of cops is a train wreck waiting to happen.

I stuff the paper that held my bagel into the plastic bag and take a gulp of orange juice, then turn to Gulinello. "I'm just not into the drinking thing. Maybe if you guys went to a restaurant or something."

"What, you can't hold your liquor? Do you get wild, dance on tables or something?" he chuckles.

I start to laugh and hold a tissue up to my mouth to keep from spitting the orange juice out.

"Have you ever seen the music video for 'Thriller' by Michael Jackson?" I say as I watch a wave of people cross Fifth Avenue.

"Yea, of course, why?" he says, blowing smoke into the air.

"That's kind of what happens to me when I drink," I say, turning away and hoping I don't have to explain further.

He makes a face like he just smelled bad milk. "Jeez, Sarge, I don't even know how to take that."

"Midtown North Sergeant on the air," the radio dispatcher calls over the receiver.

I pick up my radio and press the button. "I'm on the air."

"Sector boy is requesting you at a hotel on 48th Street between 7th and 8th for the job they're assigned to. I'll show you responding. Acknowledge?"

Never happier to have my breakfast at Tiffany's interrupted, I hold the radio up to my mouth and smile. "Show us responding."

"Hi, Boss," Officer Matthews says before holding up a piece of paper he's writing on and starts reading. "The deceased is female, last name Abnegate, and according to the hotel manager she used this license to check in, which states she is thirty years old. The medical staff told me the pills she took along with the over a dozen empty mouthwash bottles may be what caused her death."

As I look over officer Matthew's shoulder, his voice trails off. The woman is barely visible in the bed, the mattress and sheets taking over what's left of her frail body.

Before I respond, Matthews speaks louder. "Boss?"

I look at him. "Oh, yes, sorry, what were you saying?"

"I already notified the squad. They're on the way and trying to find a next of kin. Olive is out in the hall talking to the cleaning lady who found her," he says.

"Good job." I walk past him and over to the bed. I kick a few empty bottles and stop just shy of the mattress, taking quick deep breath.

She does not look peaceful at all. It looks like her body took a massive beating beyond simple starvation. I turn to the hotel manager. "How long was she here, and how was she able to get all these bottles of mouthwash?"

Gulinello walks up behind me. "Sarge, I told the guys they have to bag all the bottles and pills. I sent Matthews downstairs to grab a larger bag; there must be more than twenty empty bottles all over this room."

"She was here for three days," the manager says, wiping his

forehead with his handkerchief. "I didn't see her until now. The supply closet is right down the hall; she could have gotten them from there," he explains.

I turn to Gulinello, who is right next to me. "Would you make sure they don't forget to let us know if the squad found anything out about her family? I'll meet you at the elevator."

"I'm on it, and I'll be right behind you," Gulinello says. I don't look back as I lift my hand in acknowledgment and walk down the hall.

"Hey, you seemed off up there, like something was bothering you. Are you alright?" Gulinello asks as he closes the car door.

I watch visitors walking in and out of the hotel smiling, taking pictures, tipping the bell hops, not missing a beat in their journey. No one the wiser when it comes to the dead woman in room 1004.

"I'm okay. It's just a shame she died, alone, in the middle of what seems like the greatest city in the world. And you know what? I don't think she gave a crap where she was." I stare out the window at a family getting out of a limo.

"I just don't get how she drank all that mouthwash; she must have been desperate. I can't imagine drinking that crap. Poor lady," Gulinello says, shaking his head and lighting a cigarette.

I can imagine, I think as he hands me the cigarette he just lit.

"What really gets me is how young she is to have killed herself like that. good thing her family didn't find her like that. Right, Sarge?"

He starts the car and turns to me, "You never finished answering my question before, about coming out with the group of us. You just started to tell me why you don't drink."

I think about all the times I couldn't remember how I hooked up with the person in the bed next to me when I woke up after a night of drinking, the nights I completely forgot, the way-too-many free clinic visits, and the day I put that gun to my head.

As Gulinello starts driving, I flick the ashes out of the window. A woman waves at us, and I smile back at her.

I thought it was easy to be high and drunk, whatever put me in a state of mind to do the things I did to keep me from ever feeling shame or pain. Ms. Abnegate suffered for sure, and why I was still alive was only an act of a higher power. I truly believed that while I looked at her in that bed. I was not going to turn my back on the mercy I was given. I was not going to shut the door on my past. And I didn't want to make my future one of regret.

I turn to Gulinello and say, "I don't drink, because I am one decision away from trading places with Ms. Abnegate." I look straight ahead, holding my breath. If he thinks something is wrong with that, better to find out now than later.

"What, you're about to kill yourself with mouthwash?" he asks, stopping at a red light.

I start to laugh. "If you were a girl, I would call you Cindy. From "Three's Company.""

"Well, I feel pretty close right now," he says, chuckling, "What do you mean exactly?"

I imagine Ms. Abnegate's little self holding her hand while she went off to the afterlife before turning to say, "I don't drink, because I am an alcoholic."

It seems everything in Times Square stops. The pedestrians stop mid-cross and turn toward us, the tourists on the double decker bus glare at us with pointed fingers, and the screens plastered all over the buildings blast light right through the windshield. I can't take it back now.

Gulinello slowly turns his head toward me, smiles, and says, "You are the coolest boss ever. That is damn respectful, Sarge, and—it's an honor you told me that; I'm sure that wasn't easy."

I exhale, the tourists go back to pointing out highlights around them, and pedestrians continue rushing across the street.

I put my hand over my heart as if I just ran (and won) a marathon. I don't worry so much about what Gulinello thinks of me; I'm happy that I finally think enough of myself to keep my promise—to never act like somebody else again, no matter who is in the audience.

CHAPTER 27

I sit up with such speed I almost fall off the bed. I am panting, and my clothes and body are drenched. I look around the room. There's no one here. The room is dark except for the light from the TV and the streetlight outside the window.

I peel the sheets off my legs and rush to the kitchen. I open the cabinets one by one, slamming each shut just as quickly. I look under the sink, but nothing is there. I hear a car horn and music from the street below.

I run to the window and see that the bar across the street is in full swing. Women are standing outside smoking and drinking. I press my hands on the cool glass of the window.

My breathing is short and quick. I have got to get a drink; I can't take this anymore. I wipe the sticky hair from my face and stumble over to the dresser.

Getting pants on is a chore. My body is spewing out sweat, and I'm exhausted. I throw the pants on the floor and grab shorts.

I trip over my shoe and fall to my knee. On the floor next to my bed is the 12-Step book. I worked on step two with Nona last night. *Came to believe a power greater than myself can restore me to sanity.*

I never imagined myself as insane until I said out loud to Nona and Dr. Buzel the things I've done while drinking.

I get up and hold onto the wall. *Please don't let me go down to that bar.* Why get this far only to have this unbearable urge? I feel myself being pulled toward the apartment door. I can hear the drinks being poured into the glasses, the music floating through me, the liquor warming my insides.

Living without drinking isn't going to work. It's too scary. I can't stand the silence.

"Whenever you are having a bad urge, pick up the phone and call someone—call me," Nona would say. My clock says 2:30am. Who would bother with a call at this time?

No one will know anyway. I'll be back within an hour. The stinging and stickiness on my body is only going to subside if I drink. My head is spinning, and I need it to stop. I need the noise to shut up.

I am not having an urge; this is a full-on obsession, and I grab the doorknob. I get weak and lean up against the wall.

"There will be times when the only thing between you and a drink is the God of your understanding. The higher power you choose to let do for you, what you can't do for yourself," I hear in my head.

I gasp for air and slide down the wall.

Who freaking cares? This isn't what I imagined. It shouldn't be this hard.

I look over to where I fell the night of the gun incident. I see myself lying there, people standing around me, whispering.

My heart is beating so fast I feel like I'm going to pass out. I'm digging my fingers into the wooden floor, my nails aching. I drag myself along the floor, past the image of the gun, the dirty laundry and uniform shirt, past the self judgement and shame, past the pain. I get to the bathroom and run the shower. *Please let this pass, God, please help me,* I say as I climb inside the tub.

I bite down on a washcloth with all my might and grunt.

I then open my mouth and scream, "Take this shit from me if I am to keep at staying sober!" I am crying and forcing the words out. "If I am going to," I swallow hard, "trust you, then take this pain from me. I swear I'll go to that bar right now!"

My eyes soften from the rage spilling out of them and my crying calms. I loosen the grip on the washcloth and lean against the back of the tub. The room is silent and oddly comforting.

I raise the washcloth and start to wipe my face, arms, and neck.

I put my hand on the edge of the tub, slowly stand, and feel lighter.

I turn on the shower and cry because I know what it feels like to let myself out of the driver's seat. I am not drowning anymore. I turned everything over— not to a God I hated but to one I can trust. I was trying to keep part of my old life with me, but if I could fix things then staying sober would be worth it.

I don't have to fix anything. It's already being taken care of.

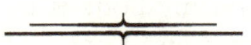

Emily and I take the train to the restaurant to meet Mom. She's been amazing. Our routine was to drink at my place or hers, or to meet at a bar. She hasn't once had a drink in front of me since I came back, and I never asked her to change her habits.

She and Mom are taking me out to celebrate my ninety days sober. Emily even went with me to a few open meetings during my first week home. Nona told me that alcohol, problems, and life overall do not go away just because I stop drinking and that my true friends will support that. I always knew Emily was a true friend.

"I'll have the rib and chicken combo and—," Emily looks at Mom and turns back to the menu, "a Coke with lemon." She closes the menu and winks at the waiter, who slowly takes the menu from her.

"I'll have the chicken and lemonade," I say, giggling.

"I'm having the same as Emily," Mom says as she gives the waiter a dollar and adds, "Make sure you put an extra rib on the plate." The waiter stares at the folded dollar.

"The mountains we must try to move," he says and walks away.

"Oh my goodness, how rude. A dollar?!" Emily screeches.

I'm slapping the table, trying to keep my water from spilling. "Where on earth did you get the idea to do that from?" I ask.

"I saw it in a movie. I don't want just three ribs, I want four," Mom says, holding up as many fingers.

"We know what four is," Emily says, pushing Mom's hand

down. "Next time, do that when you're by yourself. Now he thinks we're *all* cheap." We all laugh.

The waiter sits our drinks on the table, looks at Mom, and turns on his heels.

"Let's have a toast," Mom says.

We all raise our drinks.

"To Margarette for doing something so wonderful. I am so proud to have you as my daughter."

"Cheers, and many more ninety days to you, Margarette. I love you, girl," Emily says as we all clink glasses.

When my mother took me out after I graduated from the academy and then again after I was promoted to sergeant, I felt like I was being spoiled. I make her laugh and she seems to get such joy out of being with me.

We have yet to talk about the past. I tried, but she'd change the subject or look like she was going to cry, so I let up. After speaking to Nona, Dr. Buzel, and my friend from the Harlem meeting, Mary, we all decided that she's just not mentally ready to face what we went through.

I watch her and Emily as they chat about people in the restaurant. I want to be the person who brings a little sunshine to someone. I don't want to spend time with my friends and family rehashing the bad times and hoping they admit wrongdoing. As they say in recovery, *keep it on yourself.*

"Margarette," Mom says.

"Yea," I say, taking a bite of my chicken.

"You have come such a long way. We didn't know about the, you know, the problem, but with all you have done, getting promoted as well, I wanted to say that I know I could have done things differently, if only I had a chance to make up for it." She holds a tissue to her face and Emily leans over and hugs her.

"Mom, as much work as I'm doing and must do, one thing I know is my whole life, including things I did, had to happen for me to be here today. Instead of wishing I could change the past, I cannot repeat it today or in the future. We can start from there, right?"

"Alright with the after-school special crap. Let's eat," Emily says.

"Oh, wait," Mom says, reaching into her purse and pulling out a small envelope. "I got this for you."

I open the envelope and pull out a ninety-day sobriety coin. On it says, *To thine own self be true.*

I hold it in my hand, get up, give her a hug, and say, "Yes indeed."

The first thing I had to do when I got home from rehab was attend a meeting. Changing my old habits was imperative to keep me from having an idle mind or becoming restless.

"Have a plan before leaving the house," Dr. Buzel says.

"Window browsing always ends up in a purchase you don't need," Nona reminds me.

Sarge helped me get back my love for reading, and the literature from the program became some of my favorite to read. It gives guidance on everything from how to respond if I am offered a drink to what to say to old acquaintances.

I work the day shift, so I see Dr. Buzel right after work before I go home. If Nona's not around, I meet Mary.

We go to a meeting together a few times a week. On my days off, I go to a meeting in the morning and one in the evening. Mary and I have become "running buddies," someone you hang with and go to meetings with. Before long, she and Nona were volunteering me to speak at meetings.

When I don't see them in person because I'm stuck at work or have another job assignment, I call. I remember how awkward I felt the first time I called Nona. How nervous I was when I introduced myself to Mary.

"Don't think, just do it," Bobby Jordan said.

"Think about when you couldn't think—when you were three or four years old," Dr. Buzel said.

They said thinking is usually for survival and commonly negative. Be a kid in the sandbox who runs up to another kid and says, "You wanna play?"

That is how I feel looking at Mary and Ray as I sit in the back seat. We're going to speak at a meeting, and I'm often surprised at the fun, quality friends I've made.

Having dinner with groups of people after the meeting has become so fun that I often forget I have to work the next day. I'm worn out by the time I get home, and my new routine includes reflection and thanking God. It feels good to no longer be drinking myself into oblivion.

I sit up in bed at night and read for about an hour—either a book that I'm working through with Nona or other literature related to sobriety, sometimes a novel recommended by Sarge. I write in my journal and reflect on everything I am grateful for. After reading and journaling, I shut my eyes for a moment.

"Thank you for keeping me honest, sober, and helpful for another day," I pray, followed by the Serenity Prayer.

"God grant me the serenity to accept the things I cannot change..." I say out loud, before turning out the light.

By taking on the suggestions of these wonderful people I now love and respect, I'm creating a better life for myself, and it is already beyond my wildest dreams. My Grandma's words ring in my ear. *God takes care of us as long as we believe in Him and in loving one another.*

I have come full circle in my belief in God. He is different from the God I knew as a child, and I have a different relationship with Him, but it is there. And it is possibly the most supportive relationship I have—always there in the background, protecting me from the things I used to believe that unnecessarily tainted the miracle I am.

It feels good to no longer fear judgement, from others or from Him, knowing that He is the only person who could judge me, but doesn't.

I trust that I'm going to make the choices I'm supposed to make. My intent is to be true to myself—integrity, grace, and dignity.

It is the new me.

It's a humid August evening at the New Direction barn. It's packed to the rafters with people who are hugging, laughing, and eating cake. It's Matt's thirtieth sobriety anniversary, and I made sure I could attend. He invited his dear friend Liz to be his key speaker.

"You are one of the two who made it, like I thought you would be, kiddo," Bobby says as he hands me a cup of orange soda.

"I can't say it was easy or I got it right away, but I'm following all the suggestions, even if I don't understand everything," I reply, shoving a piece of cake into my mouth.

"This young lady is something else," Liz says, nudging my shoulder.

I take her plate and put it on the table in front of us.

"I'm so happy I'm here. What a treat getting to meet you," I say.

"Margarette, Matt says, "you were one who worried Margaret and me. There are no words for how proud we are of you." He takes my hand and holds on tight.

"I wanted to say to you all that what I see in this barn, what I see because of people living their lives with joy, no matter what road life takes, really shows how powerful this is," I say, wiping my eyes with my shirt sleeve.

Liz turns to me. "Matt told me all about you, sweetie, and I know you are a miracle. You watch the road, your life is going to knock you out. It has for me."

Liz was one of the first women in recovery, and she's become very well known, a household name for anyone who knows about 12-step programs.

"Come, sweetie. Sit closer, read this with me," Liz says as her friend Lucille hands her a magazine from the literature library.

"I'll be back," Bobby says, tossing his plate in the garbage, "I have a disease that will never be cured, and I have to go give some of it away."

"What's that?" Liz asks.

"Good-lookin-itis!" he says, strutting off laughing.

"He is one of my favorite people," I say, catching my breath.

Liz opens the magazine and we read an article about how the three pillars of unity, strength, and hope come from one individual reaching out to another, and then another, and living in the solution.

Liz writes in the magazine and hands it to me. I look at the page, and it says, *Trust that the God of your understanding has a plan for you if you just trust the process. Love, Liz.*

Matt has tears in his eyes, as do I, and as I hug Liz, I whisper in her ear, "Thank God I was spared." If I could do for one person what everyone so far has done for me, especially when they didn't have to spend a second on me, then my whole life was worth it.

Matt stands in the front of the barn and says, "Everyone, every year this anniversary gets bigger and bigger. Anniversaries are not for the people who have been here a while, they are to show newcomers that there is life after misery, that when we become an example, we can only show others what life is like without running from the hard things. We may not be able to make someone change, but every time we reach out to help someone, we save ourselves one minute, hour, day, and year at a time."

Everyone whistles, claps, and yells congrats to Matt. I think I'm the loudest.

"Make sure you call sometimes and let me know how you are doing, young lady," Liz says as I give her a huge hug and kiss.

"I will, I promise."

When I was here as a client, I could only reason with not drinking by how my physical pain had diminished. I never imagined being happy and wanting a life that I faced with courage and *without* a substance or alcohol.

I don't know when that changed, but I keep the drink away because not only do I feel good, I know I deserve the life I have.

Sharon, Susan, and Tina snap pictures with me, we all give each other kisses, and I say goodbye to Matt, Margaret, Bobby, and the rest of the staff. An hour later, I'm in my car heading home on a sober high.

Gulinello, or Chris, as I now call him, is passing out chocolate bars with custom labels that read "Margarette's 1 Year Anniversary" while I greet all the people who came to watch me speak. Mary, Ray, Tom, Nona, Mom, Emily, Rosie, and a whole group of fellowship supporters have all come to support me today to mark an occasion I never thought I'd see.

An older lady with glasses walks up and touches my arm. "What a nice young man you have over there," she says, smiling widely.

"Not to mention cute as heck," says another woman who has joined us.

All three of us lean in and giggle, and Chris must feel our eyes on him, because he looks over and winks at me.

Everyone is eating cake and drinking soda or juice, and the music is pumping loud. It looks different from the parties I attended years ago, but this is truly a celebration. I know that a year is only a start, but to think that, only a year ago, I didn't even want to be alive anymore? And now, I wake up remembering every moment of a party rather than waking to a blank memory of the previous night's events.

I remember Matt's words, that the celebration is not about me but about inspiring someone new in terms of what's possible for them. I scan the room for Leslie, who is counting days. We lock eyes and she holds up the 90-day coin I gave her during the meeting. "One day at a time," I mouth at her across the room. She puts her hand on her heart, and even from here, I can see her eyes glisten.

It's truly a gift to discover what you never thought was possible.

CHAPTER 28

I've stopped using the phrase "everything happens for a reason." I'm the type that can obsessively look for the reason, refuse to move ahead, and end up stuck on a hamster wheel. But I love the saying "Nothing happens by accident." Even something that appears to be an accident is merely another brick in the building. If I'm as honest as I can be, even if I don't know the answer, I feel good. And the better I feel, the more I want the life I am creating.

There are many events in my life that I can't immediately remember, mostly due to my brain blocking out those that were paralyzing and heartbreaking. Alcohol certainly kills the cells that render one aware of their actions.

I used to dread next-day phone calls or potential comments from friends or coworkers about my behavior the night before. I used to hate waking up, especially to the lowest depths of self-loathing. I never imagined getting out of that endless hole of terror. I never thought I would be spared the drowning without constant pain as a reminder of my choices.

At times, it is hard to believe that it has been three years since the night I was deathly drunk in my apartment. The day Tom Connor took me to rehab. And the day that changed my life.

However, almost three years after that dreaded day, when I was taken to a detox center in Long Island, I have come a long way.

The memories I'm creating are memories I'm not ashamed of, and what's most miraculous is that I'm not ashamed of anything *before* that day either.

My mom and Emily and Shelly are laughing, sitting across from me in the limo. The driver turns to give us a thumbs up, indicating that we've arrived. That thumbs up feels like I just won an award and received the cue to enter stage right.

Emily and Mom snap a few pictures and open the door. I barely notice the brutal chill of the air as it wisps inside; I'm too excited. The sun shines brightly above, only a few clouds in the sky. Mom and Emily are laughing as they tighten their coats and walk up the steps. Shelly turns and gives me a wink and thumbs up. Even though we've grown apart, she's still my sister, and it's only right that she's my Maid of Honor.

An arm reaches down toward me, and I grab it with my white silk glove. As I step out of the limo, Sarge puts his hand protectively over my arm and looks at me.

"Remember when I said two of the most beautiful things in the world is a mother and a bride?"

I hold back tears and nod.

"Well, I must add that you have become one of the most admirable and most beautiful women I know. I am looking at someone who is no villain and certainly no coward. I have truly come to adore you."

Virginia, the wedding coordinator, guides us through the door of Convent Avenue Baptist Church. She walks ahead of us and through the second set of doors. Sarge and I stand off to the side.

I look around the church entrance. The brass and gold lined walls and smell of incense remind me of the little church in North Carolina. We stand in the lobby of the castle-like building, and I feel like Cinderella. I feel the hands of the people who worked to build such a beautiful place, the building's beauty adding to the way I feel as I look through the glass windows into the audience facing the stage.

I glance up toward the balcony and see the teenage me looking down, smiling, throwing rose petals.

"I am trying so hard not to cry, Sarge," I say, holding back tears. "I adored you first." I laugh and go on, "Thank you for being here, thank you for seeing in me what I was afraid to see, and thank you for being you. This is a true honor, and I can't believe I am here, getting married and surrounded by the best people I know." I hug him so tight he lets out a cough.

About a year into my life as a sober woman, I stopped thinking about Harlem School of the Arts as a nostalgic memory and decided to attend the school again.

I felt if I started with something private, like voice lessons, I wouldn't be embarrassed if I stunk.

That is when I met Mrs. Larose Saxon and we quickly became close.

She immediately reminded me of Grandma Sarah with her soft yet confident voice and Gram with her way of reassuring me that doubt was my only enemy. She encouraged me to sing at a recital and I couldn't believe I agreed.

As I stood on that Harlem School stage, I had all sorts of flashbacks of the dance and acting performances I was a part of when I was younger.

I sang *Sister*, from *The Color Purple*, because I felt the redemption of myself through the pain of my life that had to happen. I felt the grace after it all, and receiving the warmth from the audience, the little girl in me was shining through the big girl I was proud to become.

Everyone gave me a standing ovation when I finished, including Mrs. Saxon—standing behind everyone pumping her fist in the air.

I couldn't be more grateful for her, and she was just as honored to be a part of one of the most important events of my life.

On this day, it is heartwarming to see Mrs. Saxon on the stage. She starts singing *Ave Maria*.

Emily, my bridesmaid, adjusts her boobs and winks at me. Rosie steps over to me and touches my face. "Chica, flacita, mi amor, I am so proud of you. I love you very much," she says, wiping a tear from her eye. "Shit, girl, I can't screw up my make up before everyone sees how fabulous I look!" We all laugh, and Sarge gives her son, Gibby, a pat on the head.

Rosie turns to her son, "Okay, papi, you make sure you hold

the rings on the pillow tight. Don't drop them; you are the little prince."

"Yes, Mama," he says, looking straight ahead. I bend down and kiss him on his head.

Shelly walks down the aisle first, waving at people and stopping to kiss our friends on the cheek. She is such a show queen! *Oh my goodness, how I love them*, I whisper to myself. Emily is close behind Shelly, giggling at how Shelly is doing a red carpet bounce down the aisle.

Virginia is handing the basket filled with blue rose petals to Chris's niece, Madison. We look like the princess and her maiden, her dress adorned with flowers and pearls. We both have flowers in our hair, made by Nona, whom I see sitting in one of the pews chatting it up with Christine.

I look down at my engagement ring, sapphire and diamonds, my favorite colors. Christine is a stone buyer from Israel. She and Chris secretly planned to make my rings from a photo of a set I loved. He unraveled the whole story when he proposed to me. *Life is amazing as heck!* I think as I turn to look at Madison.

She's spinning around so her dress flares out. I take her hand and we spin together. I imagine I am dancing with myself. I let little me out of her cage, and she reminds me of the innocence, love, and resilience I've always admired in her.

"Let's go, my dear. It's your turn," Virginia says as she holds the door open for Madison.

I watch her skip down the aisle, dropping petals along the way. Everyone is staring at her, some wiping their eyes and some snapping pictures of her having as much fun as if she were on a playground.

Sarge grabs my arm. "Are you ready, Allyn?"

"As Kit says to Vivian Ward in Pretty Woman, I feel like freakin' Cinderella, Sarge, of course I'm ready!" I say, letting a tear roll down my cheek.

"By the way, it's about time you call me John," he says, smiling at me.

When everyone stands up, my breath is sucked out of me. The faces looking adoringly as I reflect on myself, the person I truly am, and the love and support I earned from each person in the room.

Canon in D is playing, and I look around the room. The pews are draped in blue and white roses, and there is a white lace runner on the floor. Rosie and Emily have their arms locked, both crying. Dr. Buzel gives me a wink and a wave as I nod my head.

There is no bride side or groom side. Everyone is standing amongst each other as if we were in a cozy living room. There are people from my support group here, Chris's childhood friends, Fuzz, Weiss, Dixon, and other coworkers from my Hell's Kitchen Precinct. I couldn't be prouder. My mom is next to Chris's mom, and our friends are joined together watching a day that I will truly remember in its entirety.

Chris stands next to his brother, and I smile at him. His eyes are filled with tears. When John and I reach the front, Chris walks to us, and they shake hands.

"She is a daughter to me, and now I can say I am proud to have you as a son—as long as you don't screw it up," John says. They both laugh and hug.

I remember when I met Mary at a meeting. *Do the opposite*, I thought. Instead of shying away and wondering if we would ever be friends, I approached her and asked if we could go jogging together. She was wearing a jogging suit at the time, so that was the best thing I could come up with.

She agreed to hang out with me. We always joke that I really didn't want to go jogging and she certainly didn't want to go jogging with me.

We have become so close; I consider her like a big sister.

I take Chris's hand, and we turn to face Mary, today our pastor, who opens her book and straightens her collar. "You look absolutely beautiful, my friend," she says.

Grandma is here, I know it, and I stand here utterly thankful and proud that this is what she's watching. This is my life, a life filled with people I deserve.

"We are gathered here today to celebrate, and I truly mean celebrate, these two people, Chris and Margarette's, union in marriage. I have officiated many unions, and this is one that makes me especially proud," Pastor Mary says.

"Chris, do you take Margarette to be your lawfully wedded wife?"

Chris squeezes both my hands and stares deep into my eyes, then shuts his eyes tight and opens them again. I smile at him. I know he's fighting tears, so I stick my tongue out at him, and he smirks.

"To have and to hold, in sickness and in health, to love and to cherish her, until death do you part," Mary says.

"Absolutely. I mean, I do; I do!" We all laugh. I wipe his eyes and once again take his hands.

Looking around the room, I feel like I'm in the middle of the old apartment, dancing to music and listening to the laughter and chatter from the grownups who crowd the space. I want to jump into the audience like a rock star and kiss everyone who is a part of me, a part of us, a part of my life.

"Margarette, do you take Chris as your lawfully wedded husband?"

I see little me, spinning down the aisle wearing a white dress, white lace socks, and patent leather shoes. I miss the way Grandma took such care of me, how she never made me feel invisible. I smile at her, the little girl I tried so hard to erase, the girl who stuck with me no matter how much I thought I hated her. She stands next to me, her arms wrapped around my leg.

"To have and to hold, to love and to cherish, in sickness and in health, until death do you part?" Mary puts her hand over her heart and smiles.

As I glance down at little me holding onto my leg and smiling as bright as the sun shining through the stained-glass windows, I imagine hugging her back as I look into Chris's eyes.

I see my reflection in his eyes, and I love what looks back at me. A kind, loving soul. Someone who is loyal and honest. The room is filled with people we love and who have been there from the beginning. The things I don't remember may come up at some point, but on this day, a day that wouldn't have been had I not given myself a chance is a day I will never forget.

I take a deep breath and say, "I do."

266

ABOUT THE AUTHOR

Margarette Allyn is an author, speaker and dancer who believes in the healing power of making choices guided by instinct, intuition and faith.

Discovering her passion for dance at a young age, her aspirations took flight when she was accepted into Fiorello H. LaGuardia High School of Music & Art and Performing Arts in New York City's Upper West Side. She dared to dream even bigger— why not aim for The Juilliard School? It was a dream that seemed beyond reach, especially for a young woman from Harlem. But Margarette held onto the idea that the sky has no limits.

However, unforeseen circumstances, ego, and personal choices halted her burgeoning dance career, crushing her dreams of attending Juilliard and leaving her with a deep sense of loss.

At the age of 24, Margarette embarked on a new path, joining the NYPD. Despite battling an overwhelming cloud of dread, despair, and her complex relationship with alcohol, she clung fiercely to her discipline, determination, and the will to truly live. Supported by her loyal friends and colleagues, she dedicated twenty years to her police career, retiring as a Sergeant in 2019. Today, Margarette resides in Tampa, Florida, with her husband and two sons.

Grateful for the grace and mercy bestowed upon her, Margarette finds purpose in giving back to those she mentors, is dancing once again, accepts motivational and inspirational speaking engagements and looks forward to many more years of being on stage.

Visit her at www.margaretteallyn.com.

ACKNOWLEDGEMENTS

Many people helped me get here. Not just with this book but in life. Isn't it nice that there are no requirements for unconditional love?

Thanks to all of you for having the patience I only dreamed of. For the grace and mercy, I have been given.

Priyanka Biswas
Cathryn Mora
Adina Edleman
Elizabeth Lyons
Juliette Fogra

www.ingramcontent.com/pod-product-compliance
Lightning Source LLC
Chambersburg PA
CBHW020438130626
46549CB00001B/206